Sous Vide

Cookbook

for Beginners

365 Simple and Tasty Recipes

for Perfectly Cooked Meals

Alex Harwood

CONTENTS

BEEF, PORK & LAMB RECIPES 26

POULTRY RECIPES 37

VEGETARIAN & VEGAN RECIPES 67

APPETIZERS & SNACKS 74

COCKTAILS AND INFUSIONS 82

VEGETABLES & SIDES 88

OTHER FAVORITE RECIPES 97

RECIPE INDEX 105

WHAT IS SOUS VIDE (AND WHY SHOULD I CARE?)

The "sous vide" part of sous vide cooking refers to the vacuum-sealed bags that are often called for when you're using the technique. (The French phrase literally means "under vacuum.") However, these days, when someone says "sous vide cooking," they're generally referring to any kind of cooking that takes place in a precisely temperature-controlled water bath, whether you're actually using a vacuum-sealed bag or not.

Sous vide cooking offers unparalleled control over whatever it is you are trying to cook, whether it's steaks and chops, shrimp and lobster, vegetables, or even large cuts of meat like pork shoulders and legs of lamb. with fast-cooking foods, like steaks and chicken breasts, sous vide removes all the guesswork involved in traditional methods. No poking with a thermometer, no cutting and peeking, no jabbing with your finger—just perfect results every single time.

For meat like pork shoulder and ribs, which are far more forgiving of accidental overcooking and require less precise temperatures, sous vide has some less obvious benefits. But in any event, sous vide increases the flexibility of your schedule, allowing you to go about your day (or two days, as the case may be) with the circulator quietly heating away in the corner of the kitchen, slowly tenderizing a tough cut of meat, or holding your steak at a perfect medium-rare until it's ready to be finished and served.

Sous vide can also allow you to get results and textures that are impossible to achieve using traditional cooking methods. Your steaks will come out of the bath cooked to your preferred temperature from edge to edge. For pork shoulder, sous vide cooking allows us to cook at temperatures that are significantly lower and more stable than those used in traditional methods, which means that we can achieve tender results with relatively little moisture loss. (You can even cook a chicken breast so that it's rare or medium-rare and is entirely pasteurized and thus perfectly safe to eat, although I don't recommend it.)

TIPS AND TRICKS

Over the course of several years and many, many tests, I've hit upon a couple cool tricks and tips to address problems that sometimes come up when you're cooking sous vide. Here are three that I've found to be the most useful.

No Vacuum Sealer? Use Water Displacement to Seal Your Food in Zipper-Top Bags

Having an easy way to remove air from plastic bags can be handy for all sorts of applications, from marinating meat more effectively to preventing freezer burn and, of course, cooking things sous vide. Vacuum sealers are designed to do this, but good ones can be prohibitively expensive, and there's a quick, easy, inexpensive option, called the water displacement method, that requires nothing more than a zipper-lock freezer bag and a tub or pot of water.

To do it, start by placing your food inside a zipper-lock bag, then seal the bag, leaving just the last inch or so of the seal open. Next, lower the bag into a pot or tub of water. As the bag gets lowered, water pressure will push air out of the bag through the small opening you've left. Just before the bag is completely submerged, seal off that opening and pull the whole bag out of the tub.

Keep Your Sous Vide Bag Submerged with a Binder Clip

One of the most common sous vide difficulties that I get emails about is floating bags. A few things can cause a bag to float. The first is an imperfect seal, meaning the air is trapped in there to begin with. (This is especially likely to happen if you are using the water displacement method.) with high temperatures or prolonged cooks, vapor can also form inside the bag as water is heated and evaporates, or as air bubbles trapped inside meat or vegetables escape. Bags can also float if the food you're cooking is less dense than water (think sous vide bacon with extra-fatty pieces).

With sous vide cooking, it's absolutely vital that your bags stay submerged and that trapped air bubbles are pushed to the top of the bag and away from the food. This is the only way to guarantee that your food is heating properly, which is important for both food safety and quality.

So how do you get a persistently floating bag to sink? All you've got to do is clamp a large binder clip (like these ACCO clips) on the bottom of the bag, then slip a heavy spoon into the mouth of the clip. The head of the spoon will keep it from falling out, and the weight should keep your food submerged. For especially stubborn bags, you can add a few spoons.

Add Ping-Pong Balls to Your Sous Vide Water Bath

If you cook something sous vide for a long period of time, the water in the bath container can dip to such a low level that your circulator will shut off completely. This not only interrupts the cook time but can pose a serious risk to food safety. To prevent evaporation, you can cover your water bath with plastic wrap or aluminum foil, or cut a sous-vide-device-shaped hole out of an appropriately fitting lid, but I've found that the easiest solution is to dump a bunch of Ping-Pong balls in the bath.

By floating a layer of Ping-Pong balls on the water's surface, you'll simultaneously insulate your bath and help steam to condense and drip back down. The great thing is that Ping-Pong balls will conform to the shape of whatever container you're using and allow you to easily drop bags in and lift them from the bath mid-cook. They're also completely reusable. I keep about 50 of them stored with the rest of my sous vide kit.

FREQUENTLY ASKED SOUS VIDE QUESTIONS

q: What are the downsides to cooking sous vide?

None! Just kidding. Sous vide–style precision cooking is a technique, another tool in your arsenal, and, as with all techniques, there's a tradeoff. Here are a few of the most immediate:

- **It takes longer.** For instance, a traditionally cooked steak goes from fridge to plate in 15 to 20 minutes (a bit longer if you have to preheat your oven); a sous vide steak will take an hour or more. A barbecue pork shoulder on an outdoor smoker or in the oven can take six to eight hours; with sous vide, it can take over a day. However, with sous vide cooking, this time is almost 100% hands-off.

- **You will not achieve the exact same sear.** Flag-waving sous vide zealots may claim otherwise, but the rapid sear you can achieve after cooking sous vide will not be as thick or crusty as the sear you get from a traditional cooking method. Some folks prefer a thicker sear, while others prefer the thin sear achieved after sous vide cooking.
- **It often requires more equipment.** Cooking sous vide requires a precision cooker and a plastic bag or vacuum sealer, in addition to all the tools required for more traditional methods. Chances are, if you're reading this article, you already have those extra tools.

Remember this: Sous vide is not a silver bullet or a panacea meant to solve all of your cooking problems or to replace more traditional methods. It's a tool meant to expand your options.

q: Can sous vide meats get a good crust?

Sure can! I mean, just look at this baby here:

That was cooked using a combination of a ripping-hot cast iron skillet and a propane torch. It's true that the crust will not be as thick as on a traditionally cooked steak, but it's definitely browned. Similarly, the skin seared on a piece of sous vide chicken breast will not be as thin or well rendered as the skin on a pan-seared chicken breast. Whether or not this is a bug or a feature is up to you to decide.

q: When should I season my meat?

People often ask if it's ok to salt and bag meat before storing, or even freezing. Salt is more than just a flavoring agent. It can have a strong impact on the texture of meat as it dissolves muscle proteins and works its way inside. Seasoning immediately before bagging and cooking will have a minimal effect, but storing the meat with salt can alter its texture, turning it from raw and meaty to somewhat firm and ham-like with time. Some folks find this texture off-putting. I personally don't mind it, particularly in meats you would traditionally brine, like chicken, pork, or fish. To avoid this texture in red meat, it's best to season it immediately before cooking, or after cooking sous vide and before searing.

q: Time ranges in sous vide recipes seem really broad. What happens if I leave food cooking for longer than the maximum time?

Sous vide cooking is extremely forgiving! If you see a time range like "1 to 4 hours" in one of our recipes, that's because within that range, there will be little to no detectable difference in quality or safety.

What if you accidentally cook for longer? Is it dangerous? So long as you're cooking at above 130°F (54°C), there are no real health risks associated with prolonged sous vide cooking. You will, however, eventually notice a difference in texture. For best results, I don't recommend cooking any longer than the maximum recommended time for each cut and temperature range. And never cook for longer than four hours if cooking below 130°F.

q: Should I put olive oil or butter in the bag?

I've seen recipes that recommend adding fat to the bag, though none that offer plausible reasons for doing so. To test whether or not it adds anything to the process, I cooked various meats—steaks, pork chops, chicken, fish, et cetera—side by side: one with nothing added to the bag, one with olive oil, and one with butter. I also repeated the test with herbs and aromatics added to each bag.

Turns out that for meats with a naturally high amount of flavorful fat—steaks, lamb chops, heavily marbled pork—adding extra fat to the bag only ends up diluting flavor. You're better off leaving it out. For leaner meats, like fish or chicken, added fat can mean a little added flavor, though you should always ask yourself whether that extra fat is a flavor you want.

q: Can I add fresh aromatics to the sous vide bag?

Yes, you can. Fresh herbs like thyme, rosemary, or parsley sprigs, or raw aromatics like shallots and garlic, can be added to the bag before cooking. Because sous vide can concentrate flavors, start with a small amount the first time you use aromatics in sous vide cooking. (Some people don't like the flavor of sous vide garlic and prefer a small dash of garlic powder instead.) If you are searing your meat afterward, adding the same aromatics to the pan as you sear will bolster that flavor.

q: Can I add a spice rub to my bag?

Yes, you can, but spice rubs behave quite differently under sous vide conditions than under standard cooking conditions. Normally, aromatic compounds will dissipate into the air in the kitchen or over your grill. At the same time, moisture dissipates, which means that what's left of your spices sticks firmly to your meat. with sous vide cooking, there's no way for that flavor to escape the bag. Meanwhile, spices

rubbed on the surface of the meat have a tendency to get rinsed off by any juices that are being expressed.

The short answer is that it's very tough to predict exactly how spices are going to react in a sous vide bag. If you have a well-tested recipe you've enjoyed or a new recipe from a reputable source, go for it. But if you're experimenting, start with just a small amount (perhaps half of what you'd typically use), and go up from there. I've found that if I want spice flavor, it's often better to rub the spices into the meat after the sous vide cooking phase and before the final searing phase.

q: Is it dangerous to cook with garlic sous vide?

Sous vide cooking takes place in an anaerobic (oxygen-free) environment. The bacteria that cause botulism grow in oxygen-free environments. However, almost any sous vide cooking will take place at temperatures high enough to actively destroy any Clostridium botulinum bacteria. Spores can survive, however, so it is recommended that you either consume or freeze any at-risk foods immediately.

q: Should I pre-sear my meat?

After repeated testing and blind taste tests, I've found that pre-searing meats—that is, browning a steak before it goes into the sous vide bag, then browning it a second time just before serving—plays at most a very minimal role in improving flavor or texture. In most cases, the difference is imperceptible, and, in fact, pre-searing can sometimes lead to more overcooked meat around the outer edges. I prefer the ease and convenience of simply placing food in the bag raw before cooking, and leaving the searing to a single step at the end.

q: What about deep-frying instead of searing after cooking sous vide?

Deep-frying a steak or pork chop cooked sous vide can be a lot of fun, and it's true that you'll very quickly get an evenly browned crust on your meat, but there are a few downsides. First, the obvious: You need a large vessel filled with hot oil in order to deep-fry. If you're anything like me, you like to keep deep-frying at home to a minimum.

Perhaps more importantly, deep-frying has a relatively low maximum temperature that is defined by the oil's smoke point—generally around 450°F (230°C) or so. Oil in a skillet or a steak on the grill, on the other hand, can achieve temperatures a couple hundred degrees higher than this, allowing your meat to char rather than simply brown. For me, this charring and the intense flavor it brings is one of the hallmarks of a great steak experience.

q: Can I use a torch alone to finish a steak or chop?

I would strongly recommend against it. Torches are extremely intense heat sources that basically follow the inverse-square law: Their intensity dissipates with the square of the distance from the torch head. What this means is that any unevenness in the surface of your steak gets amplified—areas that are slightly elevated will singe before areas that are lower will even begin to brown properly.

While it's possible to get reasonable browning with a torch by holding it at a distance great enough that this effect is minimized, or by using a dissipator like the Searzall, and by making multiple slow passes across the surface of a steak, I find the effort and time needed to do so much more of a headache than simply cooking a steak in a hot skillet, with the torch as an added heat source. Besides, a steak cooked with a skillet-and-torch combo comes out with a better crust in the end.

q: What's the best torch for searing meat?

Standard propane torches with trigger-start ignition heads have trouble staying lit when inverted. This can be a problem when you're frantically trying to relight a torch as your steak sears in a hot skillet. Adding a Searzall unit will not only ensure that the flame stays lit but will also diffuse the flame, allowing you to get a more even sear.

Want to keep things on the cheap? I find that a standard butane gas canister used with a high-intensity torch head, like the Iwatani Torch Burner, does a more than adequate job. It's what I pack in my travel cooking kit.

q: Will food acquire any off aromas when finished with a torch?

Finishing a steak or chop with nothing but the naked flame of a propane or butane torch can indeed leave an off, gasoline-like aroma on the surface of the meat due to imperfect combustion. However, if you are using the skillet/torch combination method, the added heat from the skillet will help the fuel combust more completely, while the dilution of any un-combusted fuel by the fat and juices in the pan will render it completely imperceptible.

If, for some reason, you do choose to sear with a torch alone, a Searzall unit will improve combustion efficiency and completely eliminate those odors.

q: Can I chill and reheat my food after cooking it sous vide if I haven't opened the bag?

It's true that given a high enough temperature (130°F/54°C or higher) and a long enough time period (several hours), the contents of a sealed sous vide bag should be close to sterile, which means that rapid chilling via an ice bath, followed by rapid reheating, should pose no significant health risks. (See the note on botulism above.) But in some cases, it can adversely affect results. with traditionally slow-cooked meats, like chicken thighs, pork shoulders, or pork belly, it poses no real problem; the texture will be largely unaffected. But with quick-cooking meats, like steaks, chops, chicken breasts, shrimp, and fish, repeatedly heating and cooling can lead to dry texture. I strongly recommend cooking those foods immediately before searing and serving.

Word of warning: Never chill and reheat any food that has been cooked or held at a temperature lower than 130°F. These temperatures are not high enough to destroy dangerous bacteria.

q: Can I cook bagged food straight from the freezer?

Yes! Just make sure to add a little extra time to account for thawing. For a thick steak or chop, that may be an extra half hour to hour. For small shrimp or thin chicken breasts, an extra 15 minutes should do.

q: Does sous vide meat need to rest?

Traditionally cooked steaks need to rest. That is, they need to be placed aside for five to 10 minutes before cutting and serving. This resting period is to allow time for the temperature gradient within the steak to even out. The cooler center is gently heated by the hotter outer edges, while the edges in turn lose some of their heat to the outside world. Even temperature is important: It's what prevents a steak from leaking its juices everywhere the moment it's been sliced open.

Because a sous vide steak cooks from edge to edge with more or less perfect evenness, there is no temperature gradient inside. A medium-rare steak should be 130°F from the very center to the outer edge, with only the outer surfaces hotter after searing. Sous vide steaks can be served immediately after searing. The very minimal resting they need will happen on the way from the kitchen to the table.

BREAKFAST RECIPES

Sous Vide Easy Polenta

Ingredients: Servings: 2   Cooking Time: 2 Hours 10 Mins. Cooking Temperature: 190 F / 87

1/2 C. ground polenta	2 C. milk
4 oz. Parmesan cheese, grated	3 tbsp. butter
	Pepper
	Salt

Directions:
Fill and preheat sous vide water oven at 190 F/ 87   Add milk, butter and polenta in large zip-lock bag and remove all air from bag before closing.   Place zip-lock bag into the preheated water bath and cook for 2 hours, Remove bag from water bath. Open and pour into the bowl.   Add grated Parmesan cheese and stir well. Season with pepper and salt.   Serve and enjoy.

Nutrition: Info Calories 596, Fat 38 g, Carbohydrates 45 g, Protein 23 g, Sugar 14 g, Cholesterol 106 mg

Egg And Chorizo Toast

Ingredients: Servings: 2 To 4   Cooking Time: 20 Mins Cooking Temperature: 167°f

2 tbsp. of cream	2 medium links of precooked chorizo or pork sausage, sliced into rounds
2 tbsp. of milk	
2 tbsp. of melted butter	
6 large eggs	4 slices of precooked French toast
salt and pepper	
For Serving:	sliced green onions

Directions:
Attach the sous vide immersion circulator to a Cambro container or pot with water using an adjustable clamp and preheat the water to 167°F.   Add the cream, milk, and melted butter to a large mixing bowl, and whisk until well combined. Whisk in the eggs, season with salt and pepper, and stir until the ingredients are well incorporated.   Pour the mixture into a cooking pouch, remove excess air and seal the pouch. Immerse the bag into the water bath and set the cooking time to 15 minutes. Gently massage the bag every 5 Mins. to evenly distribute the ingredients and prevent the formation of clumps. Remove from the water bath and gently massage the egg mixture to break into smaller pieces. While cooking the eggs, reheat the sausage and French toast in a skillet and set aside.   Place a slice of toast on one serving plate, add a layer of sliced chorizo, and top with eggs. Garnish with green onions and serve immediately.

Parmesan Omelette

Ingredients: Servings: 2   Cooking Time: 20 Mins Cooking Temperature: 165°f

4 large eggs	1 tbsp. unsalted butter, diced
2 tbsp. minced scallion greens	salt and pepper
2 tbsp. finely grated Parmesan cheese	fresh parsley, chopped, for serving

Directions:
Attach the sous vide immersion circulator to a Cambro container or pot with water using an adjustable clamp and preheat the water to 165°F.   In a large bowl, add all ingredients except parsley, season with salt and pepper, and whisk until well combined.   Pour the mixture into a cooking pouch, remove excess air and seal the bag. Immerse the bag in the water bath and set the cooking time to 10 minutes. Remove the bag and carefully press down to form a flat round. Return to the water bath and set the cooking time to an additional 10 minutes.   Remove the bag from the water bath and let cool for 5 Mins. before opening.   Transfer onto a serving platter, cut into two portions, and serve immediately with minced parsley on top.

Sous Vide Coconut Congee

Ingredients: Servings: 3   Cooking Time: 1 Hour 40 Mins. Cooking Temperature: 190 F / 88

1/2 C. short grain rice	1/2 C. sugar
1/2 tbsp. pumpkin pie spice	2 C. coconut milk
	2 C. water
	Salt

Directions:
Fill and set sous vide water oven at 190 F/ 88   Add rice, water, coconut milk, sugar and pumpkin pie spice in large ziplock bag and remove all air from bag before sealing.   Place zip-lock bag into the water oven and cook for 1 hour 30 minutes.   Remove bag from water bath. Open and transfer in bowl.   Season with salt and serve.

Nutrition: Info Calories 609, Fat 35 g, Carbohydrates 65 g, Protein 9 g, Sugar 38 g, Cholesterol 0 mg

Jalapeno Egg Cups

Ingredients: Servings: 4   Cooking Time: 1½ Hours Cooking Temperature: 172°f

6 large eggs
¼ C. milk or cream
4 strips precooked pancetta bacon

1 jalapeño, seeded and sliced
¼ C. Cheddar cheese

Directions:

Attach the sous vide immersion circulator to a Cambro container or pot with water using an adjustable clamp and preheat the water to 172°F. Lightly grease four canning or mason jars with oil or cooking spray and set aside. Add the milk and eggs to a bowl and whisk until well combined. Set aside. Add a slice of bacon on the bottom of each jar, divide the egg mixture into four equal portions, and pour into the jars. Sprinkle with jalapeño and top with cheese. Cover with lids or seal the jars and immerse into the water bath. Set the cooking time to 1½ hours. Remove the jars when ready and let rest for about 5 Mins. before removing the egg C. from the jars. Transfer onto a serving platter and serve immediately

Fragrant Canadian Bacon

Ingredients: Servings: 6   Cooking Time: 9 Hours

1 tsp. sage
½ tsp. ground ginger
½ tsp. ground white pepper
1 tbsp. sugar

2 tbsp. olive oil
2-lb. Canadian ham
1 tbsp. dried parsley

Directions:

Slice the Canadian bacon. Then combine the ground ginger, ground white pepper, sugar, olive oil and dried parsley in the bowl. Mix it up with the help of the fork. After this, sprinkle the sliced bacon with the prepared spicy mixture. Put the sliced bacon in the zipper lock bag. Seal it. Set the Sous Vide to 146 F and put the sealed bag with the bacon there. Cook the bacon for 9 hours. When the time is over – discard the bacon from the sealed bag and chill it little. Serve the bacon immediately. Enjoy!

Nutrition: Info Calories 215, fat 7, fiber 0, carbohydrates 85, protein 31

French Scrambled Eggs

Ingredients: Servings: 4 To 6   Cooking Time: 30 Mins Cooking Temperature: 165°f

6 large eggs
4½ tbsp. unsalted butter, melted and slightly cooled

¼ C. heavy cream
1 tsp. kosher salt, or to taste
1 tsp. ground pepper, or to taste

Directions:

Attach the sous vide immersion circulator to a Cambro container or pot with water using an adjustable clamp and preheat the water to 165°F. Add all ingredients to a large bowl and whisk until well combined. Transfer to a cooking pouch, remove excess air and seal the bag before submerging into the water bath. Set the cooking time to 30 minutes. After 20 minutes, remove the bag and gently massage the mixture to thoroughly mix the ingredients and return the bag to the water bath to continue cooking. Remove the bag from the water bath, briefly massage the egg mixture, and transfer the scrambled egg onto a large plate before serving.

Basic Steel Cut Oats

Ingredients: Servings: 4   Cooking Time: 8 Hours Cooking Temperature: 155°f

1 C. of steel cut oats, rolled oats, or oat groats

3 C. of water
¼ tsp. salt

Directions:

Attach the sous vide immersion circulator to a Cambro container or pot with water using an adjustable clamp and preheat the water to 155°F. Combine all ingredients in a cooking pouch, remove any excess air and seal the bag. Immerse bag into the water bath and set the cooking time to 8 hours. Remove from the water bath and let rest for about 5 Mins. before opening. Divide the oats into four equal portions and transfer into separate serving bowls. Top with desired ingredients and serve warm.

French Toast

Ingredients: Servings: 2   Cooking Time: 1 Hour Cooking Temperature: 147°f

2 large eggs
125 mL (½ cup) milk
4 slices of stale bread

½ tsp. ground cinnamon
butter, for frying
sugar, for serving

Directions:

Attach the sous vide immersion circulator to a Cambro container or pot with water using an adjustable clamp and preheat the water to 147°F. Add the milk, eggs, and cinnamon to a mixing bowl and whisk until well combined. Dip the bread slices into the milk-egg mixture until fully coated. Place a slice of bread in a small cooking pouch and repeat the procedure with rest of the bread slices, placing each piece of bread in a separate bag. Vacuum seal the bags and set the cooking time to 1 hour. Remove bread from the bags and carefully transfer to a plate. While waiting, preheat a skillet over medium-high heat and lightly grease the bottom with butter. In batches, fry the bread slices for 2 to 3 Mins. or until lightly golden on each side. Remove from heat, transfer to a serving plate, and sprinkle with sugar before serving.

Sous Vide Yummy Cream Topped Banana

Ingredients: Servings: 2   Cooking Time: 40 Mins. Cooking Temperature: 176 F / 80

3 ripe bananas, peeled and cut into pieces	1 cinnamon stick 1/2 C. brown sugar
3 cloves	Whipped cream

Directions:
Fill and preheat sous vide water oven at 176 F/ 80° Add bananas, cloves, cinnamon and brown sugar in zip-lock bag and remove all air from bag before sealing. Submerge zip-lock bag in preheated water bath and cook for 30 minutes. Remove bag from water bath and set aside to cool. Open zip-lock bag and discard cloves and cinnamon. Transfer bananas in bowl and topped with whipped cream. Serve immediately and enjoy.

Nutrition: Info Calories 295, Fat 6 g, Carbohydrates 70 g, Protein 0 g, Sugar 58 g, Cholesterol 0 mg

Yogurt

Ingredients: Servings: 4   Cooking Time: 24 Hours Cooking Temperature: 115°f

2 to 2½ C. of whole milk	40 g live-culture yogurt

Directions:
Attach the sous vide immersion circulator to a Cambro container or pot with water using an adjustable clamp and preheat the water to 115°F. In a medium pot, add the milk and heat to 180°F. Cook until the milk is just heated through while stirring and scraping the bottom of the pot to prevent scalding or burning. While heating the milk, prepare an ice bath and immerse the pot to stop further cooking until it cools to 110°F. Place the yogurt in a large mixing bowl, add half of the milk and stir until well combined. Add the rest of the milk and stir until smooth. Transfer the mixture into a large mason or canning jar and seal properly. Immerse into the water bath and set cooking for 24 hours. Remove the jar from the water bath. Strain the yogurt using a few layers of cheesecloth into a mixing bowl in the refrigerator for at least 4-12 hours. Serve yogurt with your favorite fruits, vegetables, or other flavorings.

Vegetable Frittata Cups

Ingredients: Servings: 4   Cooking Time: 1 Hour Cooking Temperature: 176°f

1 tbsp. extra-virgin olive oil	kosher salt 1 C. butternut squash, peeled and diced
1 medium onion, chopped	
4 cloves garlic, minced	6 oz. oyster mushrooms, trimmed and roughly chopped
1 small rutabaga, peeled and diced	
2 medium carrots, peeled and diced	¼ C. fresh parsley leaves, minced
1 medium parsnip, peeled and diced	pinch red pepper flakes
	5 large eggs
	¼ C. whole milk

Directions:
Attach the sous vide immersion circulator to a Cambro container or pot with water using an adjustable clamp and preheat the water to 176°F. Prepare four canning or mason jars and brush the inner part with oil or cooking spray. Add the oil to a large skillet over medium-high heat. Add the onion, sprinkle with salt, and cook until the onion is soft and translucent, stirring regularly. Add the garlic and cook for an additional 30 seconds, or until lightly brown and fragrant. Add the remaining vegetables except mushrooms, season with salt, and cook for about 10 Mins. or until the vegetables are soft and tender. Add the mushrooms, cook for another 3 to 5 Mins. and stir in the parsley and red pepper flakes. Remove from heat and let cool completely. While cooling the vegetables, mix the milk and eggs in a large bowl and whisk until well combined. Divide the cooled vegetables into four equal portions and transfer into the prepared jars. Pour the egg mixture into the jars to cover the vegetables fully and cover with lids. Immerse the jars into the water bath and set the cooking time for 1 hour. Remove the jars from the water bath, transfer onto a wire cooling rack and let cool completely. Carefully open the lids, let rest for 5 Mins. and transfer to a plate before serving.

Bacon And Gruyere Egg Cups

Ingredients: Servings: 4 To 6   Cooking Time: 1½ Hours Cooking Temperature: 172°f

6 eggs	¼ C. milk or cream
2 to 3 strips of	

| bacon, halved and cooked | ¼ C. Gruyere cheese |
| | ¼ C. Monterey jack cheese |

Directions:

Attach the sous vide immersion circulator to a Cambro container or pot with water using an adjustable clamp and preheat the water to 172°F. Lightly brush 4 or 6 small canning/mason jars with oil or cooking spray and set aside.   Add the milk and eggs to a mixing bowl and whisk until well combined.   Place one slice of bacon on the bottom of each jar and top with Gruyere cheese. Pour in egg mixture and add a layer of Monterey jack cheese. Cover with lid or seal the jars, immerse the jars into the water bath, and set the cooking time to 1½ hours.   Remove the jars from the water bath and let rest for about 5 Mins. before opening. Carefully transfer onto a serving platter and serve warm.

Toasted Bread Pudding

Ingredients: Servings: 4   Cooking Time: 2 Hours
Cooking Temperature: 170°f

3 C. brioche cubes, toasted	dash of cinnamon
2 large eggs	For the Toppings:
¼ C. sugar	sugar, as needed,
1 tsp. vanilla extract or paste	for brûlée topping
1 tbsp. butter	maple syrup
2 C. whole milk	½ C. heavy cream, whipped
	berries

Directions:

Preheat oven to 350 degrees.   Attach the sous vide immersion circulator to a Cambro container or pot with water using an adjustable clamp and preheat the water to 170°F.   Place the cubed brioche breads on a greased baking sheet and toast for about 6 to 8 minutes, or until golden brown. Remove from the oven and set aside.   In a mixing bowl, add eggs, sugar, and vanilla and stir until well combined. Set aside.   Combine the butter, milk, and cinnamon in a medium saucepan over medium heat and cook until the mixture starts to form steam and bubbles, stirring occasionally. Remove the saucepan from heat.   Gradually pour in the egg mixture into the milk mixture while stirring constantly, until the ingredients are well incorporated. Add the toasted brioche slowly while stirring regularly until the brioche is evenly coated with the milk mixture. Let stand for about 2 Mins. for the bread to absorb the liquid.   While soaking the bread, grease four canning or mason jars with oil or cooking spray. Divide the soaked bread into four equal portions and transfer into the greased jars. Seal the jars, immerse into the water bath and set the

cooking time to 2 hours.   Carefully remove the jars from the water bath and let rest for about 5 Mins. before opening and serving.   Transfer the bread pudding to separate serving bowls or plates and sprinkle sugar on top.   Blowtorch the sugar until caramelized and drizzle with maple syrup. Add a dollop of cream and serve with berries on top.

Brioche Buns with Cheesy Egg Topping

Ingredients: Servings: 4   Cooking Time: 45 Mins
Cooking Temperature: 149°f

4 large eggs	4 brioche buns
½ C. grated Cheddar cheese	2 scallions, green parts only, thinly sliced
½ C. grated Parmesan cheese	

Directions:

Attach the sous vide immersion circulator to a Cambro container or pot with water using an adjustable clamp and preheat the water to 149°F. Carefully immerse the eggs into the water bath and set the cooking time to 45 minutes. Remove from the water bath and set aside. While cooking the eggs, pinch out or remove the center part of the each bun to fit the size of an egg. Repeat with the rest of the bread and set aside. Preheat oven broiler to high, line a baking sheet with foil, and set aside. Carefully crack an egg on each brioche bun and add 2 tbsp. each of Cheddar and Parmesan cheese. Transfer onto the prepared baking sheet and broil for about 3 to 5 minutes, or until the cheese starts to melt and the top is lightly golden. Remove from the oven, transfer to a wire rack, and let rest for a couple of Mins. before serving.   Transfer onto a serving platter, garnish with sliced scallions, and serve immediately.

Ham And quail Egg Breakfast Sandwich

Ingredients: Servings: 4   Cooking Time: 45 Mins
Cooking Temperature: 140°f

one loaf of baguette, sliced into 8 portions (diagonal cuts or bias-cuts)	8 quail eggs
	ripe red tomatoes, sliced into rounds
	cheddar cheese, sliced
4 slices of smoked ham, cut into strips	

Directions:

Attach the sous vide immersion circulator to a Cambro container or pot with water using an adjustable clamp and preheat the water to 140°F. Carefully immerse the eggs in the water bath and set the cooking time to 30 minutes. Remove the eggs from the water bath and immerse in an ice bath for about 3 Mins. to stop further cooking. Transfer to a plate and set aside. While cooking the eggs, fry the ham in a non-stick skillet for about 3 to 4 Mins. or until golden brown. Repeat on other side. Transfer to a serving plate and set aside. Reheat the baguette slices in separate batches in the same pan until crisp and lightly golden. Remove from heat and set aside. Add a slice of cheese, a layer of ham, and tomatoes on four slices of baguette and place two eggs on top. Cover with the remaining bread and secure the sandwich by inserting a toothpick in the center. Serve immediately.

Overnight Oatmeal with Stewed Fruit Compote

Ingredients: Servings: 2   Cooking Time: 6-10 Hours Cooking Temperature: 155°f

For the Oatmeal:	pinch of cinnamon
1 C. oatmeal	For the Stewed
(quick-cooking	Fruit Compote:
rolled oats)	2 tbsp. white
3 C. water	sugar
pinch of salt	½ C. water
¾ of a C. dried	2 drops vanilla
fruit (any mix of	extract
the following –	zest of half a
cherries,	lemon, finely
blueberries,	grated
golden raisins,	zest of half an
apricots,	orange, finely
cranberries)	grated

Directions:
Attach the sous vide immersion circulator to a Cambro container or pot with water using an adjustable clamp and preheat the water to 155°F. Add all ingredients for the oatmeal mixture to a bowl and stir until well combined. Transfer into a cooking pouch, remove excess air and seal the pouch. In a separate bowl, add all ingredients for the compote and mix until well combined. Transfer into a separate pouch, remove air and seal. Immerse the bags into the water bath and set the cooking time for 6 to 10 hours. Remove bags from the water bath and gently massage to distribute the ingredients properly. Let rest for about 5 Mins. before opening and serving. Divide the oatmeal into two portions, place in serving bowls and serve with fruit compote on top.

Perfect Soft-boiled Eggs

Ingredients: Servings: 2   Cooking Time: 1½ To 2 Hrs Cooking Temperature: 145°f

4 large eggs   salt, to taste

Directions:
Attach the sous vide immersion circulator to a Cambro container or pot with water using an adjustable clamp and preheat the water to 145°F. Gently drop the eggs into the water bath and set the time to 110 mins for soft-boiled eggs with slightly runny yolks and 155 mins for soft-boiled eggs with slightly firm yolks. When the eggs are ready, immerse them in an ice bath or rinse with cool running water to stop further cooking. Gently crack the eggs or use an eggshell cutter to remove the shells. Transfer into individual egg cups, season with salt, and serve warm.

Breakfast Sausage

Ingredients: Servings: 4   Cooking Time: 3 Hours

1-lb. breakfast	½ tsp. oregano
sausages	1 tsp. salt
1 tsp. paprika	1 tsp. turmeric
¼ tsp. chili flakes	1 tsp. dried basil
1 tsp. cilantro	1 tbsp. butter

Directions:
Sprinkle the breakfast sausages with the paprika, chili flakes, cilantro, oregano, salt, turmeric, and dried basil. Mix the sausages gently and put them in the plastic bag. Seal the bag. Set the Sous Vide to 155 F and put the sealed bag with the sausages there. Cook the sausages for 3 hours. After this, remove the sealed bag with the sausages from the Sous Vide and chill it gently. Toss the butter in the skillet and preheat it to the high heat. Put the prepared sausages in the preheated skillet with the butter. Roast the sausages for 3 Mins. totally. Serve the cooked sausages hot. Enjoy!

Nutrition: Info Calories 297, fat 25, fiber 1, carbs 84, protein 18

Overnight Bacon

Ingredients: Servings: 4   Cooking Time: 8 To 48 Hours Cooking Temperature: 145°f

1 lb. thick-cut
bacon, still in its
package

Directions:
Attach the sous vide immersion circulator to a Cambro container or pot with water using an adjustable clamp and preheat the water to 145°F. Immerse the

packaged bacon into the water bath and set the cooking time for at least   Remove from water bath and let rest for 5 Mins. before opening.   While the bacon is cooling, preheat a large skillet over medium-high heat. Add one slice of bacon one at a time and cook for about 3 Mins. on each side, or until nicely browned and crisp. 5. Turn to cook the other side and transfer onto a plate lined with paper towels. Let rest for about five Mins. to drain excess oil from the bacon.   Transfer onto a serving platter and serve immediately.

DESSERTS RECIPES

Doce De Banana

Ingredients: Servings: 4   Cooking Time: 40 Mins.

5 small ripe bananas, firm but ripe, peeled and cut up into chunks	6 whole cloves Whipped cream for serving Vanilla ice-cream for serving
1 C. brown sugar 2 cinnamon sticks	

Directions:
Set up your Sous Vide immersion circulator to a temperature of 176-degrees Fahrenheit and prepare your water bath.   Put the bananas, brown sugar, cinnamon sticks, and cloves to a resealable bag.   Seal using the immersion method and cook for 30-40 minutes.   Remove the bag and allow the contents to cool.   Open the bag and remove the cinnamon sticks and cloves.   Serve warm in a bowl with a topping of whipped cream and vanilla ice cream.

Nutrition: Info   Per   serving:Calories: 310 ;Carbohydrate: 80g ;Protein: 1g ;Fat: 0g ;Sugar: 65g ;Sodium: 9mg

Sensuous White Chocolate Cheese Cake

Ingredients: Servings: 8   Cooking Time: 120 Mins.

16 oz. of cream cheese	1 tsp. of cake flour 1 tsp. of vanilla extract
¼ C. of sour cream	10 oz. of white chocolate
2 tbsp. of granulated sugar 1 large sized eggs	

Directions:
Carefully prepare your sous vide water bath to a temperature of 176° Fahrenheit using the immersion cooker   Take a medium sized bowl and mix your cream cheese, sugar, sour cream and mix everything on medium setting until combined well   with the mixer running, add your eggs one at a time, making sure to combine the previous one before adding another   Add cake flour, vanilla extract and mix everything for 3 seconds   Keep it on the side   Take a small microwave safe bowl and add white chocolate   Place your bowl in the microwave and heat it up on high settings in 30 second intervals until the whole chocolate has melted   Add your melted chocolate to the cheesecake batter and combine well   Divide the batter amongst eight 470nk glass canning jars and seal them up loosely   1 Place your jars in your water bath and let it cook for 2h ours   1 Remove the water bath   1 Place your jars in the fridge and let it chill for 4 hours   1 Serve with some toppings of seasonal fruit

Nutrition: Info Calories: 130, Protein 8g, Dietary Fiber: 4g

Balsamic Honey Shrub

Ingredients: Servings: 6   Cooking Time: 2 Hours 10 Mins.

1 C. water	½ C. honey
½ C. balsamic vinegar	Bourbon whiskey Club soda
1 tbsp. freshly grated ginger	Lime wedges

Directions:
Prepare a water bath and place the Sous Vide in it. Set to 134 F.   Place the water, vinegar, honey, and ginger in a vacuum-sealable bag. Release air by the water displacement method, seal and submerge the bag in the water bath. Cook for 2 hours.   Once the timer has stopped, remove the bag and drain the mixture. Allow chilling all night. Serve with one-part whiskey and one-part club soda with ice. Garnish with lime wedges.

Bacon Infused Bourbon

Ingredients: Servings: 8   Cooking Time: 60 Mins.

2 C. bourbon	8 oz. smoked bacon, cooked until crisp
3 tbsp. bacon fat reserved from cooking	3 tbsp. light brown sugar

Directions:
Prepare your Sous Vide water bath using your immersion circulator and raise the temperature to 150-degrees Fahrenheit.   Add all the listed ingredients to a resealable zip bag.   Seal using the immersion method. Cook for 1 hour.   Once done, take the bag out from the water bath and strain the contents through a fine-mesh strainer into a large bowl   Transfer the bourbon to the

refrigerator and chill until the pork fat solidifies on top. Skim off the fat Then, strain the bourbon a second time through a cheesecloth-lined strainer. Pass it to a storage container and store in the refrigerator.

Nutrition: Info Calories: 274 Carbohydrate: 14g Protein: 6g Fat: 19g Sugar: 13g Sodium: 316mg

Warm Vanilla quince

Ingredients: Servings: 2   Cooking Time: 50 Mins.

2 peeled quince	½ tsp. salt
1 vanilla bean	1 tbsp. butter
2 tbsp. dark brown sugar	Vanilla ice cream

Directions:
Prepare a water bath and place the Sous Vide in it. Set to 175 F. Slice the quince by the half. Remove the core. Combine the vanilla bean with brown sugar and salt. Soak vanilla seeds with the mixture. Place the quinces and the mixture in a vacuum-sealable bag. Release air by water displacement method, seal and submerge in the water bath. Cook for 45 minutes. Once the timer has stopped, remove the quinces and transfer to a bowls. Sprinkle the quinces with the butter sauce. Serve with vanilla ice cream.

Thai Basil Drink

Ingredients: Servings: 4   Cooking Time: 60 Mins.

1 bunch of Thai basil rinsed	1 C. water
	1 C. ultrafine sugar

Directions:
Prepare your Sous Vide water bath using your immersion circulator and raise the temperature to 180-degrees Fahrenheit. Add all the listed ingredients to a resealable zipper bag. Seal using the immersion method. Submerge underwater and cook for 1 hour. Once done, take the bag out from the water bath and transfer to an ice bath. Strain into a large bowl and transfer to a container Serve chilled!

Nutrition: Info Calories: 197 Carbohydrate: 19g Protein: 0g Fat: 0g Sugar: 16g Sodium: 159mg

Chocolate Chili Cake

Ingredients: Servings: 6   Cooking Time: 1 Hour 15 Mins.

4 large eggs	½ lb. chocolate chips
4oz. unsalted butter	½ tsp. chili powder
2 tbsp. cocoa powder	¼ C. brown sugar

Directions:
Preheat the Sous Vide cooker to 115F. Place the chocolate chips, and butter into Sous Vide bag. Submerge in water and cook 15 minutes. Remove the bag and set the cooker to 170F. Prepare 6 4oz. Mason jars by coating with cooking spray. Beat the eggs with brown sugar until fluffy. Stir in the chocolate, cocoa powder, and chili powder. Divide the mixture between prepared mason jars and apply the lid on finger tight only. Submerge the jars in a water bath for 1 hour. Finishing steps: Remove the jars and place onto wire rack to cool completely. Invert the cake onto a plate. Serve with raspberry ice cream

Nutrition: Info Calories 413 Total Fat 31g Total Carb 28g Dietary Fiber 9g Protein 6g

Basic Oatmeal From Scratch

Ingredients: Servings: 4   Cooking Time: 8 Hours 10 Mins.

1 C. oats	½ tsp. vanilla extract
3 C. water	Pinch of sea salt

Directions:
Prepare a water bath and place the Sous Vide in it. Set to 155 F. Combine all the ingredients in a vacumm-sealable bag. Release air by the water displacement method, seal and submerge the bag in water bath.Set the timer for 8 hours. Once the timer has stopped, remove the bag. Serve warm.

Strawberry Compote In The Easiest Way

Ingredients: Servings: 2   Cooking Time: 15 Mins.

200g of sliced strawberries	2 tsp. of vinegar
4 tbsp. of icing sugar	2 tsp. of lemon juice

Directions:
Prepare your water bath to a temperature of 182° Fahrenheit Take a bowl and add your sugar, lemon juice, balsamic vinegar and the sliced strawberries Add them to your heavy duty zip bag and seal it up using the water immersion method Cook it for 15 Mins. under water Once done, take it out and serve with some ice cream or yogurt as a fine toping

Nutrition: Info Calories: 152, Fat: 1g, Protein: 2g, Dietary Fiber: 3g

Honey Bourbon Cranberries

Ingredients: Servings: x   Cooking Time: 1 Hour
Cooking Temperature: 183°f

1 C. honey	½ oz. bourbon
7½ oz. fresh cranberries	1 tbsp. orange zest

Directions:
Attach the sous vide immersion circulator using an adjustable clamp to a Cambro container or pot filled with water and preheat to 183°F.   Into a cooking pouch, add all ingredients. Seal pouch tightly after squeezing out the excess air. Place pouch in sous vide bath and set the cooking time for 1 hour.   Remove pouch from sous vide bath and, with a towel, smash the cranberries in the pouch.   Serve warm.

Dark Chocolate Mousse

Ingredients: Servings: 4   Cooking Time: 24 Hours + 7 Hours

2/3 C. dark chocolate, chopped	½ C. double cream
½ C. milk	½ tsp. gelatin powder
	2 tbsp. cold water

Directions:
Preheat your Sous Vide machine to 194°F.   Place the chopped dark chocolate in the vacuum bag.   Seal the bag, put it into the water bath and set the timer for 6 hours.   When the time is up, pour the chocolate into a bowl and stir with a spoon.   Pour the milk into a pan and warm it over medium heat.   Soak the gelatin powder in 2 tbsp. cold water and dissolve it in the warm milk.   Carefully stir the milk-gelatin mixture into the chocolate paste until even and refrigerate for 25 minutes.   Remove from the fridge, stir again and refrigerate for another 25 minutes.   Beat the cream to peaks and combine with white chocolate mixture. Pour into single serve C. and refrigerate for 24 hours before serving.

Nutrition: Info   Per   serving:Calories   227, Carbohydrates 19 g, Fats 15 g, Protein 4 g

Brioche Bread Pudding

Ingredients: Servings: 4   Cooking Time: 120 Mins.

1 C. whole milk	¼ C. maple syrup
1 C. heavy cream	1 tsp. vanilla bean paste
½ C. granulated sugar	½ tsp. kosher salt
2 tbsp. orange	4 C. brioche, cut

juice	up into 1 inch
1 tbsp. orange zest	cubes

Directions:
Set up your Sous Vide immersion circulator to a temperature of 170-degrees Fahrenheit and prepare your water bath.   Take a large bowl and add the milk, heavy cream, sugar, maple syrup, orange zest, juice, vanilla bean paste, and salt.   Mix well and add the brioche. Toss well   Divide the mixture among 4 mason jars of 4-oz. size and gently seal them using the finger-tip method   Cook for 2 hours underwater.   Heat up your broiler and place the jars in the broiler.   Brown for 2-3 Mins. (with lids removed) and serve.

Nutrition: Info   Per   serving:Calories: 246 ;Carbohydrate: 19g ;Protein: 7g ;Fat: 16g ;Sugar: 3g ;Sodium: 164mg

Cinnamon Poached Pears with Ice Cream

Ingredients: Servings: 4   Cooking Time: 1 Hour 15 Mins.

3 peeled pears	Zest of 1 lemon
3 C. hard apple cider	1 vanilla bean, split
1 C. sugar	1 cinnamon stick
	Ice cream for serving

Directions:
Prepare a water bath and place the Sous Vide in it. Set to 194 F.   Place all the ingredients in a vacuum-sealable bag. Release air by the water displacement method, seal and submerge the bag in the water bath. Cook for 60 minutes. Once the timer has stopped, remove the pears and set aside. Drain the juices into a hot pot. Cook for 10 minutes. Cut the pears by the half and remove the seeds. Serve ice cream and top with the pears.

Carrot Muffins

Ingredients: Servings: 10   Cooking Time: 3 Hours 15 Mins.

1 C. flour	1 tsp. lemon juice
3 eggs	1 tbsp. coconut flour
½ C. butter	
¼ C. heavy cream	¼ tsp. salt
2 carrots, grated	½ tsp. baking soda

Directions:
Prepare a water bath and place the Sous Vide in it. Set to 195 F.   Whisk the wet ingredients in one bowl and

combine the dry ones in another. Gently combine the two mixtures together. Divide the mixture between 5 mason jars (Do not fill more than halfway. Use more jars if needed). Seal the jars and submerge in water bath.Set the timer for 3 hours. Once the timer has stopped, remove the jars. Cut into halves and serve.

Key Lime Pie

Ingredients: Servings: x   Cooking Time: 30 Mins
Cooking Temperature: 180°f

For Filling:	For Crust:
1 x 14-oz. can	1½ C. graham
sweetened	cracker crumbs
condensed milk	2 tbsp. granulated
½ C. fresh key	sugar
lime juice	For Topping:
4 egg yolks	½ C. heavy
⅓ C. plus 1 tsp.	whipping cream
butter, melted and	2 key limes, cut
divided	into slices

Directions:
Attach the sous vide immersion circulator using an adjustable clamp to a Cambro container or pot filled with water and preheat to 180°F.   For the filling: in a bowl, add all ingredients and beat until well-combined. Into a cooking pouch, add filling mixture. Seal pouch tightly after squeezing out the excess air. Place pouch in sous vide bath and set the cooking time for 30 minutes. Meanwhile, for the crust: evenly grease an 8-inch, round springform pan with 1 tsp. of butter.   Into a bowl, add remaining butter, graham crackers and sugar, and mix until well-combined.   Place the mixture evenly into the prepared pan.   with the back of a spoon, press crust mixture evenly to a smooth surface. Refrigerate until hard and set.   Remove the pouch from sous vide bath and carefully massage it to mix the filling mixture. Carefully open the pouch and place filling mixture evenly over crust.   Keep aside to cool for 30 minutes. After cooling, transfer the pie into refrigerator for at least 2 hours (or until set).   Into a bowl, add whipped cream and beat until soft peaks form.   Transfer whipped cream into a piping bag. with a medium nozzle, decorate pie according to your style.   Garnish with lime slices. Cut and serve.

Poached Pears

Ingredients: Servings: x   Cooking Time: 1 Hour 10 Mins Cooking Temperature: 176°f

brandy *	vanilla extract, as
white wine *	required
water *	4 pears, peeled
sugar *	and cored
2 strips orange	whipped cream, as
peel	required
cinnamon stick *	
star anise *	

Directions:
Attach the sous vide immersion circulator using an adjustable clamp to a Cambro container or pot filled with water and preheat to 176°F.   In a pan, mix brandy, wine, water, sugar, orange peel strips, cinnamon stick and star anise over a low heat and cook until heated sugar is dissolved.   Stir in vanilla extract and remove from heat. Keep aside to cool.   Into a cooking pouch, add pears and cooled syrup. Seal pouch tightly after squeezing out the excess air. Place pouch in sous vide bath and set the cooking time for 1 hour.   Remove pouches from sous vide bath and immediately plunge into a large bowl of ice water to cool.   Place pears onto a plate, transferring cooking liquid into a pan.   Place pan over stove and cook until a syrupy consistency is reached.   Pour syrup over pears and serve with a dollop of whipped cream.

Créme Brûlée

Ingredients: Servings: 6   Cooking Time: 1 Hour

6 egg yolks	1/2 tsp. salt
1/2 tsp. vanilla	2 1/2 C. heavy
extract	cream
6 tbsp. white	2 tbsp. brown
sugar /divided	sugar

Directions:
Preheat water to 175°F in a sous vide cooker or with an immersion circulator.   For the custard, whisk egg yolks, vanilla, salt and 4 tbsp. sugar until smooth. Slowly pour cream into yolk mixture, whisking constantly. Let custard mixture stand for about 30 Mins. to allow mixture to settle, then skim any remaining bubbles.   Slowly pour custard into six 4-oz. canning jars. Gently stir custard if necessary to remove any bubbles. Close jars fingertip tight, submerge in water and cook for 1 hour.   Remove jars from water and let stand until cool enough to touch. Tighten jar lids and chill custard overnight.   For the topping, preheat oven to broil. In a small bowl, mix brown sugar with remaining 2 tbsp. white sugar. Remove jar lids and evenly sprinkle sugar mixture over custard. Place jars under broiler until sugar melts, about 2 minutes, watching carefully so sugar doesn't burn. Carefully remove jars from oven and serve immediately. Enjoy!

Nutrition: Info Calories: 284; Total Fat: 23g; Saturated Fat: 13g; Protein: 4g; Carbs: 17g; Fiber: 0g; Sugar: 15g

Vanilla Berry Pudding

Ingredients: Servings: 6   Cooking Time: 2 Hours 32 Mins.

1 C. mixed fresh berries	2 C. heavy cream
4 slices challah, cubed	1 C. milk
6 egg yolks	2 tsp. almond extract
1⅛ C. superfine sugar	1 vanilla pod, halved, seeds reserved

Directions:
Prepare a water bath and place the Sous Vide in it. Set to 172 F.   Preheat the oven to 350 F. Place bread cubes in a baking tray and toast for 5 minutes. Set aside. with an electric mixer, mix the egg yolks and sugar until creamy.   Heat a saucepan over medium heat and pour in cream and milk. Cook until boiled. Add in almond extract, vanilla pod seeds and vanilla pod. Lower the heat and cook for 4-5 minutes. Set aside and allow to cool for 2-3 minutes.   Once the vanilla mixture has cooled, pour a small amount of the cream into the egg mixture and combine. Repeat the process with each egg. Combine the bread cubes with the egg-cream mixture and let the bread absorb the liquid. Add the berries and combine well. Divide the mixture into six mason jars. Seal with a lid and submerge the jars in the water bath. Cook for 2 hours.

Sweet Potatoes with Maple & Cinnamon Sauce

Ingredients: Servings: 8   Cooking Time: 2 Hours 45 Mins.

2 lb. sweet potatoes, sliced	¼ C. maple syrup
½ C. butter	1 C. chopped walnuts
2 lemons, juice and zest	1 cinnamon stick
	¼ C. brown sugar

Directions:
Prepare a water bath and place the Sous Vide in it. Set to 155 F. Place the potatoes and 1/4 C. of butter in a vacuum-sealable bag. Release air by water displacement method, seal and submerge in the water bath. Cook for 2 hours. Once done, remove the potatoes and pat them dry. Transfer to a baking tray.   Preheat the oven to 350 F. Heat a saucepan and stir 1/4 C. of butter, brown sugar, maple syrup, lemon zest and juice, walnuts, salt, and cinnamon stick. Pour the sauce over the potatoes and discard the cinnamon stick. Bake for 30 minutes. Serve warm.

Cheesy Egvfgg Bites

Ingredients: Servings: 6   Cooking Time: 1 Hour

6 pieces of eggs	¼ tsp. of salt
½ ac up of grated hard cheese	6 pieces of 4 oz. canning jars
¼ C. of cream cheese	

Directions:
Prepare your sous vide water bath and heat it to a temperature of 172° Fahrenheit   Take a blender and add all of the ingredients and blend them to a smooth cream   Divide the mix evenly amongst your jars   Attach the lids using only the pressure from your fingertips and close the jar, make sure to keep them a little lose to allow air pressure to exit   Place them in your water bath and cook for 1 hour   Remove them from the bath using tongs and open the lid to enjoy! Or, you can invert the jars and pop them out of the jar onto your plate and serve!

Nutrition: Info Calories: 357, Protein: 13g, Dietary Fiber 3g, Fat: 24g

Grand Marnier

Ingredients: Servings: 12   Cooking Time: 90 Mins.

Zest of 8 large orange	2 C. brandy
	½ C. ultrafine sugar

Directions:
Prepare your Sous Vide water bath using your immersion circulator and raise the temperature to 180-degrees Fahrenheit.   Add all the listed ingredients to a resealable zip bag.   Seal using the immersion method. Cook for 90 minutes.   Strain and discard the orange zest.   Allow it to chill and serve when needed!

Nutrition: Info Calories: 191 Carbohydrate: 39g Protein: 4g Fat: 2g Sugar: 31g Sodium: 31mg

Rhubarb & Thyme Syrup

Ingredients: Servings: 12   Cooking Time: 1 Hour 30 Mins.

2 C. diced rhubarb	1 C. water
1 C. ultrafine sugar	5 sprigs thyme

Directions:
Prepare your Sous Vide water bath using your immersion circulator and raise the temperature to 180-degrees Fahrenheit.   Add all the listed ingredients to a heavy duty zip bag   Seal using the immersion method Submerge underwater and cook for 1 ½ hour.   Remove

the bag and strain the contents to a bowl. Transfer to liquid storage, chill and serve!

Nutrition: Info Calories: 190 Carbohydrate: 47g Protein: 1g Fat: 0g Sugar: 43g Sodium: 5mg

Cheesecake

Ingredients: Servings: 6   Cooking Time: 90 Mins.

12 oz. cream cheese at room temperature	2 eggs
	Zest of 1 lemon
½ C. sugar	½ tbsp. vanilla extract
¼ C. creole cream cheese	

Directions:
Set up your Sous Vide immersion circulator to a temperature of 176-degrees Fahrenheit and prepare your water bath. Take a bowl and add both cream cheeses, and sugar and whisk them well Gradually add the eggs one by one and keep beating until well combined. Add the zest and vanilla and mix well. Pour the cheesecake mixture into 6 different jars of 6 oz. and distribute evenly Seal the jars with a lid. Place the jars underwater and let them cook for 90 minutes. Once done, remove from the water bath and chill until they are cooled Serve chilled with a topping of fresh fruit compote.

Nutrition: Info Per serving:Calories: 615 ;Carbohydrate: 56g ;Protein: 8g ;Fat: 41g ;Sugar: 40g ;Sodium: 418mg

Simple Lemon Jam

Ingredients: Servings: 6   Cooking Time: 2 Hours 55 Mins.

1 C. sugar	6 egg yolks
8 tbsp. butter, melted	¼ C. lemon juice

Directions:
Prepare a water bath and place the Sous Vide in it. Set to 182 F. Blend all the ingredients for 20 seconds. Place in a vacuum-sealable bag. Release air by the water displacement method, seal and submerge the bag in the water bath. Cook for 45 minutes. Shake a few times. Once the timer has stopped, remove the bag and transfer into an ice-water bath. Allow chilling for 2 hours and serve.

Chocolate & Ricotta Mousse

Ingredients: Servings: 8   Cooking Time: 60 Mins.

2 quarts' whole milk	¼ C. powdered sugar
6 tbsp. white wine vinegar	Grand Marnier liquor
4 oz. semisweet chocolate chips	1 tbsp. orange zest
	2 oz. ricotta

Directions:
Set up your Sous Vide immersion circulator to a temperature of 172-degrees Fahrenheit and prepare your water bath. Put the milk and vinegar to a resealable zip bag. Seal using the immersion method and cook for 1 hour. Once done, remove the bag and skim the curds from top and transfer to a strainer lined with cheesecloth. Discard any remaining liquid. Let it sit and drain the curd for about 10 minutes. Then chill for 1 hour. Prepare your double broiler by setting a bowl over a small saucepan filled with 1 inch of water Bring the water to a low simmer over medium heat. Add the chocolate chips to a bowl of the double boiler and cook until it has melted. Transfer to a food processor. Add the sugar, orange zest, grand mariner, ricotta, and then process until smooth Transfer to individual bowls and serve!

Nutrition: Info Per serving:Calories: 472 ;Carbohydrate: 37g ;Protein: 6g ;Fat: 35g ;Sugar: 34g ;Sodium: 103mg

Citrus Yogurt

Ingredients: Servings: 4   Cooking Time: 180 Mins.

½ C. yogurt	½ tbsp. lime zest
½ tbsp. orange zest	4 C. full cream milk
½ tbsp. lemon zest	

Directions:
Set up your Sous Vide immersion circulator to a temperature of 113-degrees Fahrenheit and prepare your water bath. Heat the milk on stove top to a temperature of 180-degrees Fahrenheit. Transfer to an ice bath and allow it to cool down to 110-degrees Fahrenheit. Stir in yogurt. Fold in the citrus zest. Pour the mixture into 4-oz. canning jars and lightly close the lid. Submerge underwater and cook for 3 hours. Remove the jars and serve immediately!

Nutrition: Info Per serving:Calories: 175 ;Carbohydrate: 35g ;Protein: 6g ;Fat: 2g ;Sugar: 32g ;Sodium: 66mg

Zucchini Bread

Ingredients: Servings: x   Cooking Time: 3 Hours Cooking Temperature: 195°f

½ C. packed dark brown sugar
2 tbsp. extra-virgin olive oil
½ tsp. vanilla extract
¾ C. all-purpose flour
12 oz. zucchini, grated and squeezed

1 large egg
¼ C. whole wheat flour
½ tsp. baking soda
½ tsp. baking powder
1½ tsp. ground cinnamon
¾ tsp. salt

Directions:
Attach the sous vide immersion circulator using an adjustable clamp to a Cambro container or pot filled with water and preheat to 195°F. Generously grease 4 half-pint canning jars. Into a bowl, add sugar, egg, oil and vanilla extract and beat until well-combined. Fold in zucchini. In another bowl, mix together flour, baking soda, baking powder, cinnamon and salt. Add zucchini mixture into flour mixture, and mix until well-combined. Divide mixture into prepared jars evenly. (Each jar should be not more than half-full.) with a damp towel, wipe off sides and tops of jars. Tap the jars onto a counter firmly to remove air bubbles. Cover each jar with the lid tightly. Place jars in sous vide bath and set the cooking time for 3 hours. Remove the jars from sous vide bath and carefully remove the lids. Place jars onto a wire rack to cool completely. Carefully, run a knife around the inside edges of the jars to loosen the bread from the walls. Cut into slices and serve.

Rich Orange Curd

Ingredients: Servings: 2   Cooking Time: 60 Mins.

6 tbsp. butter, melted and cooled
4 orange juice

6 large egg yolks at room temperature
1 C. sugar

Directions:
Prepare a water bath and place the Sous Vide in it. Set to 179 F. Combine the sugar, butter and orange juice. Stir until the sugar dissolved and add the egg yolks. Mix well. Place the egg mix in a vacuum-sealable bag. Release air by the water displacement method, seal and submerge the bag in the water bath. Cook for 45 minutes. Once the timer has stopped, remove the bag and transfer into an ice bag. Shake well. Allow chilling all night.

Apple & Cinnamon Pie

Ingredients: Servings: 4   Cooking Time: 2 Hours 20 Mins.

2 lb. green, cored, peeled and sliced
3/4 C. sugar
2 tbsp. cornstarch

2 tbsp. butter
2 tsp. ground cinnamon
1 pack puff pastry
2 tbsp. milk
2 tbsp. sugar

Directions:
Preheat the water bath to 160°F. Put the sliced apples, cornstarch, sugar, cinnamon and butter in the vacuum bag and set the cooking time for 1 hour 30 minutes. When the time is up, cool down the filling to the room temperature. In the meantime, preheat the oven to 375°F, grease a baking pan, and roll out 1 sheet of the pastry. Pour the filling over the sheet, and cover it with another sheet, seal the sheets on the edges with your fingers. Bake in the preheated oven for 35 minutes.

Nutrition: Info Per serving:Calories 276, Carbohydrates 30 g, Fats 16 g, Protein 3 g

Honey Baked Cheese

Ingredients: Servings: 6   Cooking Time: 50 Mins.

2 C. milk
6 tbsp. white wine vinegar
2 large eggs

2 tbsp. olive oil
Salt and black pepper to taste
2 tbsp. honey to serve

Directions:
Prepare a water bath and place the Sous Vide in it. Set to 172 F. Place the vinegar and milk in a vacuum-sealable bag. Release air by the water displacement method, seal and submerge the bag in the water bath. Cook for 60 minutes. Preheat the oven to 350 F. Once the timer has stopped, remove the bag and strain the cuds. Allow to draining for 10 minutes. Transfer to a blender and mix with the eggs, salt, olive oil and pepper for 20 seconds. Put the ricotta in 6 oven ramekins and bake for 30 minutes. Sprinkle with honey.

BEEF, PORK & LAMB RECIPES

Pork Steaks with Creamy Slaw

Ingredients: Servings: x   Cooking Time: 24 Hours Cooking Temperature: 160°f

For Pork Steaks:
2 (1-inch thick) pork shoulder steaks
1 tsp. kosher salt
½ tsp. freshly ground black

¼ tsp. fine sea salt
½ tsp. freshly ground black pepper
2 tbsp. olive oil
2 tbsp. mayonnaise

pepper
1 tsp. vegetable oil
For Creamy Slaw:
½ small, purple
cabbage head,
cored and thinly
sliced

Fresh juice of 1
lemon
1 tsp. Dijon
mustard

Directions:

Attach the sous vide immersion circulator to a Cambro container or pot with water using an adjustable clamp and preheat water to 160°F. For pork steaks: season pork steaks evenly with salt and black pepper. Divide pork steaks into two cooking pouches. Seal pouches tightly after removing the Cover the sous vide bath with plastic wrap to minimize water evaporation. Add water intermittently to keep the water level up. For slaw: in a large bowl, place cabbage, sea salt, and black pepper and toss to coat well. In a small bowl, add remaining slaw ingredients and beat until well combined. Pour mustard mixture over cabbage and toss to coat well. Remove pouches from the sous vide bath and open carefully. Remove pork steaks from pouches and pat dry with paper towels. In a cast iron skillet, heat oil over medium heat and sear pork steaks for 1 Min. on each side. Cut each steak into 2 pieces of equal size. Divide pork pieces onto serving plates and serve alongside creamy slaw.

Pork Medallions

Ingredients: Servings: 4   Cooking Time: 1 Hr.

1 tbsp. olive oil
1 pinch salt
1 tsp. ground
cumin

1 pinch black
pepper
¼ C. chopped
fresh parsley
1 ¾ lb. pork
tenderloin

Directions:

Preheat the Sous Vide cooker to 145 degrees F. Cut the pork tenderloin in medallions. Season with salt, pepper, and cumin. Place the seasoned pork into Sous Vide bag and add parsley. Vacuum seals the bag and submerge in water. Cook the medallions 1 hour. Heat olive oil in a large skillet. Remove the medallions from the cooker. Sear on both sides. Serve warm.

Nutrition: Info Calories: 317 Protein: 51gCarbs: 5gFat: 16g

Brined Pork Belly

Ingredients: Servings: x   Cooking Time: 12 Hours 10 Mins. Cooking Temperature: 158°f

4 C. water
½ C. light brown
sugar
½ C. kosher salt
2 tbsp. whole
black peppercorns

6 fresh thyme
sprigs
1 lb. skinless pork
belly
1 tbsp. vegetable
oil

Directions:

Add water, brown sugar, salt, peppercorns, and thyme to a large pan and bring to a boil. Remove from heat and refrigerate for at least 5 hours. After 5 hours, place pork belly in brine, cover, and refrigerate again for 24 hours. Attach the sous vide immersion circulator to a Cambro container or pot with water using an adjustable clamp and preheat water to 158°F. Remove pork belly from brine and place in a large cooking pouch. Seal pouch tightly after removing the excess air. Place pouch in sous vide bath and set the cooking time for 12 hours. Cover the sous vide bath with plastic wrap to minimize water evaporation. Add water intermittently to keep the water level up. Remove pouch from the sous vide bath and immediately plunge into a large bowl of ice water. Set aside to cool completely. Transfer the pouch to the refrigerator for at least 4 hours. After 4 hours, remove pork belly from pouch and cut into ¾-inch thick slices. In a large, non-stick skillet, heat oil over medium heat and sear pork pieces for 10 minutes. Serve immediately.

Beef Bourguignon

Ingredients: Servings: x   Cooking Time: 25 Hours Cooking Temperature: 180°f

For Beef:
Vegetable oil, as
required
¼ C. small bacon,
cubed
2 lb. beef, cubed
1 bottle nice
burgundy wine
1 tbsp. butter,
divided
1 lb. mushrooms,
chopped roughly
20 pearl onions
2 celery stalks,
finely chopped
2 carrots, peeled
and finely
chopped
1 white onion,
finely chopped
2 garlic cloves,
mashed

1 bay leaf
Sugar, to taste
½ tbsp. all-
purpose flour
½ tbsp. cold water
Salt and freshly
ground black
pepper, to taste
1 rosemary sprig
Chopped fresh
parsley, for
garnishing
For Mashed
Potatoes:
2 russet potatoes,
peeled and cubed
3 tbsp. heavy
cream
Butter, as required
Salt, to taste

Directions:

In a wide cast iron pan, heat enough vegetable oil to cover the bottom of the pan and cook bacon cubes until just browning. Add beef and sear until browned completely. Transfer beef and bacon to a bowl, reserving fat in a separate small bowl. Add some wine and scrape the brown bits from bottom and sides of the pan. Cook until a thick glaze is formed. Move glaze to a small bowl and set aside to cool. In the same pan as used for glaze, melt ½ tbsp. of butter over medium-high heat. Add mushrooms and cook for 5 minutes. Cover and cook for 1-2 minutes. Transfer mushrooms to a bowl. Add more wine to the now-empty pan and scrape the brown bits from bottom and sides of the pan. Cook until a thick glaze is formed. Add glaze to the bowl of reserved glaze and set aside to cool. Melt remaining ½ tbsp. of butter over medium-high heat in the same pan. Add pearl onions and cook for 5 minutes. Transfer the onions into the bowl of mushrooms. Add some wine to the pan and scrape the brown bits from bottom and sides. Cook until a thick glaze is formed. Transfer glaze into the bowl of reserved glaze and set aside to cool. For wine reduction: In the same pan, cook reserved bacon fat over medium-high heat and add celery, carrot, and white onion for 7-10 minutes. Add 3¼ C. of wine, garlic, bay leaf, some cooked bacon, and reserved glaze and cook for 30 minutes, stirring occasionally. Strain wine reduction through a fine strainer. Return strained sauce to the pan and bring to a gentle boil. In a small bowl, dissolve flour into cold water. Add flour mixture to strained wine reduction and cook for 3 minutes. Remove from heat and stir in sugar, salt, and black pepper. Set aside to cool. Attach the sous vide immersion circulator to a Cambro container or pot with water using an adjustable clamp and preheat water to 180°F. Place beef, bacon, mushrooms, pearl onions, rosemary sprigs, and wine reduction in a large cooking pouch. Seal pouch tightly after removing the excess air. Place pouch in sous vide bath and set the cooking time for 24 hours. Cover the sous vide bath with plastic wrap to minimize water evaporation. Add water intermittently to keep the water level up. For mashed potatoes: cook potatoes in a pan of boiling water for 10 minutes. Remove from heat and drain potatoes. Return potatoes to the pan. Add heavy cream and some butter and mash until well combined. Season with salt. Remove pouch from the sous vide bath and open carefully. Remove beef, mushrooms, and pearl onions from pouch, reserving the cooking liquid in a pan. Discard rosemary sprigs. Place pan with reserved liquid over stove and cook for 5-10 Mins. or until desired thickness of sauce is reached. Remove from heat and stir in beef, mushrooms, and pearl onions. Serve with mashed potatoes.

quail Legs

Ingredients: Servings: 2   Cooking Time: 180 Mins.

8 quail legs, bone-in, skin-on	Kosher salt as needed
Fresh ground black pepper as needed	1 tbsp. extra-virgin olive oil

Directions:

Prepare the Sous Vide water bath using your immersion circulator and raise the temperature to 145-degrees Fahrenheit Take the quail and season it carefully with pepper and salt, transfer the quail to a heavy duty zipper bag Seal using the immersion method, and cook for 3 hours Once done, remove the quail and pat dry with kitchen towels Rub the quail with olive oil Take an iron skillet and place it over high heat and allow it to heat for 5 minutes, then add the quail and sear until the skin turns golden brown (30 seconds per side) Arrange on a platter and serve

Nutrition: Info Per serving:Calories: 290 ;Carbohydrate: 18g ;Protein: 27g ;Fat: 18g ;Sugar: 1g ;Sodium: 74mg

Peppercorn Veal Chops with Pine Mushrooms

Ingredients: Servings: 5   Cooking Time: 3 Hours 15 Mins.

1 lb. veal chops	5 peppercorns
1 lb. Pine mushrooms, sliced	3 tbsp. vegetable oil
½ C. freshly squeezed lemon juice	2 tbsp. extra virgin olive oil
1 tbsp. bay leaves, crushed	Salt and black pepper to taste

Directions:

Prepare a water bath, place Sous Vide in it, and set to 154 F. Season the chops with salt and pepper. Place in a vacuum-sealable bag in a single layer along with lemon juice, bay leaves, peppercorns, and olive oil. Seal the bag. Submerge the bag in the water bath and cook for 3 hours. Remove from the water bath and set aside. Heat up the vegetable oil in a large skillet. Add pine mushrooms and stir-fry with a pinch of salt over medium heat until all the liquid evaporates. Add veal chops along with its marinade and continue to cook for 3 more minutes. Serve immediately.

Boneless Pork Ribs

Ingredients: Servings: 4   Cooking Time: 8 Hours

1/3 C. unsweetened coconut milk	1 tbsp. Sriracha sauce
2 tbsp. peanut butter	1 inch peeled fresh ginger
2 tbsp. soy sauce	2 tsp. sesame oil
2 tbsp. light brown sugar	12 oz. boneless country style pork ribs
2 tbsp. dry white wine	Chopped up fresh cilantro and steamed basmati rice for serving
2-inch fresh lemongrass	
2 garlic cloves	

Directions:

Prepare the Sous Vide water bath using your immersion circulator and increase the temperature to 134-degrees Fahrenheit.   Add the coconut milk, peanut butter, soy sauce, brown sugar, wine, lemongrass, ginger, Sriracha sauce, sesame oil and garlic to a blender, blend until smooth.   Add the ribs to a resealable zip bag alongside the sauce and seal using the immersion method. Cook for 8 hours.   Once done, remove the bag and take the ribs out from the bag, transfer to plate.   Pour the bag contents to a large skillet and place it over medium-high heat, bring to a boil and lower heat to medium-low. Simmer for 10-15 minutes.   Then, add the ribs to the sauce and turn well to coat it.   Simmer for 5 minutes. Garnish with fresh cilantro and serve with the rice!

Nutrition: Info   Per   serving:Calories: 840 ;Carbohydrate: 24g ;Protein: 53g ;Fat: 59g ;Sugar: 12g ;Sodium: 534mg

Yummy Smoked Beef Brisket

Ingredients: Servings: 8   Cooking Time: 33 Hours 50 Mins.

1/4 tsp. liquid hickory smoke	1 tsp. dried parsley
8 tbsp. honey	1 tsp. garlic powder
Salt and black pepper to taste	1 tsp. onion powder
1 tsp. chili powder	1/2 tsp. ground cumin
	4 lb. beef brisket

Directions:

Prepare a water bath and place the Sous Vide in it. Set to 156 F.   Combine the honey, salt, pepper, chili powder, parsley, onion and garlic powder, and cumin. Reserve 1/4 of the mixture. Brush the brisket with the mixture.   Place the brisket in a sizeable vacuum-sealable bag with the liquid smoke. Release air by the water displacement method, seal and submerge the bag in the water bath. Cook for 30 hours. Once the timer has stopped, remove the bag and allow to chill for 1 hour. Preheat the oven to 300 F.   Pat dry with kitchen towels the brisket and brush with the reserved sauce. Discard the cooking juices. Transfer the brisket to a baking tray, put into the oven and roast for 2 hours.   Once the time has stopped, remove the brisket and cover it with aluminium foil for 40 minutes. Serve with baked beans, fresh bread, and butter.

Red Cabbage & Potatoes with Sausage

Ingredients: Servings: 4   Cooking Time: 2 Hours 20 Mins.

1/2 head red cabbage, sliced	2 tbsp. cider vinegar
1 apple, cut up into small dices	2 tbsp. brown sugar
24 oz. red potatoes, cut up into quarters	Black pepper to taste
1 small onion, sliced	1 lb. pre-cooked smoked pork sausage, sliced
1/4 tsp. celery salt	1/2 C. chicken broth
	2 tbsp. butter

Directions:

Prepare a water bath and place the Sous Vide in it. Set to 186 F. Combine the cabbage, potatoes, onion, apple, cider, brown sugar, black pepper, celery, and salt. Place the sausages and the mixture in a vacuum-sealable bag. Release air by water displacement method, seal and submerge the bag in the water bath. Cook for 2 hours.   Heat butter in a saucepan over medium heat. Once the timer has stopped, remove the bag and transfer the contents to a saucepan. Cook until the liquid evaporates. Add in cabbage, onion and potatoes and cook until browned. Divide the mixture into serving platters.

Thyme Pork Chops

Ingredients: Servings: 4   Cooking Time: 70 Mins.

4 pork chops	Salt and black pepper to taste
2 tsp. fresh thyme	
1 tbsp. olive oil	

Directions:

Prepare a water bath and place the Sous Vide in it. Set to 145 F. Combine the pork with the remaining ingredients in a vacuum-sealable bag. Release air by the water displacement method, seal and submerge the bag in water bath. Set the timer for 60 minutes. Once done, remove the bag and sear it in a pan for a few seconds each side to serve.

Carnitas Tacos

Ingredients: Servings: 4   Cooking Time: 16 Hrs.

2 lbs. pork shoulder	2 bay leaves
1 tsp. salt	Corn tortillas for serving
1 tsp. pepper	Fresh cilantro for serving
1 onion, chopped	Lime for serving
3 cloves garlic	
½ tsp. ground cumin	

Directions:
Preheat the water bath to 185 degrees F. Rub pork with salt, pepper, and cumin. Seal into the bag with onion, garlic, and bay leaves. Place into the water bath and cook 16 hours.   When pork is cooked, remove from bag and shred with two forks or your hands. To serve, place a small amount of pork in a tortilla and top with cilantro and a squeeze of lime.

Nutrition: Info Calories: 623 Protein: 543gCarbs: 9gFat: 424g

Cilantro-garlic Beef Roast

Ingredients: Servings: 8   Cooking Time: 24 Hours 30 Mins.

4 tbsp. olive oil	1 C. soy sauce
2 lb. beef chuck	½ C. freshly squeezed orange juice
Salt and black pepper to taste	
1 tsp. thyme	½ C. Worcestershire sauce
1 tsp. cilantro	
½ C. freshly squeezed lemon juice	¼ C. yellow mustard
	3 garlic cloves, minced

Directions:
Prepare a water bath and place the Sous Vide in it. Set to 141 F. Prepare the roast and truss it using butcher's twine. Season with salt, pepper, thyme, and cilantro. Put a cast iron pan over high heat. In the meantime, baste the roast with 2 tbsp. of olive oil using a soft brush. Place the meat on the pan to sear for 1 Min. on both sides. Combine Worcestershire sauce, mustard, garlic, soy sauce, lemon and orange juice in one vessel.   Slide the beef in a vacuum-bag, mix it with the previously made marinade and close the bag using water displacement method. Cook in water bath for 24 hours. Once ready, open the bag and pour the liquid over to a small saucepan. Cook for 10 Mins. over high heat until you reach half of the volume.   Add 2 tbsp. of olive oil and preheat the iron-cast pan over high heat. Gently put the meat on the pan and sear one Min. each side. Take the roast out of the pan and let cool down for about 5 minutes. Slice and add the sauce on top.

Saucy Veal with Port Wine

Ingredients: Servings: 6   Cooking Time: 2 Hours 5 Mins.

3 tbsp. butter	1 leek, white part only, chopped
¾ C. vegetable broth	Salt and black pepper to taste
½ C. Port wine	
¼ C. sliced shiitake mushrooms	8 veal cutlets
	1 fresh rosemary sprig
3 tbsp. olive oil	
4 garlic cloves, minced	

Directions:
Prepare a water bath and place the Sous Vide in it. Set to 141 F. Combine broth, Port wine, mushrooms, butter, olive oil, garlic, leek, salt, and pepper. Place the veal in a large vacuum-sealable bag. Add in rosemary and the mixture. Release air by the water displacement method, seal and submerge the bag in the water bath. Cook for 1 hour and 45 minutes.   Once done, remove the veal and pat dry. Discard the rosemary and transfer the cooking juices to a saucepan. Cook for 5 minutes. Add the veal and cook for 1 minute. Top with sauce to serve.

Amazing Prime Rib

Ingredients: Servings: 12   Cooking Time: 6 Hours

Kosher salt	3-pound, bone-in beef Ribeye roast
1 tablespoon, black peppercorn coarsely ground	1 tablespoon, dried celery seeds
1 tablespoon, green peppercorn coarsely ground	2 tablespoon, dried garlic powder
1 tablespoon, pink peppercorn coarsely ground	4 sprigs, rosemary
	1 quart, beef stock
	2 egg whites

Directions:
Season the beef with kosher salt and chill for 12 hours Prepare the Sous Vide water bath by dipping the immersion cooker and waiting until the temperature

has been raised to 132°F   Transfer beef to zip bag and seal using immersion method   Cook for 6 hours Preheat your oven to 425°F and remove the beef, pat it dry   Take a bowl and whisk together peppercorn, celery seeds, garlic powder and rosemary   Brush the top of your cooked roast with egg white and season with the mixture and salt   Place the roast on a baking rack and roast for 10-15 minutes. Allow it to rest 10-15 Mins. and carve   Take a large saucepan and add the cooking liquid from the bag, bring to a boil and simmer until half. Carve the roast and serve with the juice

Nutrition: Info Per serving:Calories 532, Carbohydrates 10 g, Fats 40 g, Protein 33 g

Pork & Bean Stew

Ingredients: Servings: 8   Cooking Time: 7 Hours 20 Mins.

2 tbsp. vegetable oil	1 tbsp. butter
1 trimmed pork loin, cubed	2 tbsp. all-purpose flour
Salt and black pepper to taste	1 C. dry white wine
2 C. frozen pearl onions	2 C. chicken stock
2 large parsnips, chopped	1 can white beans, drained and rinsed
2 minced cloves garlic	4 fresh rosemary sprigs
	2 bay leaves

Directions:
Prepare a water bath and place the Sous Vide in it. Set to 138 F.   Heat a non-stick pan over high heat with butter and oil. Add the pork. Season with pepper and salt. Cook for 7 minutes. Put in onions and cook for 5 minutes. Mix the garlic and wine until bubble. Stir in beans, rosemary, stock, and bay leaves. Remove from the heat.   Place the pork in a vacuum-sealable bag. Release air by the water displacement method, seal and submerge the bag in the water bath. Cook for 7 hours. Once the timer has stopped, remove the bag and transfer into a bowl. Garnish with rosemary.

Chili Lamb Steaks with Sesame Seed Topping

Ingredients: Servings: 2   Cooking Time: 3 Hours 10 Mins.

2 lamb steaks	2 tbsp. avocado oil
2 tbsp. olive oil	1 tsp. sesame seeds
Salt and black pepper to taste	Pinch of red pepper flakes

Directions:
Prepare a water bath and place the Sous Vide in it. Set to 138 F. Place the lamb with olive oil in a vacuum-sealable bag. Release air by the water displacement method, seal and submerge the bag in water bath. Cook for 3 hours.   Once done, pat the lamb dry. Season with salt and pepper. Heat avocado oil in a skillet over high heat and sear the lamb. Chop into bites. Garnish with sesame seeds and pepper flakes.

Rolled Beef

Ingredients: Servings: 8   Cooking Time: 37 Hrs.

Beef:	4oz. peas
8 4oz. sliced beef	1 sprig thyme
Salt and pepper, to taste	1 pinch sugar
¼ C. vegetable oil, to fry	4oz. carrots, chopped
Filling:	8 tsp. Dijon mustard
	16 slices bacon

Directions:
Preheat Sous Vide cooker to 176 degrees F. Place the peas in a Sous Vide bag. Add the carrots, a pinch of sugar and salt to taste. Vacuum seal the bag and place in a water bath. Cook the veggies 30 minutes. Remove from the bag.   Cover the beef slices with parchment paper. lb. with a meat tenderizer to make the beef this. Spread the mustard over meat, and top each slice with two pieces bacon. Roll the meat into roulade, then roll the meat over veggies and secure the roulades with a kitchen twine. Season with salt and pepper. Heat the oil in a skillet and sear the roulades on all sides. Cool the roulades and transfer in a Sous Vide bag. Vacuum seal the beef and cook 37 hours at 153 degrees F.   Remove the meat from the cooker. Allow cooling completely before removing from the bag. Remove the kitchen twine and slice before serving.

Nutrition: Info Calories: 287 Protein: 12gCarbs: 4gFat: 23g

Sweet Lamb with Mustard Sauce

Ingredients: Servings: 4   Cooking Time: 1 Hour 10 Mins.

1 lamb of rack, trimmed	Salt to taste
3 tbsp. runny honey	2 tbsp. avocado oil
2 tbsp. Dijon mustard	1 tbsp. thyme
1 tsp. sherry wine vinegar	Toasted mustard seeds for garnish
	Chopped green onion

Directions:

Prepare a water bath and place the Sous Vide in it. Set to 135 F. Combine all the ingredients, except the lamb. Place the lamb in a vacuum-sealable bag. Release air by the water displacement method, seal and submerge the bag in the water bath. Cook for 1 hour. Once the timer has stopped, remove the lamb and transfer to a plate. Heat the oil in a frying pan over high heat and sear the lamb for 2 Mins. each side. Chop and top with cooking juices. Garnish with green onion and toasted mustard seeds.

Herby Skirt Steak

Ingredients: Servings: 6   Cooking Time: 3 Hours 20 Mins.

2 tbsp. butter	¼ tsp. onion
3 lb. skirt steak	powder
2 tbsp. extra-virgin oil	¼ tsp. cayenne
	pepper
1½ tsp. garlic	¼ tsp. dried
powder	parsley
Salt and black	¼ tsp. dried sage
pepper to taste	¼ tsp. crushed
	dried rosemary

Directions:

Prepare a water bath and place the Sous Vide in it. Set to 134 F. Brush the steak with olive oil.   Combine the garlic powder, salt, pepper, onion powder, cayenne pepper, parsley, sage, and rosemary. Rub the steak with the mixture.   Place the steak in a large vacuum-sealable bag. Release air by the water displacement method, seal and submerge the bag in the water bath. Cook for 3 hours.   Once the timer has stopped, remove the steak and pat dry with kitchen towel. Heat the butter in a skillet over high heat and sear the steak for 2-3 Mins. on all sides. Allow to rest for 5 Mins. and cut to serve.

Lamb Chops & Mint Pistachio

Ingredients: Servings: 4   Cooking Time: 120 Mins.

2 full racks lamb sliced into chops	½ C. unsalted pistachio nuts,
Kosher salt and	shelled
black pepper as	3 tbsp. lemon
needed	juice
1 C. packed fresh	2 cloves garlic,
mint leaves	minced
½ C. packed fresh	6 tbsp. extra-virgin olive oil
parsley	
½ C. scallion,	
sliced	

Directions:

Prepare the Sous Vide water bath using your immersion circulator and raise the temperature to 125-degrees Fahrenheit   Season the lamb with salt and pepper   Put in a zip bag and seal using the immersion method. Cook for 2 hours   After 20 minutes, take the lamb out and set the grill to high   Add the mint, parsley, pistachios, scallions, garlic, and lemon juice in a food processor and form a paste   Drizzle 4 tbsp. of olive oil as you process, and keep going until you have a smooth paste   Season with salt and pepper   Brush your cooked lamb with 2 tbsp. of olive oil and grill for 1 Min. per side   Serve the chops with pesto

Nutrition: Info   Per   serving:Calories: 474 ;Carbohydrate: 0g ;Protein: 18g ;Fat: 44g ;Sugar: 0g ;Sodium: 368mg

Standing Rib Roast

Ingredients: Servings: x   Cooking Time: 24-36 Hours Cooking Temperature: 130°f

1 x 3-rib standing	kosher salt and
rib roast (6-8	freshly cracked
pounds) (a.k.a.	black pepper, to
prime rib roast)	taste
1-2 oz. dried morel	3 oz. garlic-infused olive oil
mushrooms	

Directions:

Attach the sous vide immersion circulator using an adjustable clamp to a Cambro container or pot filled with water and preheat to 130°F.   Into a cooking pouch, add rib roast and mushrooms. Seal pouch tightly after squeezing out the excess air. Place pouch in sous vide bath and set the cooking time for at least 24 and up to 36 hours.   Remove pouch from sous vide bath and carefully open it. Transfer rib roast onto a cutting board, reserving mushroom and cooking liquid into a bowl. with paper towels, pat rib roast completely dry.   Rub rib roast with salt and black pepper evenly.   Heat cast iron pan to medium high heat and place the rib roast in, fat cap down. Sear for 1-2 Mins. per side (or until browned on all sides).   Meanwhile, season reserved mushroom mixture with garlic oil, a little salt, and black pepper.   Transfer rib roast onto a cutting board, bone side down.   Carefully, remove rib bones and cut rib roast into ½-inch-thick slices across the grain.   Serve immediately with mushroom mixture.

Pork Osso Bucco

Ingredients: Servings: 2   Cooking Time: 24 Hrs.

2 pork shanks	1 tsp. salt
1 tbsp. olive oil	1 tsp. pepper
½ sweet onion,	½ C. white wine

finely chopped
1 carrot, finely chopped
1 stalk celery, finely chopped
4 cloves garlic, minced

7 oz. whole tomatoes, crushed
2 bay leaves
2 sprigs rosemary
2 sprigs thyme
Crusty bread for serving

Directions:

Preheat the water bath to 175 degrees F. Meanwhile, prepare the sauce. Heat 1 tbsp. olive oil in a saucepan. Add onions, carrots, and celery and cook until onion is translucent. Add garlic and stir. Pour in wine and tomatoes and cook until sauce is reduced and alcohol smell has evaporated. Remove from heat. Season the shanks with salt and pepper. Place each shank into a separate bag and add half the sauce to each bag. Divide the herbs between the bags. Seal and place into the water bath. Cook 24 hours. Serve with crusty bread.

Nutrition: Info Calories: 683 Protein: 102gCarbs: 125gFat: 271g

Sherry Braised Pork Ribs

Ingredients: Servings: 4   Cooking Time: 18 Hours 10 Mins.

2 lb. pork ribs, chopped into bone sections
1 tbsp. ginger root, sliced
½ tsp. ground nutmeg

2 tbsp. soy sauce
1 tsp. salt
1 tsp. white sugar
1 anise star pod
¼ C. dry sherry
1 tbsp. butter

Directions:

In a small bowl, combine salt, sugar and ground nutmeg, and rub the pork ribs with this mixture. Put the ribs into the vacuum bag, add sliced ginger root, soy sauce, anise star and sherry wine. Preheat your sous vide machine to 176°F. Set the cooking time for 18 hours. When the time is up, carefully dry the ribs with the paper towels. Sear the ribs in 1 tbsp. butter on both sides for about 40 seconds until crusty.

Nutrition: Info Per serving:Calories 284, Carbohydrates 32 g, Fats 12 g, Protein 12 g

Baby Ribs with Chinese Sauce

Ingredients: Servings: 4   Cooking Time: 4 Hours 25 Mins.

1/3 C. hoisin sauce
1/3 C. dark soy sauce
1/3 C. sugar

1-inch piece fresh grated ginger
1 ½ tsp. five-spice powder

3 tbsp. honey
3 tbsp. white vinegar
1 tbsp. fermented bean paste
2 tsp. sesame oil
2 crushed garlic cloves

Salt to taste
½ tsp. fresh ground black pepper
3 lb. baby back ribs
Cilantro leaves for serving

Directions:

Prepare a water bath and place the Sous Vide in it. Set to 168 F. Combine in a bowl hoisin sauce, dark soy sauce, sugar, white vinegar, honey, bean paste, sesame oil, five-spice powder, salt, ginger, white and black pepper. Reserve 1/3 of the mixture and allow chilling. Brush the ribs with the mixture and share among 3 vacuum-sealable bag. Release air by the water displacement method, seal and submerge the bags in the water bath. Cook for 4 hours. Preheat the oven to 400 F. Once the timer has stopped, remove the ribs and brush with the remaining mixture. Transfer to a baking tray and put in the oven. Bake for 3 minutes. Take out and allow resting for 5 minutes. Cut the rack and top with cilantro.

Pork Carnitas

Ingredients: Servings: 8   Cooking Time: 18 To 24 Hours

1 tbsp. salt, plus more to taste
1 tbsp. ground cumin
1 tbsp. dried oregano
1 tsp. freshly ground black pepper, plus more to taste
1/2 tsp. cayenne pepper, plus more to taste

1 boneless pork shoulder /about 3 pounds
8 garlic cloves /minced
1 can /12 oz. cola /not diet, made with real sugar
2 tbsp. lime juice
2 tbsp. orange juice

Directions:

Preheat water to 165°F in a sous vide cooker or with an immersion circulator. Mix salt, cumin, oregano, black pepper and cayenne pepper and rub into pork shoulder. Vacuum-seal pork, garlic, cola and lime juice in a sous vide bag or use a plastic zip-top freezer bag /remove as much air as possible from the bag before sealing. Submerge bag in water and cook for 18 to 24 hours. Remove pork from cooking bag, reserving cooking juices. Shred pork with two forks, season to taste with salt, black pepper and cayenne pepper and set aside. Preheat oven broiler. Spray a rimmed baking sheet with cooking spray and spread pork on baking sheet. Drizzle orange juice and about 1 C. of the liquid from the cooking bag over pork and broil until pork is crispy and lightly browned, watching carefully, 8 to 10 minutes. Transfer pork to a large bowl and drizzle with additional cooking liquid if desired. Serve and enjoy!

Nutrition: Info Calories: 268; Total Fat: 6g; Saturated Fat: 2g; Protein: 45g; Carbs: 6g; Fiber: 0g; Sugar: 4g

Chili Beef Meatballs

Ingredients: Servings: 3   Cooking Time: 55 Mins.

1 lb. lean ground beef	¼ tsp. chili pepper
2 tbsp. all-purpose flour	3 garlic cloves, crushed
¼ C. milk	1 tsp. olive oil
½ tsp. freshly ground black pepper	1 tsp. salt
	½ C. celery leaves, finely chopped

Directions:
Prepare a water bath, place Sous Vide in it, and set to 136 F.   In a large bowl, combine the ground beef with flour, milk, black pepper, chili pepper, garlic, salt, and celery. Mix with your hands until all of the ingredients are thoroughly combined. Shape bite-sized balls and place in a large vacuum-sealable bag in a single layer. Submerge the sealed bag in the water bath and cook for 50 minutes. Take the meatballs out of the bag, and pat dry. Sear the meatballs in a medium-hot skillet with the olive oil, turning to brown on all sides.

Beef Burgers

Ingredients: Servings: 4   Cooking Time: 60 Mins.

10 oz. ground beef	2 hamburger buns
2 slices American cheese	Condiments for topping
Salt and pepper as needed	Butter for toasting

Directions:
Prepare the Sous Vide water bath using your immersion circulator and raise the temperature to 137-degrees Fahrenheit   Shape the beef into patties and season them with salt and pepper   Put in a zip bag and seal using the immersion method. Cook for 1 hour   Toast the buns in a warm cast iron pan and butter   Once the burgers are cooked, place them in the pan and sear for 30 seconds per side   Add the cheese on top and allow it to melt   Assemble the burger with topping and condiments   Serve!

Nutrition: Info Per serving:Calories: 287 ;Carbohydrate: 34g ;Protein: 11g ;Fat: 12g ;Sugar: 5g ;Sodium: 362mg

Apple Butter Pork Tenderloin

Ingredients: Servings: 3   Cooking Time: 120 Mins.

1 pork tenderloin	Salt and pepper, as needed
1 jar apple butter	
Fresh rosemary sprigs	

Directions:
Prepare the Sous Vide water bath using your immersion circulator and raise the temperature to 145-degrees Fahrenheit.   Season the pork with salt and pepper. Spread apple butter on pork.   Transfer to a resealable zip bag and add the rosemary sprigs.   Seal using the immersion method and cook for 2 hours.   Once done, remove the pork from the bag and pat dry.   Season with salt and pepper and apply apple butter generously. Sear on hot grill.   Slice and serve!

Nutrition: Info Per serving:Calories: 520 ;Carbohydrate: 84g ;Protein: 12g ;Fat: 28g ;Sugar: 38g ;Sodium: 330mg

Pork Knuckles

Ingredients: Servings: 4   Cooking Time: 24 Hrs.

2 10oz. pork knuckles	½ C. raw apple cider vinegar
Salt and pepper, to taste	2 ¾ C. apple juice
4 cloves garlic, chopped	½ C. brown sugar
½ C. mustard	4 sprigs thyme
	1 bay leaf

Directions:
Preheat Sous Vide cooker to 158 degrees F. Generously season pork knuckles with salt and pepper. Heat some oil in a large skillet. Sear pork 2 Mins. per side. Remove from the skillet. Toss the remaining ingredients into a skillet, and cook until reduced by half. Place aside to cool. Place the pork knuckles in Sous Vide bag along with the prepared sauce. Vacuum seal the bag. Submerge bag in a water bath. Cook 24 hours. Remove shanks from the bag and place aside. Strain cooking juices into a saucepan. Simmer over medium heat until thickened. Pour the sauce over shanks and serve.

Nutrition: Info Calories: 358 Protein: 29gCarbs: 42gFat: 6g

Garlic Rack Of Lamb

Ingredients: Servings: 4   Cooking Time: 1 Hour 30 Mins.

2 tbsp. butter	1 tbsp. sesame oil
2 racks of lamb, frenched	4 fresh basil sprigs, halved
1 tbsp. olive oil	Salt and black pepper to taste
4 garlic cloves, minced	

Directions:

Prepare a water bath and place the Sous Vide in it. Set to 130 F. Season the rack lamb with salt and pepper. Place in a large vacuum-sealable bag. Release air by the water displacement method, seal and submerge the bag in the water bath. Cook for 1 hour and 15 minutes. Once the timer has stopped, remove the rack and pat dry with kitchen towel. Heat sesame oil in a skillet over high heat and sear the rack for 1 Min. per side. Set aside. Put 1 tbsp. of butter in the skillet and add in half of garlic and half of basil. Top over the rack. Sear the rack for 1 minute. Turn around and pour in more butter. Repeat the process for all racks. Cut into pieces and serve 4 pieces in each plate.

Cuban Shredded Beef

Ingredients: Servings: x   Cooking Time: 24 Hours Cooking Temperature: 140°f

2-lb. center-cut chuck eye roast	2 garlic cloves, minced
Kosher salt and freshly ground black pepper, to taste	2 tsp. ground cumin
	½ tsp. red pepper flakes, crushed
4 tbsp. canola oil, divided	½ C. orange juice
1 onion, thinly sliced	2 tbsp. fresh lime juice

Directions:

Attach the sous vide immersion circulator to a Cambro container or pot with water using an adjustable clamp and preheat water to 140°F.   Season chuck roast evenly with salt and pepper.   Place roast in a cooking pouch. Seal pouch tightly after removing the excess air. Place pouch in sous vide bath and set the cooking time for 24 hours. Cover the sous vide bath with plastic wrap to minimize water evaporation. Add water intermittently to keep the water level up.   Remove pouch from the sous vide bath and open carefully. Remove roast legs from pouch and transfer to a cutting board. Shred roast into bite-sized pieces with two forks. In a large skillet, heat 2 tbsp. of oil over medium-high heat and cook onion for 5 minutes, stirring occasionally. Add garlic and spices and cook for 2 minutes. Stir in both juices and cook for 2 minutes. Stir in salt and black pepper and transfer to a bowl.   In the same skillet, heat remaining oil and cook shredded beef until browned and crisp, stirring occasionally.   Stir in cooked onion mixture, salt, and pepper and serve.

Pulled Pork(2)

Ingredients: Servings: 6   Cooking Time: 24 Hrs.

2lb. pork shoulder, trimmed	2 tbsp. maple syrup
1 tbsp. ketchup	2 tbsp. soy sauce
4 tbsp. Dijon mustard	

Directions:

Preheat your Sous Vide cooker to 158 degrees F. In a bowl, combine ketchup, mustard, maple syrup, and soy sauce. Place the pork with prepared sauce into Sous Vide bag. Vacuum seal the bag and submerge in water. Cook the pork 24 hours.   Open the bag and remove pork. Strain cooking juices into a saucepan. Torch the pork to create a crust. Simmer the cooking juices in a saucepan until thickened.   Pull pork before serving. Serve with thickened sauce.

Nutrition: Info Calories: 471 Protein: 36gCarbs: 1gFat: 38g

Tamari Steak with Scramble Eggs

Ingredients: Servings: 4   Cooking Time: 1 Hour 55 Mins.

¼ C. milk	1 tsp. onion powder
1 C. Tamari sauce	Salt and black pepper to taste
½ C. brown sugar	
⅓ C. olive oil	2 ½ lb. skirt steak
4 garlic cloves, chopped	4 eggs

Directions:

Prepare a water bath and place the Sous Vide in it. Set to 130 F. Combine the Tamari sauce, brown sugar, olive oil, onion powder, garlic, sea salt and pepper. Place the steak in a vacuum-sealable bag with the mixture. Release air by the water displacement method, seal and submerge the bag in the water bath. Cook for 1 hour and 30 minutes.   In a bowl, combine eggs, milk, and salt. Stir well. Scramble the eggs in a skillet over medium heat . Set aside. Once the timer has stopped, remove the steak and pat it dry. Heat a skillet over high heat and sear the steak for 30 seconds per side. Cut into tiny strips. Serve with the scrambled eggs.

Flank Steak with Chimichurri Sauce

Ingredients: Servings: x   Cooking Time: 36 Hours Cooking Temperature: 134°f

For Steak:	½ C. fresh mint
2-lb. flank steak	leaves
Salt and freshly	2 tsp. fresh lemon
ground black	zest
pepper, to taste	½ C. extra-virgin
For Chimichurri	olive oil
Sauce:	2 tbsp. fresh
¼ medium red	lemon juice
onion, chopped	1 tbsp. white
3 garlic cloves,	vinegar
chopped	⅓ tsp. red pepper
2 C. fresh parsley	flakes
leaves	Salt, to taste

Directions:
Attach the sous vide immersion circulator to a Cambro container or pot with water using an adjustable clamp and preheat water to 134°F.   Season flank steak evenly with salt and black pepper.   Place flank steak in a cooking pouch. Seal pouch tightly after removing the excess air. Place pouch in sous vide bath and set the cooking time for 30-36 hours. Cover the sous vide bath with plastic wrap to minimize water evaporation. Add water intermittently to keep the water level up. Preheat the grill to high heat.   For Chimichurri Sauce: add all sauce ingredients to a food processor and pulse until smooth.   Remove pouch from the sous vide bath and open carefully. Remove steak from pouch and pat dry with paper towels.   Grill flank steak for 45 seconds on each side. Remove flank steak from grill and set aside for 5 Mins. before slicing.   Cut into ½-inch slices, across the grain. Serve with a topping of chimichurri sauce.

Sunday Roast

Ingredients: Servings: 6   Cooking Time: 24hr. 20min

3lbs. chuck roast	1 large sprig fresh
2 tbsp. coarse salt	rosemary
1 tbsp. coarse	1 tbsp. olive oil
pepper	

Directions:
Preheat the water bath to 140 degrees F. Season the beef with salt and pepper. Seal it into a bag with the rosemary. Place in water bath and cook 24 hours. After 24 hours, remove beef from bag and pat dry. Sear in olive oil in a hot pan until brown on all sides.

Nutrition: Info Calories: 305 Protein: 475gCarbs: 74gFat: 101g

Sous Vide Burgers

Ingredients: Servings: 4   Cooking Time: 30mins.

2lb. ground beef	For Serving:
1 large egg	Burger Buns
1 tbsp. dried	Salad
parsley	Onion rings
1 tsp. black pepper	Tomatoes
Salt, to taste	Cheese Slices

Directions:
Heat your Sous vide cooker to 133 degrees F. In a bowl, combine beef, egg, parsley, black pepper, and desired amount of salt. Shape the mixture into patties. Use a kitchen scale to portion meat into 7oz. patties. Place two patties into Sous Vide Bag and vacuum seal. Cook the patties for 15 Mins. up to 30 minutes.   Remove the patties from the cooker. Place the patties on a large plate and set aside until cooled to a room temperature. Preheat your grill. Sear the patties 30 seconds per side. Serve with desired additions.

Nutrition: Info Calories: 216 Protein: 32gCarbs: 5gFat: 8g

Pork & Zucchini Ribbons

Ingredients: Servings: 2   Cooking Time: 3 Hours

2 (6-ounce) bone-	2 tsp. red wine
in pork loin chops	vinegar
Salt and black	2 tsp. honey
pepper as needed	2 tbsp. rice bran
3 tbsp. extra-	oil
virgin olive oil	2 medium
1 tbsp. freshly	zucchini, sliced
squeezed lemon	into ribbons
juice	2 tbsp. pine nuts,
	toasted up

Directions:
Prepare the Sous Vide water bath using your immersion circulator and raise the temperature to 140-degrees Fahrenheit.   Take the pork chops and season it with salt and pepper, transfer to a heavy duty zip bag and add 1 tbsp. of oil .   Seal using the immersion method and cook for 3 hours.   Prepare the dressing by whisking lemon juice, honey, vinegar, 2 tbsp. of olive oil and season with salt and pepper.   Once cooked, remove the bag from the water bath and discard the liquid.   Heat up rice bran oil in a large skillet over high heat and add the pork chops, sear until browned (1 Min. per side) Once done, transfer it to a cutting board and allow to rest for 5 minutes.   Take a medium bowl and add the

zucchini ribbons with dressing Thinly slice the pork chops and discard the bone. Place the pork on top of the zucchini. Top with pine nuts and serve!

Nutrition: Info Per serving:Calories: 174 ;Carbohydrate: 4g ;Protein: 19g ;Fat: 9g ;Sugar: 2g ;Sodium: 302mg

Paprika Tenderloin with Herbs

Ingredients: Servings: 4   Cooking Time: 2 Hours 20 Mins.

1 tbsp. chopped fresh basil + additional for serving	1 lb. pork tenderloin, trimmed
1 tbsp. chopped fresh parsley + additional for serving	Salt and black pepper to taste 1 tbsp. paprika 2 tbsp. butter

Directions:
Prepare a water bath and place the Sous Vide in it. Set to 134 F. For the herbs mixture, combine the basil, paprika, and parsley. Season the tenderloin with salt, pepper and herb mixture. Place in a vacuum-sealable bag. Add in 1 tbsp. of butter. Release air by the water displacement method, seal and submerge the bag in water bath. Cook for 2 hours. Once done, remove the tenderloin and transfer to a heated with butter and herb mixture skillet. Sear for 1-2 Mins. each side. Remove and allow resting for 5 minutes. Cut the tenderloin into medallions.

Bacon Strips & Eggs

Ingredients: Servings: 2   Cooking Time: 60 Mins.

2 slices British-style bacon rashers cut up into ½ inch by 3-inch slices	4 egg yolks 4 slices crisp toasted bread

Directions:
Prepare the Sous Vide water bath using your immersion circulator and raise the temperature to 143-degrees Fahrenheit. Gently place each of your egg yolks in the resealable zipper bag and seal it using the immersion method. Submerge it underwater and cook for about 1 hour. In the meantime, fry your bacon slices until they are crisp. Drain them on a kitchen towel. Once the eggs are cooked, serve by carefully removing the yolks from the zip bag and placing it on top of the toast. Top with the slices of bacon and serve!

Nutrition: Info Per serving:Calories: 385 ;Carbohydrate: 49g ;Protein: 16g ;Fat: 16g ;Sugar: 4g ;Sodium: 514mg

Pork Chop with Spiced Coffee Sauce

Ingredients: Servings: 4   Cooking Time: 2 Hours 50 Mins.

4 bone-in pork chops 1 tbsp. paprika powder 1 tbsp. ground coffee	1 tbsp. brown sugar 1 tbsp. garlic salt 1 tbsp. olive oil

Directions:
Prepare a water bath and place the Sous Vide in it. Set to 146 F. Place the pork in a vacuum-sealable bag. Release air by the water displacement method, seal and submerge the bag in water bath. Cook for 2 hours and 30 minutes. Meanwhile, prepare the sauce mixing well the paprika powder, ground coffee, brown sugar, and garlic salt. Once the timer has stopped, remove the pork and dry it. Drizzle the pork with the sauce. Heat oil in a skillet over high heat and sear the pork for 1-2 Mins. per side. Allow resting for 5 minutes. Cut the pork in slices and serve.

POULTRY RECIPES

Crispy Chicken with Mushrooms

Ingredients: Servings: 4   Cooking Time: 1 Hour 15 Mins.

4 boneless chicken breasts 1 C. panko bread crumbs 1 lb. sliced Portobello mushrooms	Small bunch of thyme 2 eggs Salt and black pepper to taste Canola oil to taste

Directions:
Prepare a water bath and place the Sous Vide in it. Set to 149 F. Place the chicken in a vacuum-sealable bag. Season with salt and thyme. Release air by the water displacement method, seal and submerge in water bath. Cook for 60 minutes. Meanwhile, heat a skillet over medium heat. Cook the mushrooms until the water has evaporated. Add in 3-4 sprigs of thyme. Season with salt and pepper. Once the timer has stopped, remove the bag. Heat a frying pan with oil over medium heat. Mix the panko with salt and pepper. Layer the chicken in

panko mix. Fry for 1-2 Mins. per side. Serve with mushrooms.

Turkey Breast with Crispy Skin

Ingredients: Servings: x   Cooking Time: 3 Hours 30 Mins. Cooking Temperature: 145°f

For Turkey Breast: 5-lb. whole skin-on, bone-in turkey breast	1 large carrot, peeled and roughly chopped
Kosher salt and freshly ground black pepper, to taste	1 large onion, roughly chopped
For Gravy:	4 C. low-sodium chicken broth
1 tbsp. vegetable oil	1 tsp. soy sauce
2 celery ribs, roughly chopped	2 bay leaves
	3 tbsp. butter
	¼ C. flour

Directions:

Attach the sous vide immersion circulator to a Cambro container or pot with water using an adjustable clamp and preheat water to 145°F.   Carefully remove turkey skin in a single piece and set aside. with a sharp boning knife, carefully remove meat from breastbone and set breastbone aside after chopping it into 1-inch chunks. Season turkey breast generously with salt and black pepper. Place 1 breast half onto a smooth surface with the cut side facing up. Place second breast half with the cut side facing down and the fat end aligning with the skinny end of the first breast half. Gently roll up breast halves into an even cylinder and tie at 1-inch intervals with kitchen twine.   Place turkey roll in a cooking pouch. Seal pouch tightly after removing the excess air. Place pouch in sous vide bath and set the cooking time for 2½ hours.   Preheat oven to 400°F. Arrange a rack in the center position of the oven. Line a rimmed baking sheet with parchment paper.   For crispy skin: spread skin evenly onto prepared baking sheet. Season generously with salt and black pepper. Arrange a second parchment paper over the turkey skin and carefully squeeze out any air bubbles with the side of your hand. Place another rimmed baking sheet on top of the parchment paper.   Roast for 30-45 minutes. Remove from oven and set aside to cool in room temperature. For gravy: heat oil over high heat in a medium pan. Add chopped breastbone, celery, carrot, and onion and cook for 10 minutes, stirring occasionally.   Add broth, soy sauce, and bay leaves and bring to a boil. Reduce heat and simmer for 1 hour. Through a fine-mesh strainer, strain mixture. The broth should be a little over 4 cups. Discard solids from mixture and keep broth, setting aside.   in another medium pan, melt butter over medium heat. Add flour and cook for 3 minutes, stirring continuously. Slowly add broth, beating continuously, and bring to a boil. Reduce heat and simmer until mixture reduces to 3 cups. Season with salt and pepper. Remove pouch from the sous vide bath and open carefully. Remove turkey roll from pouch and carefully remove kitchen twine.   Cut roll into ¼-½ inch slices. Break skin into serving-sized pieces. Place turkey slices onto a warmed serving platter with skin pieces arranged around and serve alongside gravy.

Herby Chicken with Butternut Squash Dish

Ingredients: Servings: 2   Cooking Time: 1 Hour 15 Mins.

6 chicken tenderloin	2 tbsp. olive oil
4 C. butternut squash, cubed and roasted	4 tbsp. red onion, chopped
4 C. rocket lettuce	1 tbsp. paprika
4 tbsp. sliced almonds	1 tbsp. turmeric
Juice of 1 lemon	1 tbsp. cumin
	Salt to taste

Directions:

Prepare a water bath and place the Sous Vide in it. Set to 138 F.   Place the chicken and all seasonings in a vacuum-sealable bag. Release air by the water displacement method, seal and submerge in water bath. Cook for 60 minutes.   Once the timer has stopped, remove the bag and transfer the chicken to a hot skillet. Sear for 1 Min. per side. In a bowl, combine the remaining ingredients. Serve the chicken with the salad.

Greek Meatballs

Ingredients: Servings: 4   Cooking Time: 120 Mins.

1 tbsp. extra-virgin olive oil	1 lb. ground chicken
2 garlic cloves, minced	½ tsp. grated lemon zest
1 tsp. fresh oregano, minced	½ tsp. freshly ground black pepper
1 tsp. kosher salt	¼ C. panko bread crumbs
	Lemon wedges for serving

Directions:

Prepare your Sous Vide water bath, using your immersion circulator, and raise the temperature to 146-degrees Fahrenheit   Add the garlic, olive oil, chicken, oregano, lemon zest, salt, and pepper in a medium-sized bowl   Mix well everything using your hands and gently mix in the panko bread crumbs   Form the mixture into 14 balls   Put the balls in a resealable bag and seal using the immersion method   Submerge the bag and cook for 2 hours   Remove the bag and transfer the balls to a baking sheet /lined with foil   Set your broiler to high heat   Broil the balls for 5-7 Mins. until they turn brown   Serve with lemon wedges

Nutrition: Info Calories: 238 Carbohydrate: 3g Protein: 8g Fat: 21g Sugar: 2g Sodium: 332mg

Cheesy Chicken Balls

Ingredients: Servings: 6   Cooking Time: 1 Hour 15 Mins.

1 lb. ground chicken	32 small, diced cubes of
2 tbsp. onion, finely chopped	mozzarella cheese
¼ tsp. garlic powder	1 tbsp. butter
Salt and black pepper to taste	3 tbsp. panko
2 tbsp. breadcrumbs	½ C. tomato sauce
1 egg	½ oz. grated Pecorino Romano cheese
	Chopped parsley

Directions:
Prepare a water bath and place the Sous Vide in it. Set to 146 F. In a bowl, mix the chicken, onion, salt, garlic powder, pepper, and seasoned breadcrumbs. Add in egg and combine well. Form 32 medium-size balls and fill with a cube of cheese, make sure the mix covers the cheese well.   Place the balls in a vacuum-sealable bag and let chill for 20 minutes. Then, release air by the water displacement method, seal and submerge the bag in the water bath. Cook for 45 minutes.   Once the timer has stopped, remove the balls. Melt butter in a skillet over high heat and add panko. Cook until toast. As well cook the tomato sauce. In a serving dish, place the balls and glaze with the tomato sauce. Top with the panko and cheese. Garnish with parsley.

Duck Breast A La Orange

Ingredients: Servings: x   Cooking Time: 3 Hours 40 Mins. Cooking Temperature: 135°f

2 (6-ounce) duck breasts	4 fresh thyme sprigs
1 shallot, quartered	Salt and freshly ground black pepper, to taste
4 garlic cloves, crushed	1 tbsp. sherry

Juice and zest of 1 orange	vinegar
1 tbsp. black peppercorns	1 C. chicken broth
	2 tbsp. cold, unsalted butter

Directions:
Attach the sous vide immersion circulator to a Cambro container or pot with water using an adjustable clamp and preheat water to 135°F.   Place duck breasts, shallot, garlic, thyme, orange zest, juice from orange, and the peppercorns in a cooking pouch. Seal pouch tightly after removing the excess air. Place pouch in sous vide bath and set the cooking time for 3½ hours. Remove pouch from the sous vide bath and open carefully. Remove the duck breasts from pouch, reserving the remaining pouch ingredients and liquid. Pat dry the duck breasts with paper towels. Using a sharp knife, score a wide crisscross pattern on the top skin of both breasts. Season breasts evenly with salt and pepper.   Heat a non-stick sauté pan over medium heat and sear breasts for 5 minutes. Transfer the duck breasts to a plate, discarding the duck fat left in the pan. For sauce: in the same pan, add vinegar over medium-high heat and scrape browned bits from bottom of pan. Add the broth and the reserved orange mixture from pouch and simmer until sauce reduces to ¼ cup. Add cold butter and beat until well combined. Stir in desired amount of salt and black pepper and remove from heat. Cut duck breasts into desired slices and serve alongside orange sauce.

Rosemary Chicken Stew

Ingredients: Servings: 2   Cooking Time: 4 Hours 15 Mins.

2 chicken thighs	2 bay leaves
6 garlic cloves, crushed	¼ C. dark soy sauce
¼ tsp. whole black pepper	¼ C. white vinegar
	1 tbsp. rosemary

Directions:
Prepare a water bath and place the Sous Vide in it. Set to 165 F. Combine the chicken thighs with all the ingredients. Place in a vacuum-sealable bag. Release air by the water displacement method, seal and submerge in water bath. Cook for 4 hours.   Once the timer has stopped, remove the chicken, discard bay leaves and reserve the cooking juices. Heat canola oil in a skillet over medium heat and sear the chicken. Add in cooking juices and cook until you have reached the desired consistency. Filter the sauce and top the chicken.

Duck Leg Confit

Ingredients: Servings: 2   Cooking Time: 12 Hours 10 Mins.

2 duck legs	Salt and pepper to
1 tbsp. dried	taste
thyme	Cranberry sauce
2 big bay leaves,	for serving
crushed	
6 tbsp. duck fat	

Directions:
Preheat your Sous Vide machine to 167°F.   Mix the bay leaves with salt, pepper and thyme, and season the duck legs with the mixture.   Refrigerate overnight.   In the morning, rinse the legs with cold water and carefully put them into the vacuum bag.   Add 4 tbsp. duck fat, seal the bag removing the air as much as possible, put it into the water bath and set the cooking time for 12 hours. Before serving, roast the legs in 2 remaining tbsp. of duck fat until crispy.   Serve with cranberry sauce.

Nutrition: Info Per serving:Calories 529, Carbohydrates 15 g, Fats 37 g, Protein 34 g,

Sweet & Sour Chicken Wings

Ingredients: Servings: 2   Cooking Time: 2 Hours 15 Mins.

12 chicken wings	2 tbsp. brown
Salt and black	sugar
pepper to taste	¼ C. mirin
1 C. chicken fry	Sesame seeds for
mix	garnish
½ C. water	Cornstarch slurry
½ C. tamari sauce	(mixed 1 tbsp.
½ minced onion	cornstarch and 2
5 garlic cloves,	tbsp. water)
minced	Olive oil for frying
2 tsp. ginger	
powder	

Directions:
Prepare a water bath and place the Sous Vide in it. Set to 147 F.   Place the chicken wings in a vacuum-sealable bag and season with salt and pepper. Release air by the water displacement method, seal and submerge the bag in the water bath. Cook for 2 hours. Once the timer has stopped, remove the bag. Heat a frying pan with oil.   In a bowl, combine 1/2 C. of fry mix and 1/2 C. of water. Pour the remaining fry mix in another bowl. Soak the wings in the wet mix, then in the dry mix. Fry for 1-2 Mins. until crispy and golden brown.   For the sauce, heat a saucepan and pour all the ingredients; cook until bubbly. Stir in the wings. Top with sesame seeds and serve.

Thyme & Rosemary Turkey Legs

Ingredients: Servings: 4   Cooking Time: 8 Hours 30 Mins.

5 tsp. butter,	1 tbsp. cumin
melted	1 tbsp. thyme
10 garlic cloves,	2 turkey legs
minced	
2 tbsp. dried	
rosemary	

Directions:
Prepare a water bath and place the Sous Vide in it. Set to 134 F.   Combine the garlic, rosemary, cumin, thyme, and butter. Rub the turkey with the mixture.   Place the turkey in a vacuum-sealable bag. Release air by the water displacement method, seal and submerge the bag in the water bath. Cook for 8 hours   Once the timer has stopped, remove the turkey. Reserve cooking juices. Heat a grill over high heat and put the turkey. Sprinkle with cooking juices. Turn around and sprinkle with some more juices. Set aside and allow to cool. Serve.

Lemon Chicken with Mint

Ingredients: Servings: 3   Cooking Time: 2 Hours 40 Mins.

1 lb. chicken	¼ C. oil
thighs, boneless	1 tsp. ginger
and skinless	½ tsp. cayenne
1 tbsp. freshly	pepper
squeezed lemon	1 tsp. fresh mint,
juice	finely chopped
2 garlic cloves,	½ tsp. salt
crushed	

Directions:
In a small bowl, combine olive oil with lemon juice, garlic, ground ginger, mint, cayenne pepper, and salt. Generously brush each thigh with this mixture and refrigerate for at least 30 minutes.   Remove thighs from the refrigerator. Place in a large vacuum-sealable bag and cook for 2 hours at 149 F. Remove from the vacuum-sealable bag and serve immediately with spring onions.

Cheesy Chicken Salad with Chickpeas

Ingredients: Servings: 2   Cooking Time: 1 Hour 30 Mins.

6 chicken breast tenderloins, boneless, skinless
4 tbsp. olive oil
2 tbsp. hot sauce
1 tsp. ground cumin
1 tsp. light brown sugar
1 tsp. ground cinnamon
Salt and black pepper to taste
1 can drained chickpeas
½ C. crumbled feta cheese
½ C. crumbled queso fresco cheese
½ C. torn basil
½ C. freshly torn mint
4 tsp. pine nuts, toasted
2 tsp. honey
2 tsp. freshly squeezed lemon juice

Directions:

Prepare a water bath and place the Sous Vide in it. Set to 138 F. Place the chicken breasts, 2 tbsp. of olive oil, hot sauce, brown sugar, cumin, and cinnamon in a vacuum-sealable bag. Season with salt and pepper. Release air by the water displacement method, seal and submerge the bag in the water bath. Cook for 75 minutes. Meanwhile, combine in a bowl the chickpeas, basil, queso fresco, mint, and pine nuts. Pour in honey, lemon juice and 2 tbsp. of olive oil. Season with salt and pepper. Once the timer has stopped, remove the chicken and chop in bites. Discard cooking juices. Stir the salad and chicken, mix well and serve.

Pheasant Confit

Ingredients: Servings: x   Cooking Time: 4-8 Hours 45 Mins. Cooking Temperature: 170-180°f

2 tsp. fresh lemon zest, minced
1 tbsp. dried thyme, crushed
1 tbsp. freshly ground black pepper
¼ C. kosher salt
6 pheasant legs with thighs
2 bay leaves
6 tbsp. olive oil or melted butter

Directions:

In a large bowl, mix together lemon zest, thyme, salt, and black pepper. Add pheasant legs and toss to coat with mixture. Refrigerate for 6-24 hours. Attach the sous vide immersion circulator to a Cambro container or pot with water using an adjustable clamp and preheat water to 170-180°F. Remove pheasant legs from the refrigerator and rinse under cold running water. Pat dry each leg with paper towels. Place 3 legs, 1 bay leaf, and 2-3 tbsp. of oil or butter in a cooking pouch. Repeat with remaining legs, bay leaf, and oil or butter so that you have 2 cooking pouches. Seal pouches tightly after removing the excess air. Place pouches in sous vide bath and set the cooking time for 4-8 hours, flipping every 30 minutes. Young, tender pheasant will only need 4 hours cooking time, but older pheasant will need 8 hours. Prepare a greased baking sheet. Remove pouches from the sous vide bath and immediately plunge into a large bowl of ice water. Remove pheasant legs from the pouches and pat dry with paper towels. Set the oven temperature to 400°F. Preheating isn't required. Place pheasant legs onto greased baking sheet, skin side up, and roast for 15-45 Mins. or until legs reach desired crispness.

Classic Chicken Cordon Bleu

Ingredients: Servings: 4   Cooking Time: 1 Hour 50 Mins. + Cooling Time

½ C. butter
4 boneless, skinless chicken breasts
Salt and black pepper to taste
1 tsp. cayenne pepper
4 garlic cloves, minced
8 slices ham
8 slices Emmental cheese

Directions:

Prepare a water bath and place the Sous Vide in it. Set to 141 F. Season the chicken with salt and pepper. Cover with plastic wrap and rolled. Set aside and allow to chill. Heat a saucepan over medium heat and add some black pepper, cayenne pepper, 1/4 C. of butter, and garlic. Cook until the butter melts. Transfer to a bowl. Rub the chicken on one side with the butter mixture. Then place 2 slices of ham and 2 slices of cheese and cover it. Roll each breast with plastic wrap and transfer to the fridge for 2-3 hours or in the freezer for 20-30 minutes. Place the breast in two vacuum-sealable bags. Release air by the water displacement method, seal and submerge the bags in the water bath. Cook for 1 hour and 30 minutes. Once the timer has stopped, remove the breasts and take off the plastic. Heat the remaining butter in a skillet over medium heat and sear the chicken for 1-2 Mins. per side.

Aji Amarillo Chicken Wings

Ingredients: Servings: x   Cooking Time: 4 Hours 15 Mins. Cooking Temperature: 160°f

For Sauce:
½ white onion, chopped
3 Aji Amarillo peppers, seeded and roughly
1 tsp. olive oil
Salt and freshly ground black pepper, to taste
For Wings:
40 split chicken

chopped	wings
2 garlic cloves, chopped	Salt and freshly ground black
2 tbsp. white vinegar	pepper, to taste

Directions:

Attach the sous vide immersion circulator to a Cambro container or pot with water using an adjustable clamp and preheat water to 160°F. For sauce: in a pan, heat oil over medium heat and sauté onion, peppers, and garlic until onion is translucent and peppers softened. Transfer mixture to a blender, add vinegar, salt, and black pepper, and pulse until smooth. Reserve 1 tbsp. of sauce in a bowl. Season chicken wings lightly with salt and black pepper. Place chicken wings and all but the 1 tbsp. of reserved sauce in a cooking pouch. Seal pouch tightly after removing the excess air. Place pouch in sous vide bath and set the cooking time for 4 hours. Preheat the oven broiler to high. Line a baking sheet with parchment paper. Remove pouch from the sous vide bath and open carefully, removing chicken wings from pouch. Arrange chicken wings onto the prepared baking sheet in a single layer. Broil for 10-15 minutes, flipping once halfway through the cooking time. Remove from oven and transfer into bowl of reserved sauce. Toss to coat well and serve immediately.

Chicken Breast with Lemon And French Herbs

Ingredients: Servings: 2   Cooking Time: 3 Hours 20 Mins.

2 chicken breast fillets	1 tbsp. unsalted butter
Salt and pepper to taste	1 C. button mushrooms,
1 tsp. olive oil	coarsely chopped
For the sauce:	2 tbsp. white wine
1 onion, sliced	½ C. chicken
2 garlic cloves, minced	broth
1 tbsp. olive oil	1 C. cream
	Salt and pepper to taste

Directions:

Preheat your sous vide machine to 145°F. Carefully put the chicken breasts into the vacuum bag. Add the butter, salt, pepper and halved garlic cloves and seal the bag removing the air as much as possible. Put it into the water bath and set the cooking time for 3 hours. While the chicken is cooking, make the sauce. Heat olive oil in a medium skillet, and cook the chopped onion for about 2-3 minutes. Add the butter and minced garlic and cook for 2 more minutes. Add the chopped mushrooms and cook at the medium heat until the liquid evaporates. Add the white wine, cook until the liquid almost evaporates and add the chicken broth and cream. Continue cooking until the sauce thickens, add salt and pepper if needed. Set the sauce aside. Remove the cooked chicken from the sous vide machine and roast it in a skillet on both sides until light brown. Add the sauce and wait just till it heats to the desired temperature. Serve with mashed potato.

Nutrition: Info   Per   serving:Calories   261, Carbohydrates 12 g, Fats 9 g, Protein 33 g

Teriyaki Chicken

Ingredients: Servings: x   Cooking Time: 56 Mins. Cooking Temperature: 145°f

For Chicken Bowl:	Salt, to taste
1 tsp. garlic, minced	1 tbsp. corn flour
1 tsp. fresh ginger, minced	1 tbsp. water
4 tbsp. sake	4 eggs
4 tbsp. soy sauce	2 C. white rice
2 tbsp. rice wine vinegar	For Pickled Veggies:
1 tbsp. brown sugar	3 C. veggies (2-parts carrot and cucumber, 1-part
¼ tsp. chili powder	red onion and daikon), sliced finely
Freshly ground black pepper, to taste	1 C. water
	1 C. vinegar
4 medium chicken thighs	2 tbsp. brown sugar
	1 tbsp. salt

Directions:

Attach the sous vide immersion circulator to a Cambro container or pot with water using an adjustable clamp and preheat water to 145°F. In a bowl, add garlic, ginger, sake, soy sauce, vinegar, brown sugar, chili powder, and black pepper and mix until well combined. Place chicken thighs in a cooking pouch with the ginger mixture. Seal pouch tightly after removing the excess air. Place pouch in sous vide bath and set the cooking time for 50 minutes. Gently place the eggs in the same sous vide bath for 50 minutes. Prepare white rice according to the package's directions   For pickled veggies: add all ingredients in a pan over high heat and bring to a boil. Remove from heat and set aside until chicken cooks, keeping the pan covered. Remove pouch and eggs from the sous vide bath. Carefully open pouch and remove chicken thighs, reserving the cooking liquid in a bowl. Pat dry chicken thighs with paper towels. Lightly season chicken thighs with salt.   In a small bowl, dissolve corn flour into water. Add the flour mixture to the bowl of reserved cooking liquid and stir to combine. Heat a non-stick skillet over medium heat and sear chicken thighs for 2 Mins. on each side. Add reserved liquid mixture to the skillet for the last Min. of cooking and toss chicken thighs to coat.   with a slotted spoon, transfer chicken thighs to a platter. Continue cooking sauce in the skillet, stirring continuously, until it reaches desired thickness. Remove sauce from heat. Drain pickled veggies and cut chicken thighs into desired slices.   Divide cooked rice into serving bowls and top with chicken slices. Pour sauce over chicken slices and place pickled veggies on the side. Crack the egg over rice and chicken. Season with salt and pepper and serve.

Sriracha Chicken Breasts

Ingredients: Servings: 4   Cooking Time: 1 Hour 55 Mins.

1 lb. boneless skinless chicken breasts	8 tbsp. butter, cubed
Salt and black pepper to taste	1 tsp. nutmeg
	1½ C. sriracha sauce

Directions:
Prepare a water bath and place the Sous Vide in it. Set to 141 F.   Season the breasts with salt, nutmeg and pepper and. place in two vacuum-sealable bags with sriracha sauce. Release air by the water displacement method, seal and submerge the bags in the water bath. Cook for 1 hour and 30 minutes.   Once the timer has stopped, remove the chicken and pat dry with kitchen towel. Discard the cooking juices. Heat butter in a skillet over high heat and cook the breasts for 1 Min. per side. Cut the breasts into tiny pieces.

Hawaiian Chicken

Ingredients: Servings: x   Cooking Time: 3 Hours 5 Mins. Cooking Temperature: 147°f

For Glaze:	For Chicken:
2 C. chicken broth	6 lb. boneless, skinless chicken thighs
1½ C. soy sauce	
¾ C. light brown sugar	1 (3-inch) piece fresh ginger, peeled and cut into three pieces
½ C. plus 1 tbsp. water, divided	
½ C. mirin	
1 tbsp. fish sauce	6 large garlic cloves, minced
3 tbsp. cornstarch	
1 tbsp. water	For Garnishing:

1 C. scallions, thinly sliced

Directions:
Attach the sous vide immersion circulator to a Cambro container or pot with water using an adjustable clamp and preheat water to 147°F.   In a large bowl, add chicken broth, soy sauce, brown sugar, ½ C. water, mirin, and fish sauce and beat until well combined for the glaze.   Divide the glaze, chicken, ginger, and garlic into three cooking pouches. Seal the pouches tightly after removing the excess air. Place pouches in sous vide bath and set the cooking time for 3 hours.   Remove the pouches from the sous vide bath and open carefully. Strain half of the cooking liquid into a pan. Transfer all chicken into a new cooking pouch and seal it. Return pouch to sous vide bath with the sous vide turned off. Place pan of reserved cooking liquid on stove and bring to a boil. In a small bowl, dissolve cornstarch into 1 tbsp. of water. Add the cornstarch mixture to the cooking liquid, stirring continuously. Cook until the glaze becomes thick.   Place chicken on a platter and top with glaze. Garnish with scallions and serve.

Greek Flavored Chicken Meatballs

Ingredients: Servings: x   Cooking Time: 2 Hours Cooking Temperature: 146°f

1-lb. ground chicken	½ tsp. fresh lemon zest, finely grated
2 garlic cloves, minced	1 tbsp. extra-virgin olive oil
1 tsp. fresh oregano, minced	¼ C. panko breadcrumbs
1 tsp. kosher salt	
½ tsp. freshly ground black pepper	Lemon wedges, for serving

Directions:
Attach the sous vide immersion circulator to a Cambro container or pot with water using an adjustable clamp and preheat water to 146°F.   In a bowl, add all ingredients except for the breadcrumbs and lemon wedges and mix with your hands until well combined. Add breadcrumbs and gently mix. Make 12-14 equal-sized meatballs from the mixture.   Place the meatballs in a cooking pouch. Seal pouch tightly after removing the excess air. Place pouch in sous vide bath and set the cooking time for 2 hours.   Preheat the oven broiler to high. Line a rimmed baking sheet with a piece of foil. Remove the pouch from the sous vide bath and open carefully, removing the meatballs from pouch. Arrange meatballs onto the prepared baking sheet.

Broil meatballs for 5-7 minutes, flipping once halfway through cooking time. Serve alongside lemon wedges.

Sticky Duck Wings

Ingredients: Servings: 6   Cooking Time: 2 Hours

3lb. duck wings	¼ C. ketchup
1 tbsp. mustard	2 tbsp. Cajun spice
½ C. honey	blend
1 tbsp. soy sauce	¼ C. butter
1 tbsp. hot sauce	Salt and pepper,
	to taste

Directions:
Preheat Sous Vide cooker to 150F.   Cut the wings into portions and rub with Cajun blend. Season with some salt and pepper.   Transfer the wings into cooking bags and add butter.   Vacuum seal the wings and submerge in water.   Cook the wings 2 hours.   Finishing steps: Preheat your broiler.   Combine remaining ingredients in a bowl.   Remove the wings from the cooker and toss with prepared sauce.   Arrange the wings on baking sheet and broil 10 minutes, basting with any remaining sauce during that time.   Serve warm.

Nutrition: Info Calories 305 Total Fat 11g Total Carb 27g Dietary Fiber 7g Protein 18g

Chicken with Cherry Marmalade

Ingredients: Servings: 4   Cooking Time: 4 Hours 25 Mins.

2 lb. bone-in skin-on chicken	2 tbsp. ground nutmeg
4 tbsp. cherry marmalade	Salt and black pepper to taste

Directions:
Prepare a water bath and place the Sous Vide in it. Set to 172 F. Season the chicken with salt and pepper and combine with the remaining ingredients. Place in a vacuum-sealable bag. Release air by the water displacement method, seal and submerge the bag in the water bath. Cook for 4 hours.   Once the timer has stopped, remove the bag and move into a baking dish. Heat the oven to 450 F. and roast for 10 Mins. until crispy. Transfer to a plate and serve.

Thai Green Curry Noodle Soup

Ingredients: Servings: 2   Cooking Time: 90 Mins.

1 chicken breast, boneless and skinless	1½ tbsp. palm sugar
Salt and pepper as needed	½ C. Thai basil leaves, roughly chopped
1 can /15 oz. coconut milk	2 oz. cooked egg noodle nests
2 tbsp. Thai Green Curry Paste	1 C. cilantro, roughly chopped
1¾ C. chicken stock	1 C. bean sprouts
1 C. enoki mushrooms	2 tbsp. fried noodles
5 kaffir lime leaves, torn in half	2 red Thai chilis, roughly chopped
2 tbsp. fish sauce	

Directions:
Prepare your water bath using your Sous Vide immersion circulator, and raise the temperature to 140-degrees Fahrenheit   Take the chicken and season it generously with salt and pepper and place it in a medium-sized, resealable bag with 1 tbsp. of coconut milk   Seal it using the immersion method and submerge. Cook for 90 Mins.   After 35 minutes, place a medium-sized saucepan over a medium heat   Add the green curry paste and half the coconut milk   Bring the mix to a simmer and cook for 5-10 Mins. until the coconut milk starts to show a beady texture   Add the chicken stock and the rest of the coconut milk and bring the mixture to a simmer once again, keep cooking for about 15 Mins.   Add the kaffir lime leaves, enoki mushrooms, palm sugar and fish sauce   Lower the heat to medium-low and simmer for about 10 Mins. Remove from the heat and season with palm sugar and fish sauce, stir in the basil   Once the chicken is cooked fully, transfer it to a cooking board. Let it cool for few Mins. and then cut into slices   Serve the chicken with the curry sauce and a topping of cooked egg noodles   Garnish the chicken with some bean sprouts, cilantro, Thai chilies and fried noodles. Serve!

Nutrition: Info Calories: 237 Carbohydrate: 21g Protein: 15g Fat: 11g Sugar: 5g Sodium: 567mg

Chicken with Sun-dried Tomatoes

Ingredients: Servings: 3   Cooking Time: 1 Hour 15 Mins.

1 lb. chicken breasts, skinless and boneless	1 tbsp. fresh mint, finely chopped
½ C. sun-dried tomatoes	1 tbsp. minced shallots
1 tsp. raw honey	1 tbsp. olive oil
2 tbsp. fresh lemon juice	Salt and black pepper to taste

Directions:

Rinse the chicken breasts under cold running water and pat dry with a kitchen paper. Set aside. In a medium bowl, combine lemon juice, honey, mint, shallots, olive oil, salt, and pepper. Mix together until well incorporated. Add chicken breasts and sun-dried tomatoes. Shake to coat all well. Transfer all to a large vacuum-sealable bag. Press the bag to remove the air and seal the lid. Cook en Sous Vide for 1 hour at 167 F. Remove from the water bath and serve immediately.

Mediterranean Chicken

Ingredients: Servings: 2   Cooking Time: 90 Mins.

2 chicken breast fillets	2 tbsp. oil, from the sun-dried tomatoes
½ C. sun-dried tomatoes, packed in oil	1 sprig basil
Salt and black pepper, to taste	1 tbsp. olive oil

Directions:
Preheat the Sous Vide Cooker to 140ºF. Season the chicken with salt and pepper. Heat the olive oil in a skillet. Add chicken breasts and cook for 1 Min. per side. Transfer immediately into Sous Vide bag, and add remaining ingredients. Vacuum seal the bag and submerge in water. Cook the chicken 90 minutes. Remove the bag with chicken from the Cooker. Open the bag and transfer the chicken to a warmed plate. Serve.

Nutrition: Info Per serving:Calories 400, Carbohydrates 17.8 g, Fats 21.7 g, Protein 33.4 g

Chicken Parmigiana

Ingredients: Servings: x   Cooking Time: 12 Hours Cooking Temperature: 141°f

For Chicken:	¼ C. Parmesan cheese, grated
4 chicken breasts	
½ tsp. garlic powder	¾ C. dried Italian breadcrumbs
Salt and freshly ground black pepper, to taste	2 tbsp. fresh parsley, chopped
4 fresh rosemary sprigs	For Cooking: Oil, as required
4 fresh thyme sprigs	For Topping:
For Coating:	½ C. fresh basil, chopped
¾ C. flour	1 C. fresh mozzarella cheese, shredded
2 tsp. salt	
1 tsp. ground black	¼ C. Parmesan cheese, grated

pepper
2 eggs

Directions:
Season chicken breasts with garlic powder, salt, and black pepper evenly. Divide chicken breasts and herb sprigs into two cooking pouches. Seal pouches tightly after removing the excess air. Refrigerate pouches for up to 2 days. Attach the sous vide immersion circulator to a Cambro container or pot with water using an adjustable clamp and preheat water to 141°F. Place pouches in sous vide bath and set the cooking time for 2-12 hours. Preheat the oven broiler. Remove the pouches from the sous vide bath and open carefully. Remove the chicken breasts and pat dry chicken breasts completely with paper towels. In a shallow dish, mix together flour, salt, and black pepper for coating. In a second shallow dish, beat eggs. In a third shallow dish, mix together Parmesan cheese, breadcrumbs, and parsley. Coat chicken breasts evenly with flour mixture, then dip in egg mixture before coating with parmesan mixture. In a deep skillet, heat ½-inch of oil to 350°F and sear chicken breasts until crust is golden brown then turn and repeat on other side. Transfer chicken breasts to a sheet pan. Top each breast with the basil, Parmesan, and mozzarella cheese for topping. Broil until cheese is bubbly. Serve immediately.

Turkey Breast with Cloves

Ingredients: Servings: 6   Cooking Time: 1 Hour 45 Mins.

2 lb. turkey breast, sliced	2 tbsp. lemon juice
2 garlic cloves, minced	1 tsp. fresh rosemary, finely chopped
1 C. olive oil	
2 tbsp. Dijon mustard	1 tsp. cloves, minced
	Salt and black pepper to taste

Directions:
In a large bowl, combine olive oil, with mustard, lemon juice, garlic, rosemary, cloves, salt, and pepper. Mix until well incorporated and add turkey slices. Soak and refrigerate for 30 Mins. before cooking. Remove from the refrigerator and transfer to 2 vacuum-sealable bags. Seal the bags and cook en Sous Vide for one hour at 149 F. Remove from the water bath and serve.

Zucchini Mini Chicken Bites

Ingredients: Servings: 2   Cooking Time: 75 Mins.

1 chicken breast, boneless, skinless, butterflied
Salt and pepper as needed
3 tbsp. extra-virgin olive oil

1 tbsp. pesto
1 zucchini, sliced into ¼ inch pieces
¼ C. water
1 avocado
1 C. fresh basil leaves

Directions:

Prepare your Sous Vide water bath using your immersion circulator, and raise the temperature to 140-degrees Fahrenheit lb. the chicken breast with mallet until it has an even thickness, season with pepper and salt and place in a zip bag Add 1 tbsp. of oil and the pesto and seal using the immersion method and cook for 75 Mins. After 60 minutes, heat 1 tbsp. of olive oil in large skillet over a medium-high heat, and add the zucchini and water Cook until the water has evaporated Once cooked, carefully remove the bag from the water bath and take out the chicken Heat the remaining oil over a medium/high heat. Allow it to shimmer Add in the chicken and sear for 2 Mins. per side Transfer the chicken on a cutting board and allow it to cool for 5 Mins. Slice it into pieces, roughly the same size as the zucchini Slice the avocado to the same size Serve by stacking slices of avocado on top of the chicken and topping them with a slice of zucchini and a basil leaf Secure with toothpicks and drizzle olive oil over and then serve!

Nutrition: Info Calories: 260 Carbohydrate: 36g Protein: 11g Fat: 7g Sugar: 3g Sodium: 416mg

Chicken Breast with Mushroom Sauce

Ingredients: Servings: x   Cooking Time: 4 Hours Cooking Temperature: 140°f

For Chicken:
2 boneless, skinless chicken breasts
⅛ tsp. salt
1 tsp. vegetable oil
For Mushroom Sauce:
3 French shallots, finely chopped
2 large garlic cloves, finely chopped

1 tsp. olive oil
2 tbsp. butter
1 C. button mushrooms, sliced
2 tbsp. port wine
½ C. chicken broth
1 C. cream
Salt, to taste
¼ tsp. cracked black pepper

Directions:

Attach the sous vide immersion circulator to a Cambro container or pot with water using an adjustable clamp and preheat water to 140°F. Season chicken breasts lightly with salt. Place chicken breasts in a large cooking pouch. Seal pouch tightly after removing the excess air. Place pouch in sous vide bath and set the cooking time for 1½-4 hours. For the mushroom sauce: heat olive oil in a skillet over medium heat and sauté shallots for 2-3 minutes. Stir in butter and garlic and sauté for 1 minute. Increase the heat to medium-high. Stir in mushrooms and cook until all liquid is absorbed. Add wine. Cook until all liquid is absorbed then add broth and cook for 2 minutes. Stir in cream and reduce heat back to medium. Once the sauce becomes thick, stir in the black pepper and desired amount of salt and remove from heat. Remove pouch from the sous vide bath and open carefully. Remove chicken breasts from pouch and pat dry chicken breasts completely with paper towels. Coat chicken breasts evenly with vegetable oil. Heat a grill pan over high heat and cook chicken breasts for 1 Min. per side. Divide onto serving plates once cooked, top with mushroom sauce, and serve.

Chicken Cacciatore

Ingredients: Servings: 4   Cooking Time: 3 Hours

4 boneless, skinless chicken breasts
½ can /14 oz. whole tomatoes, crushed
1 small onion, sliced
1 red bell pepper, cut into strips

2 sprigs fresh thyme
1 bay leaf
3 cloves garlic, minced
1 tsp. salt
1 tsp. pepper to
Cooked pasta for serving

Directions:

Preheat the water bath to 145°F. Combine chicken, tomatoes, onion, bell pepper, thyme, bay leaf, garlic, and salt and pepper in a bag. Seal using water method. Place in water bath and cook 3 hours.

Nutrition: Info Calories – 336 Total Fat –87 g Total Carb – 128 g Dietary fiber – 3 g Protein –542 g

Oregano Chicken Meatballs

Ingredients: Servings: 4   Cooking Time: 2 Hours 20 Mins.

1 lb. ground chicken
1 tbsp. olive oil
2 garlic cloves, minced
1 tsp. fresh

1 tbsp. cumin
½ tsp. grated lemon zest
½ tsp. black pepper
¼ C. panko

oregano, minced breadcrumbs
Salt to taste Lemon wedges

Directions:

Prepare a water bath and place Sous Vide in it. Set to 146 F. Combine in a bowl ground chicken, garlic, olive oil, oregano, lemon zest, cumin, salt, and pepper. Using your hands make at least 14 meatballs. Place the meatballs in a vacuum-sealable bag. Release air by the water displacement method, seal and submerge the bag in the water bath. Cook for 2 hours. Once the timer has stopped, remove the bag and transfer the meatballs to a baking sheet, lined with foil. Heat a skillet over medium heat and sear the meatballs for 7 minutes. Top with lemon wedges.

Chicken Stew with Mushrooms

Ingredients: Servings: 2   Cooking Time: 1 Hour 5 Mins.

2 medium-sized chicken thighs, skinless	1 small carrot, chopped
½ C. fire-roasted tomatoes, diced	1 small onion, chopped
½ C. chicken stock	1 tbsp. fresh basil, finely chopped
1 tbsp. tomato paste	1 garlic clove, crushed
½ C. button mushrooms, chopped	Salt and black pepper to taste
1 medium-sized celery stalk	

Directions:

Make a water bath, place Sous Vide in it, and set to 129 F. Rub the thighs with salt and pepper. Set aside. Chop the celery stalk into half-inch long pieces. Now, place the meat in a large vacuum-sealable bag along with onion, carrot, mushrooms, celery stalk, and fire roasted tomatoes. Submerge the sealed bag in the water bath and set the timer for 45 minutes. Once the timer has stopped, remove the bag from the water bath and open it. The meat should be falling off the bone easily, so remove the bones. Heat up some oil in a medium-sized saucepan and add garlic. Briefly fry for about 3 minutes, stirring constantly. Add the contents of the bag, chicken stock, and tomato paste. Bring it to a boil and reduce the heat to medium. Cook for 5 more minutes, stirring occasionally. Serve sprinkled with the basil.

Chili Chicken

Ingredients: Servings: 2   Cooking Time: 2 Hours 15 Mins.

4 chicken thighs	3 tbsp. basil, chopped
2 tbsp. olive oil	3 tbsp. cilantro, chopped
Salt and black pepper to taste	2 red chilis (deseeded), chopped
1 garlic clove, crushed	1 tbsp. sweet chili sauce
3 tbsp. fish sauce	1 tbsp. green chili sauce
¼ C. lime juice	
1 tbsp. sugar	

Directions:

Prepare a water bath and place the Sous Vide in it. Set to 149 F. Roll the chicken in cling film and let it chill. Place in a vacuum-sealable bag with olive oil, salt and pepper. Release air by the water displacement method, seal and submerge the bag in the water bath. Cook for 2 hours. Once the timer has stopped, remove the chicken and chop into 4-5 pieces. Heat veggie oil in a skillet over medium heat and sear until crispy. In a bowl, combine all the dressing ingredients and set aside. Serve the chicken, season with salt and top with the dressing.

Chili Chicken & Chorizo Tacos with Cheese

Ingredients: Servings: 8   Cooking Time: 3 Hours 25 Mins.

2 pork sausages, castings removed	1 tsp. salt
1 poblano pepper, stemmed and seeded	¾ tsp. ground cumin
½ jalapeño pepper, stemmed and seeded	4 skinless, boneless chicken breasts, sliced
4 scallions, chopped	1 tbsp. vegetable oil
1 bunch fresh cilantro leaves	½ yellow onion, sliced thinly
½ C. chopped fresh parsley	8 corn taco shells
3 garlic cloves	3 tbsp. Provolone cheese
2 tbsp. lime juice	1 tomato
¾ tsp. ground coriander	1 Iceberg lettuce, shredded

Directions:

Put the ½ C. water, poblano pepper, jalapeño pepper, scallions, cilantro, parsley, garlic, lime juice, salt, coriander, and cumin in a blender and mix until smooth. Place the chicken strips and pepper mixture in a vacuum-sealable bag. Transfer to the fridge and allow to chill for 1 hour. Prepare a water bath and place Sous Vide in it. Set to 141 F. Place the chicken mix in the bath. Cook for 1 hour and 30 minutes. Heat oil in a skillet over medium heat and sauté onion for 3 minutes. Add in chorizo and cook for 5-7 minutes. Once the timer has stopped, remove the chicken. Discard cooking juices. Add in chicken and mix well. Fill the tortillas with chicken-chorizo mixture. Top with cheese, tomato and lettuce. Serve.

Spicy Adobo Chicken

Ingredients: Servings: 2   Cooking Time: 120 Mins.

2 chicken leg quarters	Salt as needed
2 garlic cloves, crushed	1 tbsp. canola oil
¼ tsp. whole black peppercorns	½ Worcestershire sauce
½ tbsp. molasses	1 bay leaf
¼ C. dark soy sauce	¼ C. white vinegar

Directions:
Mix the soy sauce, Worcestershire, peppercorns, molasses, garlic, bay leaf and salt. Add the chicken legs in a Sous Vide bag with the marinade and refrigerate for 12 hours or overnight. Prepare your Sous Vide water bath, using your immersion circulator, and raise the temperature to 165-degrees Fahrenheit Submerge the chicken and cook for 2 hours Remove the chicken legs from the bag and air dry for 10-15 minutes. Sear over medium heat in a nonstick pan with canola oil Add the sauce from the bag to the pan and keep cooking until you have reached the desired consistency Serve the chicken with sauce!

Nutrition: Info Calories: 320 Carbohydrate: 33g Protein: 16g Fat: 14g Sugar: 3g Sodium: 255mg

Lemon Thyme Chicken Breasts

Ingredients: Servings: x   Cooking Time: 2 Hours Cooking Temperature: 141°f

Leaves of 6-7 fresh thyme sprigs	1½ tbsp. olive oil
2-3 garlic cloves, finely chopped	1 lemon, thinly sliced
Salt and freshly ground black	Chopped fresh thyme, for

pepper, to taste	garnishing
2 chicken breasts	1 lemon, halved

Directions:
In a bowl, mix together thyme leaves, garlic, oil, salt, and black pepper. Add chicken breasts and coat generously with mixture. Cover and refrigerate for 2 hours. Attach the sous vide immersion circulator to a Cambro container or pot with water using an adjustable clamp and preheat water to 141°F. Place chicken breasts in a large cooking pouch. Place lemon slices over chicken breasts. Seal pouch tightly after removing the excess air. Place pouch in sous vide bath and set the cooking time for 2 hours. Remove pouch from the sous vide bath and open carefully. Remove chicken breasts from pouch and pat dry with paper towels. Heat a cast iron skillet and sear chicken breasts until golden brown on both sides. Serve hot, garnishing with chopped thyme and lemon halves.

Duck Breast with Balsamic Fig Jam

Ingredients: Servings: 4   Cooking Time: 3 Hours

2 boneless duck breasts	½ C. water
1 tsp. salt	½ C. raw sugar
1 tsp. pepper	¼ C. balsamic vinegar
6 oz. dried figs	

Directions:
Preheat the water bath to 140°F. Season duck breasts with salt and pepper. Seal into bags. In a separate bag, combine figs, water, sugar, and vinegar. Seal using water method. Place all bags into the water bath. Cook 3 hours. When the duck is cooked, remove from bag and transfer to a pan, skin-side down. Cook on medium high until skin is crisp. Remove to plate, skin-side up. Pour jam into the bowl and break up any large fig chunks. Serve in a dish alongside the duck.

Nutrition: Info Calories 400 Total Fat 142g Total Carb 377g Dietary Fiber 2g Protein 38g

Chicken Marsala

Ingredients: Servings: 2   Cooking Time: 2 Hours 30 Mins.

2 boneless, skinless chicken breasts	2 cloves garlic, minced
1 tsp. salt	1 C. chicken stock
1 tsp. pepper	1 C. marsala wine
1 lb. fresh mushrooms, sliced	½ tbsp. flour
1 shallot or ½ small onion, diced	1 tbsp. butter
	Cooked pasta for serving

Directions:

Preheat the water bath to 140℉. Salt and pepper the chicken breasts. Place in bag and add mushrooms. Cook 2 hours. When chicken is almost cooked, prepare the sauce. Melt butter in a pan and cook garlic for 30 seconds. Add flour and cook until bubbling subsides, then pour in the stock wine. Cook until sauce reduces by half. Season to taste with salt and pepper. Remove the cooked chicken from the bag and slice across the grain. Stir chicken and mushrooms into sauce. Serve over pasta.

Nutrition: Info Calories 556 Total Fat 142g Total Carb 219g Dietary Fiber 3g Protein 617g

Green Chicken Curry with & Noodles

Ingredients: Servings: 2   Cooking Time: 3 Hours

1 chicken breast, boneless and skinless	2 tbsp. fish sauce
	1½ tbsp. sugar
	½ C. Thai basil
Salt and black pepper to taste	leaves, roughly chopped
1 can (13.5 oz) coconut milk	2 oz. cooked egg noodle nests
2 tbsp. green curry paste	1 C. cilantro, roughly chopped
1¾ C. chicken stock	1 C. bean sprouts
1 C. shiitake mushrooms	2 tbsp. fried noodles
5 kaffir lime leaves, torn in half	2 red chilis, roughly chopped

Directions:

Prepare a water bath and place the Sous Vide in it. Set to 138 F. Season the chicken with salt and pepper. Place it in a vacuum-sealable bag. Release air by the water displacement method, seal and submerge the bag in the water bath. Cook for 90 minutes. Passed 35 minutes, heat a saucepan over medium heat and stir in green curry paste and half coconut milk. Cook for 5-10 Mins. until the coconut milk starts to thicken. Add in chicken stock and the rest of the coconut milk. Cook for 15 minutes. Lower the heat and add in kaffir lime leaves, shiitake mushrooms, sugar and fish sauce. Cook for at least 10 minutes. Remove from the heat and add the basil. Once the timer has stopped, remove the bag and allow cooling for 5 Mins. then chop in tiny slices. Serve in a soup bowl the curry sauce, cooked noodles and chicken. Top with bean sprouts, cilantro, chilis and fried noodles.

Vegetable Chicken with Soy Sauce

Ingredients: Servings: 4   Cooking Time: 6 Hours 25 Mins.

1 whole bone-in chicken, trussed	2 dried bay leaves
	2 C. sliced carrots
1-quart low sodium chicken stock	2 C. sliced celery
	½ oz. dried mushrooms
2 tbsp. soy sauce	3 tbsp. butter
5 sprigs fresh sage	

Directions:

Prepare a water bath and place the Sous Vide in it. Set to 149 F. Combine the soy sauce, chicken stock, herbs, veggies, and chicken. Place in a vacuum-sealable bag. Release air by the water displacement method, seal and submerge the bag in the water bath. Cook for 6 hours. Once the timer has stopped, remove the chicken and drain the veggies. Dry with a baking sheet. Season with olive oil, salt and pepper. Heat the oven to 450 F. and roast for 10 minutes. In a saucepan, stir the cooking juices. Remove from the heat and mix with butter. Slice the chicken without the skin and season with kosher salt and ground black pepper. Serve in a platter. Top with the sauce.

FISH & SEAFOOD RECIPES

Savory Creamy Cod with Parsley

Ingredients: Servings: 6   Cooking Time: 40 Mins.

For Cod	1 C. half-and-half cream
6 cod fillets	
Salt to taste	1 finely chopped white onion
1 tbsp. olive oil	
3 sprigs fresh parsley	2 tbsp. dill, chopped
For Sauce	2 tsp. black peppercorns
1 C. white wine	

Directions:

Prepare a water bath and place the Sous Vide in it. Set to 148 F. Place seasoned with salt cod fillets in vacuum-sealable bags. Add olive oil and parsley. Release air by the water displacement method, seal and submerge the bag in the water bath. Cook for 30 minutes. Heat a saucepan over medium heat, add in wine, onion, black peppercorns and cook until reduced. Stir in half-and-half cream until thickened. Once the timer has stopped, plate the fish and drizzle with sauce.

Yummy Cheesy Lobster Risotto

Ingredients: Servings: 4   Cooking Time: 55 Mins.

1 tall lobster, shell removed	¾ C. Arborio rice
Salt and black pepper to taste	2 tbsp. red wine
6 tbsp. butter	¼ C. grated Grana Padano cheese
2½ C. chicken stock	2 minced chives

Directions:

Prepare a water bath and place the Sous Vide in it. Set to 138 F. Season the lobster with salt and pepper and place in a vacuum-sealable bag with 3 tbsp. of butter. Release air by the water displacement method, seal and submerge the bag in the water bath. Cook for 25 minutes. Heat 3 tbsp. of butter in a skillet over medium heat and cook the rice. Stir in 1/4 C. of chicken stock. Keep cooking until the stock evaporated. Add 1/4 C. of chicken stock more. Repeat the process for 15 Mins. until the rice is creamy. Once the timer has stopped, remove the lobster and chop in bites. Add the lobster to the rice. Stir the remaining chicken stock and red wine. Cook until liquid is absorbed. Top with Grana Padano cheese and season with salt and pepper. Garnish with chives and more cheese.

Salmon Soba Noodles

Ingredients: Servings: 4   Cooking Time: 20 Mins.

For Salmon	For Sesame Soba
6 oz. salmon fillets, skin-on	½ broccoli head
Salt and pepper as needed	3 tbsp. tahini
1 tsp. sesame oil	1 tsp. sesame oil
1 C. extra-virgin oil	2 tsp. extra-virgin olive oil
1 tbsp. fresh ginger, grated	¼ juiced lime
2 tbsp. honey	1 sliced stalk green onion
4 oz. dry soba noodles	¼ C. cilantro, roughly chopped
1 tbsp. grape seed oil	1 tsp. toasted sesame seeds
2 garlic cloves, chopped	Lime wedges and sesame seeds for garnishing

Directions:

Prepare your Sous-vide water bath to a temperature of 128-degrees Fahrenheit. Season the fillets with salt and pepper. Add the sesame oil, olive oil, ginger, and honey in a medium-size bowl. Whisk them well and transfer to a heavy-duty zipper bag Add the fillets and toss to coat well. Seal the bag using the immersion method, submerge the bag and cook for 20 Mins. While it is being cooked, prepare your soba noodles by

cooking according to the package label Once done, place another skillet over a medium-high heat Add the grape seed oil and allow it to heat up. Add the broccoli and garlic, and stir fry them for about 7-8 Mins. Take a small-sized mixing bowl and mix in your tahini, olive oil, sesame oil, lime juice, cilantro, green onions, and toasted sesame seeds Once done, drain your cooked noodles and add them to the fried garlic and broccoli Heat another skillet over a medium-high heat Take one piece of Parchment paper and place it on the bottom of your skillet Once cooked, take the salmon out from the bag and place it in the pan, skin side facing down. Sear for about 1 Min. Divide your soba noodles into 2 serving bowls. Garnish with some lime wedge and sesame seeds. Serve!

Nutrition: Info Calories: 346 Carbohydrate: 54g Protein: 15g Fat: 10g Sugar: 6g Sodium: 1012mg

Coconut Cream Sea Bass

Ingredients: Servings: 2   Cooking Time: 30 Mins.

For the fish	½ C. chicken broth
2 medium cod fillets	½ tsp. white sugar
2 tbsp. coconut milk	1 tsp. lime juice
Salt and pepper to taste	2 slices ginger root
For the sauce	Chopped cilantro for serving
½ C. coconut milk	

Directions:

Preheat the water bath to 135°F. Rub the sea bass fillets with salt, pepper, and coconut milk and put them into the vacuum bag. Seal the bag and set the timer for 30 minutes. While the fish is cooking, make the sauce. Combine the chicken broth and coconut milk in a pan, and simmer for about 10 Mins. over the medium heat. Add the lime juice, sugar and ginger root, mix well and take the sauce off the heat. Close the pan with the lid and set aside for a couple of minutes. Put the fish in bowls, pour the sauce over and serve topped with the freshly chopped cilantro.

Nutrition: Info Per serving:Calories 339, Carbohydrates 28g, Fats 15 g, Protein 23 g

Shrimp Salad

Ingredients: Servings: 4   Cooking Time: 24 Mins.

1 chopped red onion	⅛ tsp. white pepper
Juice of 2 limes	1 diced tomato
1 tsp. extra-virgin olive oil	1 diced avocado
	1 jalapeno, seeded

¼ tsp. sea salt

1 lb. (450 g) raw shrimp, peeled and de-veined

and diced

1 tbsp. chopped cilantro

Directions:
Prepare your Sous-vide water bath to a temperature of 148-degrees Fahrenheit   Add the lime juice, red onion, sea salt, white pepper, extra virgin olive oil, white pepper and shrimp into your heavy-duty plastic bag   Seal the bag using the immersion method   Submerge the bag underwater and cook for 24 Mins.   Remove and chill the plastic bag in an ice bath for about 10 Mins. Take a large-sized bowl and add the tomato, avocado, jalapeno and cilantro   Remove it from the bag and top it up with the salad.   Serve!

Nutrition: Info   Per   serving:Calories: 148 ;Carbohydrate: 7g ;Protein: 24g ;Fat: 2g ;Sugar: 3g ;Sodium: 548mg

Sage Salmon with Coconut Potato Mash

Ingredients: Servings: 2   Cooking Time: 1 Hour 30 Mins.

2 salmon fillets, skin-on

2 tbsp. olive oil

2 sprigs sage

3 potatoes, pelled and chopped

4 garlic cloves

¼ C. coconut milk

1 bunch rainbow chard

1 tbsp. grated ginger

1 tbsp. soy sauce

Sea salt to taste

Directions:
Prepare a water bath and place the Sous Vide in it. Set to 122 F. Place salmon, sage, garlic, and olive oil in a vacuum-sealable bag. Release air by the water displacement method, seal and submerge the bag in the water bath. Cook for 1 hour.   Heat an oven to 375 F. Brush the potatoes with oil and bake for 45 minutes. Transfer potatoes to a blender and add in coconut milk. Season with salt and pepper. Blend for 3 minutes, until smooth.   Heat olive oil in a skillet over medium heat and sauté ginger, chard and soy sauce.   Once the timer has stopped, remove the salmon and transfer to a hot pan. Sear for 2 minutes. Transfer to a plate, add the potato mash, and top with char to serve.

Herb-marinated Tuna Steaks

Ingredients: Servings: 5   Cooking Time: 1 Hour 25 Mins.

2 lb. tuna steaks, about 1-inch thick

1 tsp. dried thyme, ground

1 tsp. fresh basil, finely chopped

¼ C. finely chopped shallots

½ C. sesame seeds

2 tbsp. fresh parsley, finely chopped

1 tbsp. fresh dill, finely chopped

1 tsp. freshly grated lemon zest

4 tbsp. olive oil

Salt and black pepper to taste

Directions:
Wash the tuna fillets under cold running water and pat dry with a kitchen paper. Set aside.   In a large bowl, combine thyme, basil, shallots, parsley, dill, oil, salt, and pepper. Mix until well incorporated and then soak the steaks in this marinade. Coat well and refrigerate for 30 minutes.   Place the steaks in a large vacuum-sealable bag along with marinade. Press the bag to remove the air and seal the lid. Cook en Sous Vide for 40 Mins. at 131 degree.   Remove the steaks from the bag and transfer to a kitchen paper. Gently pat dry and remove the herbs. Preheat a skillet over high temperature. Roll the steaks in sesame seeds and transfer to the skillet. Cook for 1 Min. on each side and remove from the heat.

Crispy Tilapia with Mustard-maple Sauce

Ingredients: Servings: 4   Cooking Time: 65 Mins.

2 tbsp. maple syrup

6 tbsp. butter

2 tbsp. Dijon mustard

2 tbsp. brown sugar

1 tbsp. parsley

1 tbsp. thyme

2 tbsp. soy sauce

2 tbsp. white wine vinegar

4 tilapia fillets, skin on

Directions:
Prepare a water bath and place the Sous Vide in it. Set to 114 F.   Heat a saucepan over medium heat and put 4 tbsp. of butter, mustard, brown sugar, maple syrup, soy sauce, vinegar, parsley, and thyme. Cook for 2 minutes. Set aside and allow to cool for 5 minutes. Place tilapia fillets in a vacuum-sealable bag with maple sauce. Release air by the water displacement method, seal and submerge the bag in the water bath. Cook for 45 minutes.   Once the timer has stopped, remove the fillets and pat dry with kitchen towel. Heat the remaining butter in a skillet over medium heat and sear the fillets for 1-2 minutes.

Crab Zucchini Roulade & Mousse

Ingredients: Servings: 4   Cooking Time: 10min

3lb. crab legs and claws	Mousse:
2 tbsp. olive oil	1 tbsp. Worcestershire
1 medium zucchini	sauce
Salt and pepper, to taste	2 tbsp. crème Fraiche
1 avocado, peeled, pitted	2 tbsp. fresh lime juice
	Salt, to taste

Directions:

Preheat Sous vide cooker to 185F. Place the claws and legs in a Sous Vide bag and vacuum seal. Submerge the bag with content in a water bath. Cook the crab 10 minutes. Slice the zucchini with a vegetable peeler. This way you will have some skinny strips. Remove the crab from the water bath and crack the shell. Flake the meat and transfer into a bowl. Add olive oil, salt, and pepper, and stir to bind gently. Make the mousse; in a food blender, blend the avocado and crème Fraiche until smooth. Stir in the remaining ingredients and spoon the mixture into piping bag. Arrange the zucchini slices on aluminum foil and fill with the crab meat. Roll up the zucchinis and crab into a log and refrigerate 30 minutes. To serve; cut the roulade into four pieces. Serve onto a plate with some avocado mousse. Enjoy.

Nutrition: Info Calories: 415Protein: 43gCarbs: 6gFat: 35g

Spicy Fish Tortillas

Ingredients: Servings: 6   Cooking Time: 35 Mins.

⅓ C. whipping cream	½ sweet onion, chopped
4 halibut fillets, skinned	6 tortillas
1 tsp. chopped fresh cilantro	Shredded iceberg lettuce
¼ tsp. red pepper flakes	1 large tomato, sliced
Salt and black pepper to taste	Guacamole for garnish
1 tbsp. cider vinegar	1 lime, quartered

Directions:

Prepare a water bath and place the Sous Vide in it. Set to 134 F. Combine fillets with the cilantro, red pepper flakes, salt, and pepper. Place in a vacuum-sealable bag. Release air by the water displacement method, submerge the bag in the bath. Cook for 25 minutes.

Meantime, mix the cider vinegar, onion, salt, and pepper. Set aside. Once the timer has stopped, remove the fillets and pat dry with kitchen towel. Using a blowtorch and sear the fillets. Chop into chunks. Put the fish over the tortilla, add lettuce, tomato, cream, onion mixture and guacamole. Garnish with lime.

Crusted Tuna Fish

Ingredients: Servings: 4   Cooking Time: 25mins

3 tbsp. all-purpose flour	1 pinch chili powder
3 tbsp. ground almonds	1 pinch salt
½ tbsp. butter	1 pinch black pepper
4 5oz. tuna fillets	5 tbsp. vegetable oil
Marinade:	2 tsp. lemon juice

Directions:

Preheat Sous Vide cooker to 132 degrees F. Combine the marinade ingredients in a Sous Vide bag. Add the tuna and vacuum seal. Submerge in a water bath and cook 25 minutes. Remove the fish from Sous vide bag. Pat dry the fish. In a bowl, combine all-purpose flour and almonds. Sprinkle with a pinch of salt. Heat the butter in a large skillet. Coat the tuna with the flour-nut mixture and fry in butter until golden brown. Serve warm.

Nutrition: Info Calories: 324Protein: 32gCarbs: 4gFat: 12g

Seared Tuna Steaks

Ingredients: Servings: 4   Cooking Time: 40 Mins.

1 tsp. kosher salt	2 tuna steaks /1" thick, about 10 oz. each
1/4 tsp. cayenne pepper	
3 tbsp. olive oil /divided	1 tsp. butter
	1 tbsp. whole peppercorns

Directions:

Preheat water to 105°F in a sous vide cooker or with an immersion circulator. Season tuna steaks with salt and cayenne pepper and vacuum-seal with 1 tbsp. olive oil in a sous vide bag, or use a plastic zip-top freezer bag /remove as much air as possible from the bag before sealing. Submerge bag in water and cook for 30 minutes. Remove tuna steaks from bag and blot dry with paper towels. Heat remaining 2 tbsp. olive oil and butter in a large nonstick skillet over medium-high heat. Cook peppercorns until softened and beginning to pop, about 5 minutes. Place tuna steaks in skillet and sear until browned, about 1 Min. per side. Cut tuna steaks in half and serve with the peppercorns from the skillet. Enjoy!

Nutrition: Info Calories: 359; Total Fat: 20g; Saturated Fat: 4g; Protein: 42g; Carbs: 0g; Fiber: 0g; Sugar: 0g

Lemon Butter Sole

Ingredients: Servings: 3   Cooking Time: 45 Mins.

3 sole filets	½ tsp. lemon zest
1 ½ tbsp. unsalted butter	Lemon pepper to taste
¼ C. lemon juice	1 sprig parsley for garnishing

Directions:
Make a water bath, place Sous Vide in it, and set to 132 F. Pat dry the sole and place in 3 separate vacuum-sealable bag. Release air by the water displacement method and seal the bags. Submerge in the water bath and set the timer for 30 minutes. Place a small pan over medium heat, add in butter. Once it has melted remove from the heat. Add lemon juice and lemon zest and stir. Once the timer has stopped, remove and unseal the bag. Transfer the sole filets to serving plates, drizzle butter sauce over and garnish with parsley. Serve with a side of steam green vegetables.

Crispy Salmon with Sweet Ginger Glaze

Ingredients: Servings: 4   Cooking Time: 53 Mins.

½ C. Worcestershire sauce	½ tsp. cornstarch
6 tbsp. white sugar	4 salmon fillets
	4 tsp. vegetable oil
4 tbsp. mirin	2 C. cooked rice, for serving
2 small garlic cloves, minced	1 tsp. toasted poppy seeds
½ tsp. grated fresh ginger	

Directions:
Prepare a water bath and place the Sous Vide in it. Set to 129 F. Combine the Worcestershire sauce, sugar, mirin, garlic, cornstarch, and ginger in a hot pot over medium heat. Cook for 1 Min. until the sugar has dissolved. Reserve 1/4 C. of sauce. Allow to cool. Place the fillets salmon in 2 vacuum-sealable bags with the remaining sauce. Release air by the water displacement method, seal and submerge the bags in the water bath. Cook for 40 minutes. Once the timer has stopped, remove the fillets from the bags and pat dry with kitchen towel. Heat a saucepan over medium heat and cook the C. of sauce for 2 Mins. until thickened. Heat oil in a skillet. Sear the salmon for 30 seconds per side. Serve salmon with sauce and poppy seeds.

Swordfish & Potato Salad with Kalamata Olives

Ingredients: Servings: 2   Cooking Time: 3 Hours 5 Mins.

Potatoes	Salad
3 tbsp. olive oil	1 C. baby spinach leaves
1 lb. sweet potatoes	1 C. cherry tomatoes, halved
2 tsp. salt	¼ C. Kalamata olives, chopped
3 fresh thyme sprigs	
Fish	1 tbsp. olive oil
1 tbsp. olive oil	1 tsp. Dijon mustard
1 swordfish steak	
Salt and black pepper to taste	3 tbsp. cider vinegar
1 tsp. canola oil	¼ tsp. salt

Directions:
To make the potatoes: prepare a water bath and place the Sous Vide in it. Set to 192 F. Place the potatoes, olive oil, sea salt and thyme in a vacuum-sealable bag. Release air by the water displacement method, seal and submerge the bag in the water bath. Cook for 1 hour and 15 minutes. Once the timer has stopped, remove the bag and do not open. Set aside. To make the fish: Make a water bath and place the Sous Vide in it. Set to 104 F. Season the swordfish with salt and pepper. Place in a vacuum-sealable bag with the olive oil. Release air by the water displacement method, seal and submerge the bag in the water bath. Cook for 30 minutes. Heat canola oil in a skillet over high heat. Remove the swordfish and pat pat dry with kitchen towel. Discard the cooking juices. Transfer the swordfish into the skillet and cook for 30 seconds per side. Cut into slices and cover with plastic wrap. Set aside. Finally, make the salad: to a salad bowl, add the cherry tomatoes, olives, olive oil, mustard, cider vinegar, and salt and mix well. Add in baby spinach. Remove the potatoes and cut by the half. Discard cooking juices. Top the salad with potatoes and swordfish to serve.

Shrimp Penne

Ingredients: Servings: 4   Cooking Time: 25 Mins.

16 shrimps, peeled and deveined	3 tbsp. lemon juice
1 tbsp. lemon zest	2 tbsp. butter

Salt and pepper to taste

Cooked penne pasta for 4 persons

Directions:
Preheat your cooking machine to 125°F. Put the shrimps into the vacuum bag, add butter and salt and pepper to taste. Seal the bag, put it into the water bath and set the timer for 25 minutes. Carefully pour the cooked shrimps together with all cooking liquid into a medium pot. Add the lemon juice, lemon zest and 2 C. dry white wine to the pot. Simmer the mixture until it thickens, pour the sauce over the cooked penne and serve.

Nutrition: Info Per serving:Calories 449, Carbohydrates 55 g, Fats 17 g, Protein 19 g

Salmon Egg Bites

Ingredients: Servings: 6   Cooking Time: 60 Mins.

6 whole eggs
¼ C. crème fraiche
¼ C. cream cheese
4 spears asparagus
2 oz. smoked salmon
2 oz. chèvre
½ oz. minced shallot

2 tsp. chopped, fresh dill
Salt and pepper as needed
Tools Required:
6 x 4 oz. canning jars

Directions:
Prepare your Sous-vide water bath to a temperature of 170-degrees Fahrenheit   Add the eggs, cream fraiche, cream cheese and salt into a blender   Chop the asparagus into ½ cm chunks. Add them in a mixing bowl with the shallots   Chop the salmon into small portions and add them to your shallots   Whisk well with some minced dill   Whisk everything with a fork Lay out the canning jars and add the egg mixture between them   Divide the salmon mix into six and put one portion in each jar   Add 1/6 chèvre into the jars and lock the lid to fingertip tightness   Put them into the water bath and cook for 1 hour   Once done, take out from the water bath.   Sprinkle some salt over and serve

Nutrition: Info Calories: 589 Carbohydrate: 61g Protein: 28g Fat: 26g Sugar: 9g Sodium: 590mg

Herb Butter Lemon Cod

Ingredients: Servings: 6   Cooking Time: 37 Mins.

8 tbsp. butter
6 cod fillets
Salt and black pepper to taste
Zest of ½ lemon
1 tbsp. minced fresh dill

½ tbsp. minced fresh chives
½ tbsp. minced fresh basil
½ tbsp. minced fresh sage

Directions:
Prepare a water bath and place the Sous Vide in it. Set to 134 F. Season the cod with salt and pepper. Place the cod and lemon zest in a vacuum-sealable bag.   In a separate vacuum-sealable bag, place the butter, half of dill, chives, basil, and sage. Release air by the water displacement method, seal and submerge both bags in the water bath. Cook for 30 minutes.   Once the timer has stopped, remove the cod and pat dry with kitchen towel. Discard the cooking juices. Remove the butter from the other bag and pour over the cod. Garnish with the remaining dill.

Garlic Shrimps

Ingredients: Servings: 4   Cooking Time: 25 Mins.

16 shrimps, peeled and deveined
1 tbsp. unsalted butter, melted

1 shallot, minced
2 garlic cloves, minced

Directions:
Preheat your cooking machine to 125°F.   Put all ingredients in the vacuum bag.   Seal the bag, put it into the water bath and set the timer for 25 minutes.   Serve immediately as an appetizer or tossed with penne pasta.

Nutrition: Info Per serving:Calories 153, Carbohydrates 9 g, Fats 1 g, Protein 27 g

Dill Mackerel

Ingredients: Servings: x   Cooking Time: 25 Mins
Cooking Temperature: 122°f

2 mackerel fillets, pin boned
sea salt, to taste

fresh lemon rind, as required
oil, as required

Directions:
Attach the sous vide immersion circulator using an adjustable clamp to a Cambro container or pot filled with water and preheat to 122°F.   Season mackerel fillets evenly with a little salt.   Into a cooking pouch, add mackerel fillets and lemon zest. Seal pouch tightly after squeezing out the excess air. Place pouch in sous vide bath and set the cooking time for 20 minutes. Remove pouches from sous vide bath and carefully open it. Remove fillets from pouch. with paper towels,

pat fillets completely dry. In a skillet, heat some oil over high heat and cook fillets for 1-2 minutes. Serve immediately.

Shrimp Cocktail Slider

Ingredients: Servings: 2   Cooking Time: 15 Mins.

Kosher salt and pepper as needed	10 small-sized shrimps, peeled and de-veined
4 tbsp. fresh dill, chopped	2 tsp. ketchup
1 tbsp. unsalted butter	Tabasco sauce
4 tbsp. mayonnaise	4 small-sized, oblong dinner rolls
2 tbsp. red onions, minced	8 small-sized leaves of butter lettuce
2 tsp. freshly squeezed lemon juice	½ lemon, sliced into wedges

Directions:
Prepare your Sous-vide water bath to a temperature of 149-degrees Fahrenheit   Take a bowl and add the mayonnaise, red onion, lemon juice, ketchup and Tabasco sauce in it. Whisk them well to create the seasoning   Take the mixture and season it well with pepper and salt and divide the mixture and shrimps equally between two heavy-duty, resealable plastic bags   Add 1 tbsp. of dill and ½ tbsp. of butter to each of the bags   Seal the bags using the immersion method, submerge and cook for 15 Mins.   Preheat your oven to 400-degrees Fahrenheit and warm the rolls for about 10 Mins.   Remove them and slice in half lengthwise   Once done, remove the contents of the bag and strain over a medium bowl   Transfer the shrimps to the bowl with the dressing. Give it a nice toss   Take 2 lettuce leaves and place the shrimp mixture on top of the lettuce rolls   Serve with lemon

Nutrition: Info   Per   serving:Calories: 375 ;Carbohydrate: 15g ;Protein: 17g ;Fat: 28g ;Sugar: 8g ;Sodium: 443mg

Scallops with Lemon Meyer Glaze

Ingredients: Servings: x   Cooking Time: 40 Mins Cooking Temperature: 122°f

2 lb. sea scallops, muscles removed	2 tbsp. scallions, white and green parts separated, finely chopped (greens reserved for garnish)
4 slices Meyer lemon	
Salt and freshly ground black pepper, to taste	pinch of red chili

½ C. fresh orange juice

juice and zest of 2 Meyer lemons

2 tbsp. butter

flakes

4 tbsp. dry sherry

2 tsp. honey

Directions:
Attach the sous vide immersion circulator using an adjustable clamp to a Cambro container or pot filled with water and preheat to 122°F.   Into 2 cooking pouches, divide scallops, salt and black pepper. In each pouch, place 2 lemon slices. Seal pouches tightly after squeezing out the excess air. Place pouches in sous vide bath and set the cooking time for 30 minutes.   In a bowl, mix together orange juice and enough lemon juice to get ⅔ C. liquid. Keep aside.   Remove pouches from sous vide bath and carefully open them. Remove scallops from the pouches.   For the sauce: in a skillet, melt butter over medium-high heat and sauté white part of scallion and chili flakes until soft. with a slotted spoon, transfer scallion into a bowl and keep aside.   To the same skillet, add scallops and gently sear for 90 seconds per side. with a slotted spoon, transfer scallops onto a platter.   To the same skillet, add sherry and scrape browned pieces from bottom.   Add cooked scallion whites, juice mixture, and some of lemon zest and bring to a boil. Cook until desired thickness sauce is achieved. Add honey 1 tsp. at a time, and stir to combine.   Place sauce over scallops evenly. Garnish with scallion greens and some lemon zest, and serve immediately.

Basil Cod Stew

Ingredients: Servings: 4   Cooking Time: 50 Mins.

1 lb. cod fillet	2 tbsp. tomato paste
1 C. fire-roasted tomatoes	1 carrot, sliced
1 tbsp. basil, dried	¼ C. olive oil
1 C. fish stock	1 onion, finely chopped
3 celery stalks, finely chopped	½ C. button mushrooms

Directions:
Heat olive oil in a large skillet, over medium heat. Add celery, onions, and carrot. Stir-fry for 10 minutes. Remove from the heat and transfer to a vacuum-sealable bag along with other ingredients. Cook in sous vide for 40 Mins. at 122 F.

Savory Buttery Lobster Tails

Ingredients: Servings: 2   Cooking Time: 1 Hour 10 Mins.

2 lobster tails, shells removed
2 sprigs fresh tarragon
8 tbsp. butter
2 tbsp. sage
Salt to taste
Lemon wedges

Directions:

Prepare a water bath and place the Sous Vide in it. Set to 134 F. Place the lobster tails, butter, salt, sage and tarragon in a vacuum-sealable bag. Release air by the water displacement method, seal and submerge the bag in the water bath. Cook for 60 minutes. Once the timer has stopped, remove the bag and transfer the lobster to a plate. Sprinkle butter on top. Garnish with lemon wedges.

Grouper with Beurre Nantais

Ingredients: Servings: 6   Cooking Time: 45 Mins.

Grouper:
2 lb grouper, cut into 3 pieces each
1 tsp. cumin powder
½ tsp. garlic powder
½ tsp. onion powder
½ tsp. coriander powder
¼ C. fish seasoning
¼ C. pecan oil
Salt and white pepper to taste

Beurre Blanc:
1 lb butter
2 tbsp. apple cider vinegar
2 shallots, minced
1 tsp. peppercorns, crushed
5 oz. heavy cream, Salt to taste
2 sprigs dill
1 tbsp. lemon juice
1 tbsp. saffron powder

Directions:

Make a water bath, place Sous Vide in it, and set to 132 F. Season the grouper pieces with salt and white pepper. Place in a vacuum-sealable bag, release air by the water displacement method, seal and submerge the bag in the water bath. Set the timer for 30 minutes. Mix the cumin, garlic, onion, coriander, and fish seasoning. Set aside. Meanwhile, make the beurre blanc. Place a pan over medium heat and add, shallots, vinegar, and peppercorns. Cook to attain a syrup. Reduce heat to low and add butter, whisking continuously. Add dill, lemon juice, and saffron powder, stir continuously and cook for 2 minutes. Add cream and season with salt. Cook for 1 minute. Turn heat off and set aside. Once the timer has stopped, remove and unseal the bag. Set a skillet over medium heat, add pecan oil. Pat dry the grouper and seasoning with the spice mixture and sear them in the heated oil. Serve grouper and beurre nantais with a side of steamed spinach.

Cod In Tom Yum Broth

Ingredients: Servings: x   Cooking Time: 30 Mins
Cooking Temperature: 130°f

2 cod fillets, cut lengthwise into 2 slices
2 tbsp. olive oil
salt and freshly ground black pepper, to taste
2 kaffir lime leaves, torn
1 lemongrass stalk (white part only), cut into 3-inch segments and bruised

2 thick galangal slices
2 C. chicken broth
2 small red chilies, bruised
1 tsp. palm sugar or light brown sugar
1 tsp. fresh lime juice
1 tsp. fish sauce
1 tbsp. fresh cilantro, roughly chopped

Directions:

Attach the sous vide immersion circulator using an adjustable clamp to a Cambro container or pot filled with water and preheat to 130°F. In 2 cooking pouches, divide cod, oil, salt and black pepper. Seal pouches tightly after squeezing out the excess air. Place pouches in sous vide bath and set the cooking time for 30 minutes. Meanwhile, in a pan, add kaffir lime leaves, galangal slices, lemongrass and broth and bring to a boil. Simmer for 10 minutes. Stir in remaining ingredients (except cilantro), and remove from heat. Remove pouches from sous vide bath and carefully open them. Transfer fish pieces into serving bowls evenly and top with hot broth. Garnish with cilantro and serve.

Sweet Mango Shrimp

Ingredients: Servings: 4   Cooking Time: 15 Mins.

24 medium-sized shrimps, peeled and de-veined
4 pieces' mangoes, peeled and shredded, cut into thin strips
2 medium-sized shallots, thinly-sliced
¾ C. halved cherry tomatoes
2 tbsp. chopped, fresh Thai basil leaves

¼ C. toasted dry pan peanuts
For Thai Dressing
¼ C. freshly squeeze lime juice
6 tbsp. palm sugar
5 tbsp. fish sauce
4-8 pieces' garlic cloves
4-8 pieces small red chili

Directions:

Prepare your Sous-vide water bath to a temperature of 135-degrees Fahrenheit Take a heavy-duty, large resealable zipper bag and layer the shrimp in a single layer inside Seal the bag using the immersion method. Submerge under water and cook for 15 Mins. Put the lime juice, fish sauce, and palm sugar in a small bowl and mix well Take a mortar and pestle and lb. well the garlic Add the chilis and keep pounding Whisk well, then add the mixture to the dressing Once the shrimps are ready, take them out Transfer them to a large-sized bowl Add the green mango strips, Thai basil, shallots, tomato halves and peanuts to the bowl Top off with the dressing and serve!

Nutrition: Info Calories: 245 Carbohydrate: 11g Protein: 19g Fat: 11g Sugar: 5g Sodium: 532mg

Sweet Chili Shrimp Stir-fry

Ingredients: Servings: 6   Cooking Time: 40 Mins.

1½ lb. shrimp	1 tbsp. soy sauce
3 dried red chilis	2 tsp. sugar
1 tbsp. grated ginger	½ tsp. cornstarch
6 garlic cloves, smashed	3 green onions, chopped
2 tbsp. champagne wine	

Directions:
Prepare a water bath and place the Sous Vide in it. Set to 135 F. Combine the ginger, garlic cloves, chilis, champagne wine, sugar, soy sauce, and cornstarch. Place the peeled shrimp with the mixture in a vacuum-sealable bag. Release air by the water displacement method, seal and submerge in the water bath. Cook for 30 minutes. Place green onions in a skillet over medium heat. Add in oil and cook for 20 seconds. Once the timer has stopped, remove the cooked shrimp and transfer to a bowl. Garnish with onion. Serve with rice.

Black Cod

Ingredients: Servings: x   Cooking Time: 35 Mins Cooking Temperature: 130°f

2 medium bone-in black cod fillets	1 C. soy sauce
1 x 1-inch piece fresh ginger, grated	½ C. mirin
	2 dashes fish sauce

Directions:
Attach the sous vide immersion circulator using an adjustable clamp to a Cambro container or pot filled with water and preheat to 130°F. Into a cooking pouch, add all ingredients. Seal pouch tightly after squeezing out the excess air. Place pouch in sous vide bath and set the cooking time for 30 minutes. Preheat broiler to high. Remove pouch from sous vide bath and carefully open it. Remove fillets from pouch. with paper towels, pat fillets completely dry. Broil until golden brown.

Parsley Prawns with Lemon

Ingredients: Servings: 4   Cooking Time: 35 Mins.

12 large prawns, peeled and deveined	1 bay leaf
	1 sprig parsley, chopped
1 tsp. salt	2 tbsp. lemon zest
1 tsp. sugar	1 tbsp. lemon juice
3 tsp. olive oil	

Directions:
Make a water bath, place Sous Vide in it, and set to 156 F. In a bowl, add prawns, salt, and sugar, mix and let it sit for 15 minutes. Place prawns, bay leaf, olive oil, and lemon zest in a vacuum-sealable bag. Release air by the water displacement method and seal. Submerge in bath and cook for 10 minutes.Once the timer has stopped, remove and unseal the bag. Dish prawns and drizzle with lemon juice.

SOUPS & STEWS

Oxtail Stew

Ingredients: Servings: x   Cooking Time: 20 Hours 40 Mins Cooking Temperature: 180°f

For Stew:	For Sauce:
4 lb. oxtail pieces	1½ tbsp. butter
8 medium whole onions, unpeeled	2 celery sticks, finely chopped
1 whole garlic bulb, unpeeled	1 medium leek, thinly sliced
1 C. white wine	10 closed-cup mushrooms, thinly sliced
3½ oz. Demerara sugar	
⅛ tsp. ground cloves	2 tsp. English mustard
Pinch of cayenne pepper	2 C. reserved cooking liquid
Salt and freshly ground black pepper, to taste	4 tbsp. onion puree from oxtail
4 medium carrots, peeled and cut into half-moons	pinch of cayenne pepper
	salt and freshly ground black pepper, to taste

Directions:

Preheat the oven to 390°F and line a baking tray with a piece of foil. Arrange onion and garlic bulb onto prepared baking tray and roast for 50 minutes. After 15 minutes, remove garlic from roasting tray and keep aside. Remove onions from oven and keep aside with garlic to cool slightly, then squeeze the roasted onion pulp and garlic pulp from the skins. Transfer squeezed pulp into a small pan with wine, sugar and seasonings and bring to a boil. Simmer for 10-15 minutes. with an immersion blender, blend the onion mixture into a thick puree. Keep aside to cool completely, reserving 4 tbsp. in another bowl. Attach the sous vide immersion circulator using an adjustable clamp to a Cambro container or pot filled with water and preheat to 180°F. Into a cooking pouch, add oxtail pieces with remaining onion puree and freeze for 15 minutes. Remove pouch from freezer and seal pouch tightly after squeezing out the excess air. Place pouch in sous vide bath and set the cooking time for 20 hours. Remove pouch from sous vide bath and carefully open it. Remove oxtail pieces from pouch, reserving cooking liquid. Through a sieve, strain cooking liquid into a bowl and refrigerate to cool. After cooling, remove solidified fat from top. Flake meat from bones of warm oxtail pieces and, using 2 forks, shred meat. For the sauce: in a large pan, melt butter and sauté carrots, celery and leeks until they begin to soften. Add flaked oxtail meat, cooking liquid, reserved onion puree and mustard, and bring to a boil. Reduce heat and simmer, covered, for 15-20 minutes. Add mushrooms in the last 5 Mins. along with cayenne pepper, salt and black pepper to taste. Serve immediately.

Minestrone Soup

Ingredients: Servings: x   Cooking Time: 1 Hour Cooking Temperature: 185°f

5½ C. water	⅓ C. celery,
¾ oz. Parmesan	chopped
rind	salt, to taste
1½ C. onion,	⅓ C. cooked orzo
chopped	pasta
1 C. carrot, peeled	leaves from 1 sprig
and chopped	fresh rosemary,
2 cloves garlic,	minced
pressed	4 fresh basil
2 tsp. tomato	leaves, chopped
paste	olive oil, as
1 C. canned	required
cannellini beans,	Parmesan
rinsed and	shaving, as
drained	required

Directions:

Attach the sous vide immersion circulator using an adjustable clamp to a Cambro container or pot filled with water and preheat to 185°F. Into a large cooking pouch, place water, Parmesan rind, onion, carrot, celery, garlic, tomato paste and salt. Seal pouch tightly after squeezing out the excess air. Place pouch in sous vide bath and set the cooking time for 1 hour. Remove pouch from sous vide bath and carefully open it. Remove Parmesan rind and discard. Divide beans, pasta and herbs into hot serving bowls and top evenly with hot soup. Drizzle each bowl with olive oil generously. Garnish with Parmesan shavings and serve immediately.

Thai Coconut Chicken Curry Soup

Ingredients: Servings: x   Cooking Time: 1 Hour 10 Mins Cooking Temperature: 149°f

1 tbsp. coconut oil	¼ C. water
1 red bell pepper,	1 x 13½-oz. can
seeded and cut	full-fat coconut
into ½-inch pieces	milk
½ of yellow onion,	1 C. chicken broth
sliced into half	2 tbsp. fish sauce
moons	2 tbsp. granulated
3 cloves garlic,	sugar
thinly sliced	1 tbsp. fresh lime
1 x 1-inch piece	juice
fresh ginger,	1 oz. dried rice
minced	vermicelli noodles
2 tbsp. red curry	1 C. frozen shelled
paste	edamame
1 lb. skinless,	fresh cilantro and
boneless chicken	lime wedges, for
breasts, cut into 1-	serving
inch pieces	

Directions:

Attach the sous vide immersion circulator using an adjustable clamp to a Cambro container or pot filled with water and preheat to 149°F. In a large skillet, melt coconut oil over medium heat and sauté bell pepper, onion, garlic, ginger and curry paste for 3 minutes. Add water and with an edged wooden spoon, scrape browned bits from the bottom of skillet. Cook for 5 minutes, then remove from heat. Into a cooking pouch, place onion mixture, chicken, coconut milk, broth, fish sauce, sugar and lime juice. Seal pouch tightly after squeezing out the excess air. Place pouch in sous vide bath and set the cooking time for 1 hour. Meanwhile, boil a large pan of water and cook noodles according to directions on the packet. For the last 4 Mins. of cooking, place frozen edamame in pan. Drain rice and edamame mixture well and run under cold water for 1 minute. Remove pouch from sous vide bath and carefully open it. Divide noodle mixture into serving bowls and top evenly with hot soup. Garnish with cilantro and lime wedges and serve immediately.

Pork & White Beans Stew

Ingredients: Servings: x   Cooking Time: 10 Hours Cooking Temperature: 140°f

2 tbsp. vegetable oil	2 cloves garlic, minced
1 tbsp. unsalted butter	2 tbsp. all-purpose flour
1 x 2-lb. pork loin, trimmed and cut into 1-inch pieces	1 C. dry white wine
salt and freshly ground black pepper, to taste	1 x 15-oz. can white beans, rinsed and drained
2 large carrots, peeled and cut into ½-inch pieces	2 C. chicken broth
2 C. frozen pearl onions	4 large fresh rosemary sprigs
	2 bay leaves
	chopped fresh rosemary, for garnishing

Directions:
Attach the sous vide immersion circulator using an adjustable clamp to a Cambro container or pot filled with water and preheat to 140°F. Season pork evenly with salt and black pepper. In a large nonstick skillet, heat oil and butter over medium-high heat, and sear pork for 5-7 minutes. Add carrots and onions and cook for 5 minutes. Add garlic and cook for 1 minute. Stir in flour and cook for 2 minutes, stirring continuously. Add wine and bring to a boil, scraping up the browned bits from bottom of skillet. Stir in beans, broth, rosemary and bay leaves and remove from heat. Between 2 cooking pouches, divide pork mixture, placing 2 rosemary sprigs and 1 bay leaf in each pouch. Seal pouches tightly after squeezing out the excess air. Place pouches in sous vide bath and set the cooking time for at least 7 and no more than 10 hours. Remove pouches from sous vide bath and carefully open them. Divide stew into serving bowls and serve with the garnishing of chopped rosemary.

Oyster Stew

Ingredients: Servings: x   Cooking Time: 1 Hour 5 Mins Cooking Temperature: 120°f

4 tbsp. unsalted butter	2 C. oysters with liquid, shucked
1 small clove	2 C. whole milk
garlic, minced	1 bay leaf
1 C. thinly sliced leeks	kosher salt and freshly ground black pepper, to taste
2 C. heavy cream	

Directions:
Attach the sous vide immersion circulator using an adjustable clamp to a Cambro container or pot filled with water and preheat to 120°F. In a large skillet, melt butter over medium heat and cook garlic and leeks for 5 minutes, stirring occasionally. Into a large cooking pouch, place leek mixture, oysters, cream, milk and bay leaf. Seal pouch tightly after squeezing out the excess air. Place pouch in sous vide bath and set the cooking time for 1 hour. Remove pouch from sous vide bath and carefully open it. Divide stew into serving bowls and season with salt and black pepper. Serve hot.

Creamy Tomato Soup

Ingredients: Servings: x   Cooking Time: 1 Hour 20 Mins Cooking Temperature: 172°f

½ C. plus 2 tbsp. butter, divided	3 large cans diced tomatoes with liquid
⅓ C. flour	1-2 fresh tomatoes, chopped
4 C. milk	
1 C. heavy cream	
1 green bell pepper, seeded and chopped	2 tbsp. dried basil, crushed
½ large onion, chopped	pinch of cayenne pepper
1 clove garlic, chopped	1 tsp. salt
	1 tsp. freshly ground black pepper

Directions:
Attach the sous vide immersion circulator using an adjustable clamp to a Cambro container or pot filled with water and preheat to 172°F. For the roux: in a large pan, melt ½ C. of butter over medium heat. Slowly add flour, stirring continuously, and cook for 1-2 minutes. Stir in milk and cook for 1-2 Mins. or until mixture just starts to thicken, stirring continuously. Stir in cream and cook for 1-2 Mins. or until mixture becomes thick, stirring continuously. Remove from heat and keep aside. In another pan, melt coconut oil and sauté bell pepper, onion and garlic until onion becomes translucent. Add tomatoes with liquid and basil and bring to a gentle boil. Simmer for 30 minutes. with immersion blender, blend soup mixture slightly. Add white sauce and stir to combine. Add white sauce, cayenne pepper, salt and black pepper and cook until

well-combined. Remove from heat. Into a cooking pouch, add tomato mixture. Seal pouch tightly after squeezing out the excess air. Place pouch in sous vide bath and set the cooking time for 30-40 minutes. Remove pouch from sous vide bath and carefully open it. Divide soup into serving bowls and serve.

Lamb Stew

Ingredients: Servings: x   Cooking Time: 24 Hours 10 Mins Cooking Temperature: 149°f

1 whole lamb breast *	2-3 lamb stock cubes
dried Italian seasoning, to taste	gravy granules *
chopped seasonal vegetables of your choice *	salt and freshly ground black pepper, to taste

Directions:
Attach the sous vide immersion circulator using an adjustable clamp to a Cambro container or pot filled with water and preheat to 149°F. Season lamb breast lightly with Italian seasoning. Into a cooking pouch, place lamb breast. Seal pouch tightly after squeezing out the excess air. Place pouch in sous vide bath and set the cooking time for 24 hours. Meanwhile, in a large pan, cook vegetables according to your taste. Remove pouch from sous vide bath and carefully open it. Remove lamb neck from pouch, reserving pouch juices in a jug. Add 2 stock cubes and some boiling water and stir to combine well. (If mixture is thin, then add another stock cube or some gravy granules). Cut lamb breast into desired sized pieces and transfer into the pan with vegetables. Add gravy and mix until well-combined, and cook until heated through. This stew is great served with a delicious crusty bread roll or creamy mashed potatoes.

Butternut Squash & Apple Soup

Ingredients: Servings: x   Cooking Time: 2 Hours Cooking Temperature: 185°f

1 large Granny Smith apple, cored and sliced	1 medium butternut squash, peeled and sliced
½ of onion, sliced	1 tsp. sea salt
¾ C. light cream	

Directions:
Attach the sous vide immersion circulator to a Cambro container or pot with water using an adjustable clamp and preheat water to 185°F. Into a large cooking pouch, place apple, squash and onion. Seal pouch tightly after squeezing out the excess air. Place pouch in sous vide bath and set the cooking time for 2 hours. Remove pouch from sous vide bath and keep aside to cool slightly. Transfer squash mixture into blender. Add cream and salt, and pulse until smooth. Serve immediately.

Avgolemono Soup

Ingredients: Servings: x   Cooking Time: 6 Hours 35 Mins. Cooking Temperature: 150°f

1 x 4-lb. whole chicken, trussed	6 C. water
2 C. white onion, chopped	2 cloves garlic, minced
2 C. celery, chopped	½ C. uncooked long-grain white rice
2 C. carrots, peeled and chopped	1 egg, beaten
kosher salt and freshly ground black pepper, to taste	¼ C. fresh lemon juice
1 tbsp. extra-virgin olive oil	1 tbsp. cornstarch
½ C. white onion, finely chopped	2 tbsp. scallion, chopped
	2 tbsp. fresh parsley, chopped
	lemon wedges, for garnishing

Directions:
Attach the sous vide immersion circulator using an adjustable clamp to a Cambro container or pot filled with water and preheat to 150°F. Into a large cooking pouch, place chicken, 2 C. of onion, celery, carrot, salt and black pepper. Seal pouch tightly after squeezing out the excess air. Place pouch in sous vide bath and set the cooking time for 6 hours. Remove pouch from sous vide bath and carefully open it. Carefully, transfer chicken onto a plate and keep aside for at least 20 minutes. Through a fine-mesh strainer, strain cooking liquid into a large bowl. Discard vegetable solids. Remove chicken meat from bones and shred. Discard bones. In a Dutch oven, heat oil over medium heat and sauté finely chopped onion for 5 minutes. Add garlic and rice and sauté for 2 minutes. Add strained cooking liquid and bring to a boil. Simmer for 20 minutes. Into a small bowl, add egg, lemon juice and cornstarch and beat until well-combined. Add egg mixture into soup, beating continuously. Add shredded chicken and simmer for 5 minutes. Stir in salt and black pepper and remove from heat. Divide soup into serving bowls and serve with a garnish of scallions, parsley and lemon wedges.

Lentil Soup

Ingredients: Servings: x   Cooking Time: 2 Hours
Cooking Temperature: 180°f

3 tbsp. extra-virgin olive oil	kosher salt and freshly ground black pepper, to taste
1 yellow onion, finely chopped	
4 carrots, peeled and finely chopped	2 C. brown lentils
	8 C. chicken broth
3 celery stalks celery, finely chopped	3 fresh thyme sprigs
	1 bay leaf
2 garlic cloves, minced	1 tbsp. ground cumin
	fresh lemon juice, as required

Directions:
Attach the sous vide immersion circulator using an adjustable clamp to a Cambro container or pot filled with water and preheat to 180°F.   In a large non-stick skillet, heat oil over medium heat and cook onion, carrots, celery, garlic, salt and black pepper for 5 minutes, stirring occasionally.   Into a large cooking pouch, place onion mixture, lentils, broth, thyme, bay leaf and cumin. Seal pouch tightly after squeezing out the excess air. Place pouch in sous vide bath and set the cooking time for 2 hours.   Remove pouch from sous vide bath and carefully open it. Transfer soup into serving bowls and season with salt and black pepper. Drizzle with lemon juice and serve hot.

STOCKS & SAUCES

Provencal Tomato Sauce

Ingredients: Servings: 8   Cooking Time: 45 Mins.

1-pint cherry tomatoes	½ small onion, peeled and chopped up finely
1 shallot peeled and minced	
5-6 large chopped basil leaves	2-3 sprigs fresh thyme stripped
A handful of fresh parsley, fully stemmed and chopped up	½ tsp. sea salt
	¼ tsp. ground black pepper
	1 tbsp. olive oil

Directions:
Prepare your Sous-vide water bath to a temperature of 182-degrees Fahrenheit.   Add all the listed ingredients to your resealable zip bag and seal using the immersion method.   Submerge underwater and let it cook for 30-45 minutes.   Remove the pouch and knead the sauce through the pouch.   Serve as needed.

Nutrition: Info Calories: 117 Carbohydrate: 26g Protein: 5g Fat: 1g Sugar: 14g Sodium: 520mg

Raspberry Infused Vinaigrette

Ingredients: Servings: x   Cooking Time: 2 Hours
Cooking Temperature: 140°f

For Raspberry Vinegar:	1 tbsp. honey
	1 tbsp. orange juice
1 C. fresh raspberries	
1-1/2 C. white wine or champagne vinegar	1 shallot, finely chopped
	5 tbsp. olive oil
	salt and freshly ground black pepper, to taste
For Raspberry Vinaigrette:	
3 tbsp. infused raspberry vinegar	

Directions:
Attach the sous vide immersion circulator to a Cambro container or pot with water using an adjustable clamp and preheat water to 140°F.   Place raspberries and vinegar in a cooking pouch. Seal pouch tightly after squeezing out the excess air. Place pouch in sous vide bath and set the cooking time for 1-2 hours.   Remove pouch from the sous vide bath and immediately plunge into a bowl of ice water for about 15-20 minutes. Strain vinegar and transfer into an airtight container.   For raspberry vinaigrette: in a bowl, add infused vinegar, honey, and orange juice and beat until well combined. Stir in the shallots and let sit for about 10 minutes. Slowly add olive oil, beating continuously until well combined. Stir in salt and black pepper and serve.

Vegetable Stock

Ingredients: Servings: 10   Cooking Time: 12 Hours 35 Mins.

1 ½ C. celery root, diced	6 C. water
	1 ½ C. mushrooms
1 ½ C. leeks, diced	
½ C. fennel bulb, diced	½ C. parsley, chopped
4 cloves garlic, crushed	1 tbsp. black peppercorns
1 tbsp. olive oil	1 bay leaf

Directions:
Make a water bath, place Sous Vide in it, and set to 180 F. Preheat an oven to 450 F. Place the leeks, celery, fennel, garlic, and olive oil in a bowl. Toss them.

Transfer to a roasting pan and tuck them in the oven. Roast for 20 minutes. Place the roasted vegetables with its juices, water, parsley, peppercorns, mushrooms, and bay leaf in a vacuum-sealable bag. Release air, seal and submerge the bag into the water bath and set the timer for 12 hours. Cover the water bath's container with a plastic wrap to reduce evaporation and keep adding water to the bath to keep the vegetables covered. Once the timer has stopped, remove and unseal the bag. Strain the ingredients. Cool and use frozen for up to 1 month. Once the timer has stopped, remove and unseal the bag. Strain the ingredients.Cool and use frozen for up to 2 weeks.

Hollandaise Sauce(1)

Ingredients: Servings: 4   Cooking Time: 30 Mins.

1 C. dry white wine	6 large egg yolks
3 tbsp. champagne vinegar	1 C. unsalted butter, warm and melted
2 tbsp. shallots, minced	1 tbsp. freshly squeezed lemon juice
2 sprigs fresh thyme	

Directions:
Prepare your Sous-vide water bath to a temperature of 145-degrees Fahrenheit. Take a medium-sized saucepan and bring the vinegar, wine, shallot and thyme to a boil over medium heat. Bring the mixture to a simmer by lowering down the heat to low and let it simmer for 10 Mins. until you have syrup-like mixture. Strain the wine through a fine mesh into blender. Add the egg yolks and puree for 30 seconds. Transfer to a resealable zip bag and seal using the immersion method. Let it cook for 30 minutes. Once done, transfer the contents to a blender and blend for 30 seconds with warm butter and lemon juice. Season and serve!

Nutrition: Info Calories: 67 Carbohydrate: 1g Protein: 1g Fat: 7g Sugar: 6g Sodium: 44mg

Bell Pepper Puree

Ingredients: Servings: 4   Cooking Time: 40 Mins.

8 red bell peppers, cored	3 cloves garlic, crushed
⅓ C. olive oil	2 tsp. sweet paprika
2 tbsp. lemon juice	

Directions:
Make a water bath and place Sous Vide in it and set to 183 F. Put the bell peppers, garlic, and olive oil in a vacuum-sealable bag. Release air by the water displacement method, seal and submerge the bags in the water bath. Set the timer for 20 Mins. and cook. Once the timer has stopped, remove the bag and unseal. Transfer the bell pepper and garlic to a blender and puree to smooth. Place a pan over medium heat; add bell pepper puree and the remaining ingredients. Cook for 3 minutes.Serve warm or cold as a dip.

Soy Chili Sauce

Ingredients: Servings: 1 Cup. 8 Servings   Cooking Time: 30 Mins.

1 C. light soy sauce	¼ C. honey
2 green chilies, chopped, seeded	1 tsp. cumin

Directions:
Preheat Sous Vide cooker to 160F. Combine all ingredients in Sous Vide bag. Seal using water immersion technique. Submerge the bag into the water bath. Cook 30 minutes. Finishings steps: Remove the bag from cooker and serve sauce in a bowl.

Nutrition: Info Calories 35 Total Fat 1g Total Carb 18g Dietary Fiber 1g Protein 5g

Crème Fraiche

Ingredients: Servings: x   Cooking Time: 12 Hours Cooking Temperature: 149°f

1 C. heavy whipping cream	2 tbsp. low-fat buttermilk

Directions:
Attach the sous vide immersion circulator to a Cambro container or pot with water using an adjustable clamp and preheat water to 149°F. Place all ingredients in a mason jar. Cover with cap tightly. Place jar in sous vide bath and set the cooking time for about 8 and no more than 12 hours. Carefully remove jar from sous vide bath and open it. Transfer mixture into an airtight container. Seal tightly and refrigerate for up to 3 weeks.

Summer Corn Salsa

Ingredients: Servings: 8   Cooking Time: 30 Mins.

4 ears fresh corn, shucked and washed	2 limes, juiced
Salt, and pepper as needed	1/4 C. extra-virgin olive oil
2 cloves garlic, chopped and peeled	2 avocados, peeled, chopped, and seeded
1 deseeded and	1 bunch coriander, chopped up

finely chopped jalapeno
2 tomatoes, chopped

Tortillas for serving

Directions:
Prepare the Sous-vide water bath using your immersion circulator and raise the temperature to 182-degrees Fahrenheit. Season the corn with salt and pepper. Place the corn in a resealable zip bag and seal using the immersion method. Cook for 30 minutes. Take a large bowl and mix the finely chopped garlic, tomatoes, jalapenos, lime juice, avocado, coriander, and olive oil. Once cooked, remove the corn and allow it to cool. Cut the kernels and mix in the salsa. Season. Serve with tortillas.

Nutrition: Info Calories: 362 Carbohydrate: 77g Protein: 10g Fat: 7g Sugar: 5g Sodium: 1975mg

Orange Rosemary Vinegar

Ingredients: Servings: x   Cooking Time: 3 Hours Cooking Temperature: 153°f

4 C. white balsamic vinegar	10 fresh rosemary springs
zest of 10 blood oranges	

Directions:
Attach the sous vide immersion circulator to a Cambro container or pot with water using an adjustable clamp and preheat water to 153°F. Place all ingredients in a cooking pouch. Seal pouch tightly after squeezing out the excess air. Place pouch in sous vide bath and set the cooking time for about 2-3 hours. Remove pouch from sous vide bath occasionally and with your fingers, massage the mixture to mix. Remove pouch from the sous vide bath and carefully open it. Strain vinegar through a fine mesh strainer into a container. Discard the solids. Keep in refrigerator for up to six weeks.

Mezcal Cream

Ingredients: Servings: 8   Cooking Time: 30 Mins.

½ C. heavy cream	1 tsp. vanilla extract
½ C. mezcal	
½ C. ultrafine sugar	A pinch of kosher salt
4 large egg yolks	

Directions:
Prepare your Sous-vide water bath to a temperature of 180-degrees Fahrenheit. Add everything to your blender and puree for 30 seconds. Then, transfer the mixture to a large resealable bag. Seal using the

immersion method and cook for 30 minutes. Transfer to an ice bath and serve once cooled.

Nutrition: Info Calories: 791 Carbohydrate: 101g Protein: 12g Fat: 33g Sugar: 66g Sodium: 625mg

Persimmon Butter

Ingredients: Servings: x   Cooking Time: 1½ Hours Cooking Temperature: 185°f

2 lb. ripe fuyu persimmons, peeled, hulled and cut into ¼-inch thick wedges	¼ C. apple juice
	1 cinnamon stick
	1 tsp. vanilla
	¼ tsp. kosher salt
1 tsp. lemon juice	

Directions:
Attach the sous vide immersion circulator to a Cambro container or pot with water using an adjustable clamp and preheat water to 185°F. Place all ingredients in a cooking pouch. Seal pouch tightly after squeezing out the excess air. Place pouch in sous vide bath and set the cooking time for about 1½ hours. Remove pouch from the sous vide bath and set aside to cool slightly. In a food processor, add mixture and pulse until smooth.

Orange-thyme Maple Syrup

Ingredients: Servings: 12   Cooking Time: 60 Mins.

2 C. pure maple syrup	6 sprigs thyme
	½ tsp. fine sea salt
2 tbsp. orange zest	

Directions:
Prepare your Sous-vide water bath to a temperature of 135-degrees Fahrenheit. Add all the listed ingredients to a resealable zip bag. Seal using the immersion method. Submerge underwater and cook for 1 hour. Discard the thyme and allow the syrup to cool. Serve or you can store in container for up to 2 weeks.

Nutrition: Info Per serving:Calories: 234 ;Carbohydrate: 40g ;Protein: 4g ;Fat: 7g ;Sugar: 22g ;Sodium: 121mg

Ricotta Cheese

Ingredients: Servings: x   Cooking Time: 40 Mins Cooking Temperature: 195°f

8 C. whole milk	1 tsp. citric acid
1 C. heavy cream	
1 tsp. sea salt	

Directions:

Attach the sous vide immersion circulator to a Cambro container or pot with water using an adjustable clamp and preheat water to 195°F. Add all ingredients to a bowl that fits into a cooking pouch. Arrange bowl inside cooking pouch and seal tightly after squeezing out the excess air. Place pouch in sous vide bath and set the cooking time for about 35-40 minutes. Remove pouch from the sous vide bath and carefully open it. Remove bowl from cooking pouch. with a slotted spoon, gently scoop out curd from top and transfer into straining vessel. Strain ricotta until desired consistency of cheese is achieved.

Cinnamon-apple Flavored Balsamic Vinegar

Ingredients: Servings: 10   Cooking Time: 180 Mins.

17 oz. balsamic vinegar	2 medium apples, sliced
2 cinnamon sticks	1 tbsp. sugar

Directions:
Prepare your Sous-vide water bath to a temperature of 153-degrees Fahrenheit. Add all the listed ingredients to your resealable zip bag and seal using the immersion method. Submerge underwater and cook for 3 hours. Once done, strain the contents through a cheesecloth into a clean bottle. Serve as needed!

Nutrition: Info Calories: 232 Carbohydrate: 54g Protein: 1g Fat: 0g Sugar: 51g Sodium: 19mg

Champagne Vinegar

Ingredients: Servings: 1 Cup, 12 Servings   Cooking Time: 3 Hours

1 C. champagne vinegar	1 C. granulated sugar
1 lemon, juice and zest	

Directions:
Preheat the Sous Vide cooker to 130F. Combine all ingredients in a Sous Vide bag. Seal the bag using water immersion technique. Submerge the bag into a water bath and cook 3 hours. Finishing steps: Remove the bag from the water bath. Open and strain into a clean jar. Store in the fridge up to 2 months.

Nutrition: Info Calories 68 Total Fat 0g Total Carb 13g Dietary Fiber 1g Protein 1g

Pineapple Compote with Rum & Mint

Ingredients: Servings: 8   Cooking Time: 60 Mins.

1 lb. fresh pineapple, peeled, cored and diced	1 C. granulated sugar
½ C. dark rum	Zest of 1 lime
	2 sprigs fresh mint

Directions:
Prepare your Sous-vide water bath to a temperature of 190-degrees Fahrenheit. Add all the listed ingredients to a resealable bag and seal using the immersion method. Submerge underwater and let it cook for 1 hour. Once done, transfer to airtight container and use as needed or you can store for up to 2 weeks.

Nutrition: Info Calories: 196 Carbohydrate: 33g Protein: 1g Fat: 0g Sugar: 29g Sodium: 12mg

Seafood Stock

Ingredients: Servings: 6   Cooking Time: 10 Hours 10 Mins.

1 lb shrimp shells, with heads and tails	2 sprigs rosemary
3 C. water	½ head garlic, crushed
1 tbsp. olive oil	½ C. celery leaves, chopped
2 tsp. salt	

Directions:
Make a water bath, place Sous Vide in it, and set to 180 F. Toss the shrimp with the olive oil. Place the shrimp with the remaining listed ingredients in a vacuum-sealable bag. Release air, seal and submerge the bag into the water bath, and set the timer for 10 hours.

Basil Tomato Sauce

Ingredients: Servings: 2   Cooking Time: 1 Hour

1 can /28-oz. whole tomatoes, crushed	1 sprig rosemary
1 onion, diced	½ tsp. salt
2 cloves garlic, minced	½ tsp. pepper
1 tbsp. olive oil	1 C. fresh basil, chopped
1 bay leaf	Cooked pasta for serving

Directions:
Preheat the water bath to 185 °F. Combine all ingredients in a bag. Seal and place in water bath. Cook 1 hour. Remove bay leaves and rosemary sprig. Serve with cooked pasta.

Nutrition: Info Calories 158 Total Fat 97g Total Carb 25g Dietary Fiber 4g Protein 57g

Lemon Ginger Marmalade

Ingredients: Servings: 8   Cooking Time: 180 Mins.

4 pieces thinly sliced Meyer lemons	¼ C. chopped crystallized ginger
4 C. granulated sugar	1 tbsp. grated fresh ginger

Directions:
Prepare your Sous-vide water bath to a temperature of 190-degrees Fahrenheit.   Add the above-listed ingredients to your resealable zipper bag and seal using the immersion method. Cook for 3 hours.   Once done, transfer the bag to an ice bath and allow it to cool.   You can store in an air tight container and serve as needed.

Nutrition: Info Calories: 455 Carbohydrate: 119g Protein: 1g Fat: 0g Sugar: 110g Sodium: 11mg

Tomato Sauce

Ingredients: Servings: 6 C.   Cooking Time: 50 Mins.

2 tbsp. olive oil	2 sprigs fresh basil
2 onions, chopped	3 sprigs fresh oregano
2 cloves garlic, minced	1/3 C. fresh chopped parsley
2lb. cherry tomatoes	Salt, to taste

Directions:
Preheat Sous vide cooker to 180F.   Heat olive oil in a skillet.   Add onions and cook 5 minutes.   Toss in the garlic and cook 30 seconds. Insert the tomatoes and stir to coat with oil. Place aside to cool.   Transfer the tomatoes in Sous Vide bag.   Add the remaining ingredients and seal using water immersion technique. Cook the tomatoes 50 minutes.   Finishing steps: Remove the bag from the cooker.   Open the bag and chill 15 minutes. Peel the tomatoes and place in a food blender, with cooking juices. Discard the herbs.   Blend the tomatoes until smooth.   Serve or use later.

Nutrition: Info Calories 42 Total Fat 5g Total Carb 9g Dietary Fiber 4g Protein 1g

Ancho Chile Oil

Ingredients: Servings: 12   Cooking Time: 60 Mins.

2 dried ancho chilis, with stems and seeds	1 C. canola oil
	2 garlic cloves, crushed

removed and torn into 1-inch pieces	1 tsp. of kosher salt
1 tbsp. red wine vinegar	

Directions:
Prepare your Sous-vide water bath to a temperature of 180-degrees Fahrenheit.   Add all the listed ingredients to a resealable zipper bag.   Seal using the immersion method.   Submerge underwater and cook for 1 hour. Serve or you can store in container for up to 2 weeks.

Nutrition: Info   Per   serving:Calories: 196 ;Carbohydrate: 11g ;Protein: 3g ;Fat: 17g ;Sugar: 0g ;Sodium: 417mg

Coffee Butter

Ingredients: Servings: x   Cooking Time: 3 Hours Cooking Temperature: 194°f

500g salted butter (17.6 ounces)	250g coffee beans (8.8 ounces)

Directions:
Attach the sous vide immersion circulator to a Cambro container or pot with water using an adjustable clamp and preheat water to 194°F.   In a cooking pouch, place butter and coffee beans. Seal pouch tightly after squeezing out the excess air. Place pouch in sous vide bath and set the cooking time for about 3 hours. Remove pouch from the sous vide bath and carefully open it. with a sieve, strain the butter into a bowl. Discard coffee beans.   Place butter into sealed bag and refrigerate until serving.

Cheddar Cheese Sauce

Ingredients: Servings: 4 C.   Cooking Time: 15 Mins.

2 C. Gruyere cheese	¾ C. white Cheddar
2 ½ C. whole milk	½ tsp. salt

Directions:
Preheat Sous Vide to 167F.   Slice the cheeses and place into Sous Vide bag along with milk and salt.   Vacuum seal the bag and submerge in the water bath.   Cook 15 minutes.   Finishing steps: Remove the bag from the water bath.   Pour the content into a food blender. Blend on medium speed until the sauce is smooth. Serve.

Nutrition: Info Calories 160 Total Fat 18g Total Carb 3g Dietary Fiber 0g Protein 15g Note about vacuum sealing liquids: Vacuum sealing liquids can be challenging. It is recommended to either purchase Liquid Block heat seal vacuum seal bags, or heavy duty ziplock bags and use the displacement method /instructions in the introduction for removing the air from the bag and sealing.

Chicken Stock

Ingredients: Servings: 8   Cooking Time: 8 Hours

10 lbs. chicken bones	½ tsp. black peppercorn
1 lb. yellow onion peeled, cut in half	10 sprigs fresh thyme
8 oz. carrots, chopped	Small handful parsley stem
8 oz. celery, chopped	1-piece bay leaf

Directions:
Roast your chicken bones for about 1 ½ hours at 400°F in your oven.   Add the roasted chicken bones, onion, and the rest of the ingredients to a resealable zipper bag Add the water (reserve 1 cup) and seal using the immersion method.   Prepare the water bath to a temperature of 194-degrees Fahrenheit using your immersion circulator Submerge underwater and cook for 6-8 hours.   Strain the mixture from the zip bag through a metal mesh into a large-sized bowl Cool the stock using an ice bath and place it in your oven overnight Scrape the surface and discard fat.   Use as needed.

Nutrition: Info Per serving:Calories 2229, Carbohydrates 31 g, Protein 173 g, Fats 137 g

Pasteurized Mayonnaise

Ingredients: Servings: 8   Cooking Time: 2 Hours

1 tbsp. Dijon mustard	2 eggs
1 tbsp. lemon juice	1 C. olive oil
	½ tsp. salt
	½ tsp. pepper

Directions:
Preheat the water bath to 135°F.   Place eggs in water and cook 2 hours, then transfer to an ice bath. Cool completely.   Crack eggs into the bowl of a stand mixer. Add mustard and lemon juice and beat until combined. While the machine is running, pour in oil and beat until mixture thickens. Season with salt and pepper. Transfer to a jar and refrigerate.

Nutrition: Info Calories 273 Total Fat 249g Total Carb 62g Dietary Fiber 1g Protein 34g

Champagne Citrus Vinegar

Ingredients: Servings: 8   Cooking Time: 180 Mins.

Peels of 2 lemon	Peels of 2 orange
17 oz. champagne vinegar	1 thick sliced of orange
1 thick sliced of lemon	1 tbsp. granulated sugar

Directions:
Prepare your Sous-vide water bath to a temperature of 153-degrees Fahrenheit.   Twist the citrus peels.   Add the lemon slice, vinegar, sugar, orange slice and peels to your resealable zip bag.   Seal using the immersion method. Cook for 3 hours   Once done, take the bag out from the water bath and strain the contents through a cheesecloth into a storing jar with lid.   Serve as needed or you can store in a fridge for up to 6 weeks.

Nutrition: Info Calories: 35 Carbohydrate: 10g Protein: 4g Fat: 6g Sugar: 8g Sodium: 6mg

Blackberry Lavender Balsamic Vinegar

Ingredients: Servings: 10   Cooking Time: 180 Mins.

17 oz. balsamic vinegar	5 sprigs lavender
2 C. fresh blackberries	1 tbsp. granulated sugar

Directions:
Prepare your Sous-vide water bath to a temperature of 153-degrees Fahrenheit.   Add all the listed ingredients to Sous Vide zipper bag and seal using the immersion method.   Submerge underwater and cook for 3 hours. Halfway through your cooking, make sure to squeeze the bag to soften them up   Once cooked, strain the contents through a cheesecloth into a clean bottle. Serve as needed!

Nutrition: Info Calories: 364 Carbohydrate: 30g Protein: 23g Fat: 15g Sugar: 1g Sodium: 415mg

Cauliflower Alfredo

Ingredients: Servings: 4   Cooking Time: 2 Hours

2 C. chopped up cauliflower florets	½ C. chicken stock
2 crushed garlic cloves	2 tbsp. milk
2 tbsp. butter	Salt and pepper as needed

Directions:
Prepare your Sous-vide water bath to a temperature of 181-degrees Fahrenheit.   Add all the listed ingredients into a resealable zip bag.   Seal using the immersion method.   Submerge underwater and cook for 2 hours.

Once done, transfer it to a food processor and puree until you have a smooth texture   Serve!

Nutrition: Info Per serving:Calories: 90 ;Carbohydrate: 21g ;Protein: 9g ;Fat: 3g ;Sugar: 12g ;Sodium: 216mg

Garlic Basil Rub

Ingredients: Servings: 15   Cooking Time: 55 Mins.

2 heads garlic, crushed	A pinch salt
2 tsp. olive oil	2 lemons, zested and juiced
1 head fennel bulb, chopped	¼ sugar
	25 basil leaves

Directions:
Make a water bath, place Sous Vide in it, and set to 185 F. Place the fennel and sugar in a vacuum-sealable bag. Release air by the water displacement method, seal and submerge the bag in the water bath. Set the timer for 40 minutes.Once the timer has stopped, remove and unseal the bag.   Transfer the fennel, sugar, and remaining listed ingredients to a blender and puree to smooth. Store in a spice container and use up to a week with refrigeration.

Very Hot Chili Oil

Ingredients: Servings: 8   Cooking Time: 3 Hours

2 habanero peppers, sliced up crosswise	2 cups, milk olive oil
2 jalapeno peppers, sliced up crosswise	

Directions:
Prepare your Sous Vide water bath to a temperature of 131°F   Add the listed ingredients to your Zip bag and seal using immersion method   Cook for 3 hours Transfer bag to ice bath and allow it to cool   Discard the peppers   Store in airtight container and serve as needed.

Nutrition: Info Per serving:Calories 221, Carbohydrates 18 g, Fats 13 g, Protein 8 g

VEGETARIAN & VEGAN RECIPES

Honey Drizzled Carrots

Ingredients: Servings: 4   Cooking Time: 75 Mins.

1-lb. baby carrots	3 tbsp. honey
4 tbsp. vegan butter	¼ tsp. kosher salt
1 tbsp. agave nectar	¼ tsp. ground cardamom

Directions:
Prepare the Sous-vide water bath using your immersion circulator and increase the temperature to 185 degrees Fahrenheit   Add the carrots, honey, whole butter, kosher salt, and cardamom to a resealable bag   Seal using the immersion method. Cook for 75 Mins. and once done, remove it from the water bath.   Strain the glaze by passing through a fine mesh.   Set it aside. Take the carrots out from the bag and pour any excess glaze over them. Serve with a little bit of seasonings.

Nutrition: Info Per serving:Calories: 174 ;Carbohydrates: 42g ;Protein: 2g ;Fat: 1g ;Sugar: 31g ;Sodium: 180mg

Eggplant Lasagna

Ingredients: Servings: 3   Cooking Time: 3 Hours

1 lb eggplants, peeled and thinly sliced	1 tsp. salt
	3 tbsp. fresh basil, chopped
1 C. tomato sauce, divided into 3	Topping:
2 oz. fresh mozzarella, thinly sliced	½ tbsp. macadamia nuts, toasted and chopped
1 oz. Parmesan cheese, grated	1 oz. Parmesan cheese, grated
2 oz. Italian blend cheese, grated	1 oz. italian blend cheese, grated

Directions:
Make a water bath, place Sous Vide in it, and set to 183 F. Season eggplants with salt. Lay a vacuum-sealable bag on its side, make a layer of half the eggplant, spread one portion of tomato sauce, layer mozzarella, then parmesan, then cheese blend, then basil. Top with the second portion of tomato sauce.   Seal the bag carefully by the water displacement method, keeping it flat as possible. Submerge the bag flat in the water bath. Set the timer for 2 hours and cook. Release air 2 to 3 times within the first 30 Mins. as eggplant releases gas as it cooks.   Once the timer has stopped, remove the bag gently and poke one corner of the bag using a pin to release liquid from the bag. Lay the bag flat on a serving plate, cut open the top of it and gently slide the lasagna onto the plate. Top with remaining tomato sauce, macadamia nuts, cheese blend, and Parmesan cheese. Melt and brown the cheese using a torch.

Potato & Date Salad

Ingredients: Servings: 6   Cooking Time: 3 Hours 15 Mins.

2 lb. potatoes, cubed	1 tbsp. lemon juice
5 oz. dates, chopped	3 tbsp. butter
½ C. crumbled goat cheese	1 tsp. cilantro
	1 tsp. salt
1 tsp. oregano	1 tbsp. chopped parsley
1 tbsp. olive oil	¼ tsp. garlic powder

Directions:
Prepare a water bath and place the Sous Vide in it. Set to 190 F. Place the potatoes, butter, dates, oregano, cilantro, and salt in a vacuumm-sealable bag. Release air by the water displacement method, seal and submerge the bag in water bath.Set the timer for 3 hours. Once the timer has stopped, remove the bag and transfer to a bowl. Whisk together the olive oil, lemon juice, parsley, and garlic powder and drizzle over the salad. If using cheese, sprinkle it over.

Green Pea Cream with Nutmeg

Ingredients: Servings: 8   Cooking Time: 1 Hour 10 Mins.

1 lb. fresh green peas	¼ tsp. ground nutmeg
1 C. whipping cream	4 cloves
¼ C. butter	2 bay leaves
1 tbsp. cornstarch	Black pepper to taste

Directions:
Prepare a water bath and place the Sous Vide in it. Set to 184 F. Combine the cornstarch, nutmeg and cream into a bowl. Whisk until the cornstarch soften. Place the mixture in a vacuum-sealable bag. Release air by the water displacement method, seal and submerge the bag in the water bath. Cook for 1 hour. Once the timer has stopped, extract the bag and remove the bay leaf. Serve.

Gnocchi Pillows And Caramelized Peas with Parmesan

Ingredients: Servings: 2   Cooking Time: 30 Mins.

1 pack, store-bought gnocchi	Fresh ground black pepper
1 tablespoon, unsalted butter	½ cup, frozen peas
½, thinly sliced	¼ cup, heavy cream
sweet onion	½ cup, grated
Salt	Parmesan

Directions:
Prepare your Sous Vide water bath by dipping your immersion cooker and raising the temperature to 183°F Take a large zip bag and add gnocchi to the bag Seal using immersion method and cook for 1 and a ½ hours Take a cast iron skillet and place it over medium heat Add butter and allow the butter to melt Add onion and season with salt and Sauté for 3 Mins. Add frozen peas cream and simmer Stir in gnocchi and stir well to coat with the sauce Season with pepper and salt Transfer to a platter and serve!

Nutrition: Info   Per   serving:Calories   260, Carbohydrates 5 g, Fats 20 g, Protein 15 g

Sweet Daikon Radishes with Rosemary

Ingredients: Servings: 4   Cooking Time: 40 Mins.

½ C. lemon juice	1 large size daikon radish, sliced
3 tbsp. sugar	
1 tsp. rosemary	

Directions:
Prepare a water bath and place the Sous Vide in it. Set to 182 F. Combine the lemon juice, rosemary, salt, and sugar. Place the mixture and daikon radish in a vacuum-sealable bag. Release air by the water displacement method, seal and submerge the bag in the water bath. Cook for 30 minutes. Once the timer has stopped, remove the bag and transfer into an ice-water bath. Serve in a plate.

Ginger Tamari Brussels Sprouts with Sesame

Ingredients: Servings: 6   Cooking Time: 43 Mins.

1½ lb. Brussels sprouts, halved	1 tsp. grated ginger
2 garlic cloves, minced	¼ tsp. red pepper flakes
2 tbsp. vegetable oil	¼ tsp. toasted sesame oil
1 tbsp. tamari sauce	1 tbsp. sesame seeds

Directions:
Prepare a water bath and place Sous Vide in it. Set to 186 F. Heat a pot over medium heat and combine the garlic, vegetable oil, tamari sauce, ginger, and red pepper flakes. Cook for 4-5 minutes. Set aside. Place the brussels sprouts in a vacuum-sealable bag and pour in tamari mixture. Release air by the water

displacement method, seal and submerge the bag in the water bath. Cook for 30 minutes. Once the timer has stopped, remove the bag and pat dry with kitchen towel. Reserve the cooking juices. Transfer the sprouts to a bowl and combine with the sesame oil. Plate the sprouts and sprinkle with cooking juices. Garnish with sesame seeds.

Mustardy Lentil & Tomato Dish

Ingredients: Servings: 8   Cooking Time: 105 Mins.

2 C. lentils	1 tbsp. butter
1 can chopped tomatoes, undrained	2 tbsp. mustard
	1 tsp. red pepper flakes
1 C. green peas	2 tbsp. lime juice
3 C. veggie stock	Salt and black pepper to taste
3 C. water	
1 onion, chopped	
1 carrot, sliced	

Directions:
Prepare a water bath and place Sous Vide in it. Set to 192 F. Place all the ingredients in a large vacumm-sealable bag. Release air by water displacement method, seal and submerge in bath. Cook for 90 minutes. Once the timer has stopped, remove the bag and transfer to a large bowl and stir before serving.

Coconut Potato Mash

Ingredients: Servings: 4   Cooking Time: 45 Mins.

1 ½ lb. Yukon gold potatoes, sliced	8 oz. coconut milk
	Salt and white pepper to taste
4 oz. butter	

Directions:
Prepare a water bath and place Sous Vide in it. Set to 193 F. Place the potatoes, coconut milk, butter, and salt in a vacuum-sealable bag. Release air by water displacement method, seal and submerge in the bath. Cook for 30 minutes. Once done, remove the bag and drain. Reserve butter juices. Mash the potatoes until soft and transfer to the butter bowl. Season with pepper and serve.

Tomato & Agave Tofu

Ingredients: Servings: 6   Cooking Time: 1 Hour 45 Mins.

1 C. vegetable broth	2 tsp. sriracha sauce
2 tbsp. tomato paste	3 cloves minced garlic
1 tbsp. turmeric powder	1 tsp. soy sauce
	24 oz. silken tofu, cubed
1 tbsp. rice wine vinegar	
1 tbsp. agave nectar	

Directions:
Prepare a water bath and place the Sous Vide in it. Set to 186 F. Combine all the ingredients in a bowl, except the tofu. Place the tofu in a vacuum-sealable bag. Add the mixture. Release air by the water displacement method, seal and submerge the bag in the water bath. Cook for 1 hour and 30 minutes. Once the timer has stopped, remove the bag. Serve.

Rosemary Russet Potatoes Confit

Ingredients: Servings: 4   Cooking Time: 1 Hour 15 Mins.

1 lb. brown russet potatoes, chopped	1 tsp. chopped fresh rosemary
Salt to taste	2 tbsp. whole butter
¼ tsp. ground white pepper	1 tbsp. corn oil

Directions:
Prepare a water bath and place Sous Vide in it. Set to 192 F. Season potatoes with rosemary, salt and pepper. Combine the potatoes with butter and oil. Place in a vacuum-sealable bag. Release air by the water displacement method, seal and submerge the bag in the water bath. Cook for 60 minutes. Once the timer has stopped, remove the bag and transfer into a large bowl. Garnish with butter and serve.

Provolone Cheese Grits

Ingredients: Servings: 4   Cooking Time: 3 Hours 20 Mins.

1 C. grits	2 tbsp. butter
1 C. cream	1 tbsp. paprika
3 C. vegetable stock	Extra cheese for garnish
4 oz. grated Provolone cheese	Salt and black pepper to taste

Directions:
Prepare a water bath and place the Sous Vide in it. Set to 182 F. Combine the grits, cream and vegetable stock. Chop the butter and add to the mixture. Place the mix in a vacuum-sealable bag. Release air by the water displacement method, seal and submerge the bag in the water bath. Cook for 3 hours. Once the timer has stopped, remove the bag and transfer into a bowl. Stir the mixture with the cheese and season with salt and

pepper. Garnish with extra cheese and paprika, if preferred.

Broiled Onions with Sunflower Pesto

Ingredients: Servings: 4   Cooking Time: 2 Hours 25 Mins.

1 bunch large spring onions, trimmed and halved	2 cloves garlic, peeled
½ C. plus 2 tbsp. olive oil	3 C. loosely packed fresh basil leaves
Salt and black pepper to taste	3 tbsp. grated Grana Padano cheese
2 tbsp. sunflower seeds	1 tbsp. freshly squeezed lemon juice

Directions:
Prepare a water bath and place the Sous Vide in it. Set to 183 F.   Place the onions in a vacuum-sealable bag. Season with salt, pepper and 2 tbsp. of olive oil. Release air by the water displacement method, seal and submerge the bag in the water bath. Cook for 2 hours. Meanwhile, for the pesto sauce, combine in a processor food the sunflower seeds, garlic, and basil, and blend until finely chopped. Carefully add the remaining oil. Add in lemon juice and stop. Season with salt and pepper. Set aside.   Once the timer has stopped, remove the bag and transfer the onions to a skillet and cook for 10 minutes. Serve and top with the pesto sauce.

Delightful Tofu with Sriracha Sauce

Ingredients: Servings: 10   Cooking Time: 1 Hour 10 Mins.

1 C. vegetable broth	1 tbsp. rice wine
2 tbsp. tomato paste	1 tbsp. agave nectar
1 tbsp. grated ginger	2 tsp. Sriracha sauce
1 tbsp. ground nutmeg	3 minced garlic cloves
1 tbsp. rice wine vinegar	2 boxes cubed tofu

Directions:
Prepare a water bath and place the Sous Vide in it. Set to 186 F.   Combine well all the ingredients, except for the tofu. Place the tofu with the mixture in a vacuum-sealable bag. Release air by the water displacement method, seal and submerge the bag in the water bath.

Cook for 60 minutes. Once the timer has stopped, remove the bag and transfer into a bowl.

Lovely Kidney Bean & Carrot Stew

Ingredients: Servings: 8   Cooking Time: 3 Hours 15 Mins.

1 C. dried kidney beans, soaked overnight	1 quartered shallot
1 C. water	4 crushed garlic cloves
½ C. olive oil	2 fresh rosemary sprigs
1 carrot, chopped	2 bay leaves
1 celery stalk, chopped	Salt and black pepper, to taste

Directions:
Prepare a water bath and place the Sous Vide in it. Set to 192 F.   Strain the beans and wash them. Place in a vacuum-sealable bag with olive oil, celery, water, carrot, shallot, garlic, rosemary, and bay leaves. Season with salt and pepper. Release air by the water displacement method, seal and submerge the bag in the water bath. Cook for 180 minutes.   Once the timer has stopped, remove the beans. Discard bay leaves and the rosemary.

Buttered Asparagus with Thyme & Cheese

Ingredients: Servings: 6   Cooking Time: 21 Mins.

¼ C. shaved Pecorino Romano cheese	Salt to taste
16 oz. fresh asparagus, trimmed	1 garlic clove, minced
4 tbsp. butter, cubed	1 tbsp. thyme

Directions:
Prepare a water bath and place the Sous Vide in it. Set to 186 F.   Place the asparagus in a vacuum-sealable bag. Add the butter cubes, garlic, salt, and thyme. Release air by the water displacement method, seal and submerge the bag in the water bath. Cook for 14 minutes. Once the timer has stopped, remove the bag and transfer the asparagus to a plate. Sprinkle with some cooking juices. Garnish with the Pecorino Romano cheese.

Germany's Potato Salad

Ingredients: Servings: 6   Cooking Time: 1 ½ Hours

1 ½ pound, Yukon potatoes, sliced up into ¾ inch pieces
½ a C. of chicken stock
4-ounce, thick bacon cut up into ¼ inch thick strips
Salt
Pepper
½ a cup, chopped onion
1/3 cup, apple cider vinegar
4 thinly sliced scallions

Directions:

Prepare your Sous Vide water bath by dipping your immersion cooker and raising the temperature to 185°F Take a heavy-duty re-sealable bag and add potatoes alongside the stock   Season with some salt and seal up the bag using immersion method   Submerge the bag underwater and let it cook for 1 and a ½ hours   Take a large sized non-stick skillet and place it over medium-high heat   Add bacon and cook for about 5-7 Mins. Transfer it to a paper towel-lined plate using a slotted spoon   Make sure to keep reserved fat   Return the skillet to medium-high heat and add onions   Cook them for a 1 Min.   Once the cooking is done, remove the bag from the water and return the skillet to medium heat again   Add the bacon and add vinegar   Bring it to a simmer   Add the contents of the bag to the skillet and stir well to combine and allow the liquid to come to a simmer   Add scallions and toss well   Season with some pepper and salt   Serve warm!

Nutrition: Info Per serving:Calories 75, Carbohydrates 5 g, Fats 3 g, Protein 7 g

Perfect Curried Squash

Ingredients: Servings: 6   Cooking Time: 1 ½ Hours

1 medium-sized winter squash
2 tablespoons, unsalted butter
Fresh cilantro
1 to 2 tablespoon, Thai curry paste
½ teaspoon, kosher salt
Lime wedges

Directions:

Prepare your Sous Vide water bath by dipping your immersion cooker and raising the temperature to 185°F Slice the squash into half lengthwise and scoop out the seeds alongside inner membrane   Keep the seeds for later use   Slice the squash into wedges of 1 and ½ inch thickness   Take a large sized zip bag and add squash wedges, curry paste, butter, salt and seal using immersion method   Submerge and cook for 1 and ½ hours   Remove the bag and slight squeeze it   If soft then take out, otherwise cook for 40 Mins. more Transfer to serving platter and drizzle a bit of curry butter sauce   Top with cilantro and enjoy!

Nutrition: Info Per serving:Calories 152, Carbohydrates 5 g, Fats 12 g, Protein 6 g

Brussels Sprouts In Sweet Syrup

Ingredients: Servings: 3   Cooking Time: 75 Mins.

4 lb Brussels sprouts, halved
3 tbsp. olive oil
¾ C. fish sauce
3 tbsp. water
2 tbsp. sugar
1 ½ tbsp. rice vinegar
2 tsp. lime juice
3 red chilies, sliced thinly
2 cloves garlic, minced

Directions:

Make a water bath, place Sous Vide in it, and set to 183 F. Pour Brussels sprouts, salt, and oil in a vacuum-sealable bag, release air by the water displacement method, seal and submerge the bag in the water bath. Set the timer for 50 minutes.   Once the timer has stopped, remove the bag, unseal, and transfer the Brussels sprouts to a foiled baking sheet. Preheat a broiler to high, place the baking sheet in it, and broil for 6 minutes. Pour the Brussels sprouts in a bowl.   Make the sauce: in a bowl, add the remaining listed cooking ingredients and stir. Add the sauce to the Brussels sprouts and toss evenly. Serve as a side dish.

Allspice Miso Corn with Sesame & Honey

Ingredients: Servings: 4   Cooking Time: 45 Mins.

4 ears of corn
6 tbsp. butter
3 tbsp. red miso paste
1 tsp. honey
1 tsp. allspice
1 tbsp. canola oil
1 scallion, thinly sliced
1 tsp. toasted sesame seeds

Directions:

Prepare a water bath and place the Sous Vide in it. Set to 183 F. Clean the corn and cut the ears. Cover each corn with 2 tbsp. of butter. Place in a vacuum-sealable bag. Release air by the water displacement method, seal and submerge the bag in the water bath. Cook for 30 minutes.   Meanwhile, combine 4 tbsp. of butter, 2 tbsp. of miso paste, honey, canola oil, and allspice in a bowl. Stir well. Set aside. Once the timer has stopped, remove the bag and sear the corn. Spread the miso mixture on top. Garnish with sesame oil and scallions.

Easy Two-bean Salad

Ingredients: Servings: 6   Cooking Time: 7 Hours 10 Mins.

4 oz. dry black
beans
4 oz. dry kidney
beans
4 C. water
1 minced shallot

Salt to taste
1 tsp. sugar
1 tbsp. champagne
3 tbsp. olive oil

Directions:
Prepare a water bath and place the Sous Vide in it. Set
to 90 F. Combine the black beans, 3 C. of water and
kidney beans in 4-6 mason jars. Seal and submerge the
jars in the water bath. Cook for 2 hours. Once the
timer has stopped, remove the jars and top with shallots,
kosher salt and sugar. Allow resting. Seal and immerse
in the water bath again. Cook for 4 hours. Once the
timer has stopped, remove the jars and allow chilling for
1 hour. Add olive oil and champagne and shake well.
Transfer to a bowl and serve.

Lemon & Garlic Artichokes

Ingredients: Servings: 4   Cooking Time: 90 Mins.

4 tbsp. freshly
squeezed lemon
juice
12 pieces' baby
artichokes
4 tbsp. vegan
butter
2 fresh garlic
cloves, minced

1 tsp. fresh lemon
zest
Kosher salt, and
black pepper, to
taste
Chopped up fresh
parsley for
garnishing

Directions:
Prepare the Sous Vide water bath using your immersion
circulator and raise the temperature to 180-degrees
Fahrenheit. Take a large bowl and add the cold water
and 2 tbsp. of lemon juice. Peel and discard the outer
tough layer of your artichoke and cut them into quarters.
Transfer to a cold water bath and let it sit for a while.
Take a large skillet and put it over medium high heat.
Add in the butter to the skillet and allow the butter to
melt. Add the garlic alongside 2 tbsp. of lemon juice
and the zest. Remove from heat and season with a bit
of pepper and salt. Allow it to cool for about 5 minutes.
Then, drain the artichokes from the cold water and
place them in a large resealable bag. Add in the butter
mixture as well. Seal it up using the immersion
method and submerge underwater for about 1 and a ½
hour. Once cooked, transfer the artichokes to a bowl
and serve with a garnish of parsley.

Nutrition: Info   Per   serving:Calories:
408 ;Carbohydrates: 49g ;Protein: 12g ;Fat: 20g ;Sugar:
5g ;Sodium: 549mg

Mushroom Soup

Ingredients: Servings: 3   Cooking Time: 50 Mins.

1 lb mixed
mushrooms
2 onions, diced
3 cloves garlic
2 sprigs parsley
leaves, chopped

2 tbsp. thyme
powder
2 tbsp. olive oil
2 C. cream
2 C. vegetable
stock

Directions:
Make a water bath, place Sous Vide in it, and set to 185
F. Place the mushrooms, onion, and celery in a vacuum-
sealable bag. Release air by the water displacement
method, seal and submerge the bag in the water bath.
Set the timer for 30 minutes. Once the timer has
stopped, remove and unseal the bag. Blend the
ingredients from the bag in a blender. Put a pan over
medium heat, add olive oil. Once it starts to heat, add
pureed mushrooms and the remaining ingredients,
except for the cream. Cook for 10 minutes. Turn off heat
and add cream. Stir well and serve.

Pickled Cucumbers Pots

Ingredients: Servings: 6   Cooking Time: 30 Mins.

1 C. white wine
vinegar
½ C. sugar
Salt to taste
1 tbsp. pickling
spice
2 English
cucumbers sliced

½ white thinly
sliced onion
3 tsp. dill seeds
2 tsp. black
peppercorns
6 cloves garlic,
peeled

Directions:
Prepare a water bath and place the Sous Vide in it. Set
to 182 F. Combine sugar, vinegar, salt, pickling spice,
dill seeds, black peppercorns, cucumber, onion, and
garlic and place in a vacuum-sealable bag. Release air
by water displacement method, seal and submerge in
the water bath. Cook for 15 minutes. Once done,
transfer to an ice-water bath. Serve in mason jars.

Effortless Pickled Fennel with Lemon

Ingredients: Servings: 8   Cooking Time: 40 Mins.

1 C. apple cider
vinegar
2 tbsp. sugar
Juice and zest
from 1 lemon

Salt to taste
2 bulb fennels,
sliced
½ tsp. fennel
seeds, crushed

Directions:

Prepare a water bath and place the Sous Vide in it. Set to 182 F. Combine well the vinegar, sugar, lemon juice, salt, lemon zest and fennel seeds. Place the mixture in a vacuum-sealable bag. Release air by the water displacement method, seal and submerge the bag in the water bath. Cook for 30 minutes. Once the timer has stopped, remove the bag and transfer to an ice-water bath. Allow cooling.

Herby Mashed Snow Peas

Ingredients: Servings: 6   Cooking Time: 55 Mins.

½ C. vegetable broth	Salt and black pepper to taste
1 lb. fresh snow peas	2 tbsp. chopped fresh chives
Zest of 1 lemon	2 tbsp. chopped fresh parsley
2 tbsp. chopped fresh basil	¾ tsp. garlic powder
1 tbsp. olive oil	

Directions:
Prepare a water bath and place the Sous Vide in it. Set to 186 F.   Combine the peas, lemon zest, basil, olive oil, black pepper, chives, parsley, salt, and garlic powder and place them in a vacuum-sealable bag. Release air by the water displacement method, seal and submerge the bag in the water bath. Cook for 45 minutes. Once the timer has stopped, remove the bag and transfer into a blender and mix well.

Honey Apple & Arugula Salad

Ingredients: Servings: 4   Cooking Time: 3 Hours 50 Mins.

2 tbsp. honey	Dressing
2 apples, cored, halved and sliced	¼ C. olive oil
½ C. walnuts, toasted and chopped	1 tbsp. white wine vinegar
½ C. shaved Grana Padano cheese	1 tsp. Dijon mustard
4 C. arugula	1 garlic clove, minced
Sea salt to taste	Salt to taste

Directions:
Prepare a water bath and place the Sous Vide in it. Set to 158 F. Place the honey in a glass bowl and heat for 30 seconds, add the apples and mix well. Place it in a vacuum-sealable bag. Release air by the water displacement method, seal and submerge the bag in the water bath. Cook for 30 minutes.   Once the timer has stopped, remove the bag and transfer into an ice-water

bath for 5 minutes. Refrigerate for 3 hours. Combine all the dressing ingredients in a jar and shake well. Allow cooling in the fridge for a moment.   In a bowl, mix the arugula, walnuts, and Grana Padano cheese. Add the peach slices. Top with the dressing. Season with salt and pepper and serve.

Citrus Corn with Tomato Sauce

Ingredients: Servings: 8   Cooking Time: 55 Mins.

⅓ C. olive oil	3 tbsp. lemon juice
4 ears yellow corn, husked	1 serrano pepper, seeded
Salt and black pepper to taste	4 scallions, green parts only, chopped
1 large tomato, chopped	½ bunch fresh cilantro leaves, chopped
2 garlic cloves, minced	

Directions:
Prepare a water bath and place the Sous Vide in it. Set to 186 F. Whisk the corns with olive oil and season with salt and pepper. Place them in a vacuum-sealable bag. Release air by the water displacement method, seal and submerge the bag in the water bath. Cook for 45 minutes.   Meantime, combine well the tomato, lemon juice, garlic, serrano pepper, scallions, cilantro, and the remaining olive oil in a bowl. Preheat a grill over high heat.   Once the timer has stopped, remove the corns and transfer to the grill and cook for 2-3 minutes. Allow to cool. Cut the kernels from the cob and pour in tomato sauce. Serve with fish, salad or tortilla chips.

White Cannellini Beans

Ingredients: Servings: 5   Cooking Time: 180 Mins.

1 C. cannellini beans (dried) soaked overnight in salty cold water	1 C. water
	1 quartered shallot
	4 crushed garlic cloves
½ C. extra-virgin olive oil	2 fresh rosemary sprigs
1 peeled carrot, cut up into 1-inch dice	2 bay leaves
	Kosher salt, and pepper to taste
1 celery stalk, cut up into 1-inch dice	

Directions:
Prepare the Sous Vide water bath using your Sous-vide immersion circulator and raise the temperature to 190-degrees Fahrenheit.   Drain the soaked beans and rinse them.   Transfer to a heavy duty resealable zip bag and

add the olive oil, celery, water, carrot, shallot, garlic, rosemary, and bay leaves.   Season with pepper and salt. Seal using the immersion method and cook for 3 hours. Once cooked, remove the beans and check for seasoning. Discard the rosemary and serve!

Nutrition: Info   Per   serving:Calories: 578 ;Carbohydrates: 77g ;Protein: 31g ;Fat: 18g ;Sugar: 5g ;Sodium: 519mg

Eggplant Parmesan

Ingredients: Servings: 2   Cooking Time: 1 Hour

1 large eggplant, sliced	½ cup, bread crumbs
2 large eggs, beaten	⅓ cup, white flour
¼ C. parmesan cheese, grated	4 tbsp. olive oil
1 cup, tomato sauce	Salt/pepper

Directions:
Prepare your Sous Vide water bath by attaching the immersion circulator and setting the temperature to 183ºF.   Place the eggplants on water, pinch with a fork and let them release their bitterness in the water for 10 minutes. Drain, season with salt, pepper, and set aside. Place and distribute the eggplant slices into 2-3 pouches, while these are lying flat. Seal using the water displacement method or the vacuum sealer (while placing the pouch horizontally so that eggplants are not on top of each other).   Submerge into the water and let cook for 40 minutes.   In three separate small bowls, divide the beaten eggs, the breadcrumbs, and the flour. Season everything with salt and pepper.   Once the eggplants are cooked, dip each slice into the flour, then to the eggs and then to the breadcrumb mixture.   Heat the olive oil in a medium pan (over medium heat) and place the breaded eggplant slices. Cook for 2-3 Mins. on each side, or until golden brown.   Transfer the eggplants into a baking dish or pyrex and pour over the tomato sauce and the grated mozzarella cheese.   Pop these into the oven and cook for 15-20 Mins. (or until cheese is melted)   Serve hot

Nutrition: Info   Per   serving:Calories   679.9, Carbohydrates 66.5 g, Fats 39.1 g, Protein 15.5 g

APPETIZERS & SNACKS

Shrimp Appetizer

Ingredients: Servings: 8   Cooking Time: 75 Mins.

1 lb. shrimps	½ C. parsley
3 tbsp. sesame oil	Salt and white
3 tbsp. lemon juice	pepper to taste

Directions:
Prepare a water bath and place the Sous Vide in it. Set to 140 F.   Place all ingredients in a vacuum-sealable bag. Shake to coat the shrimp well. Release air by the water displacement method, seal and submerge the bag in water bath.Set the timer for 1 hour. Once the timer has stopped, remove the bag. Serve warm.

Easy Spiced Hummus

Ingredients: Servings: 6   Cooking Time: 3 Hours 35 Mins.

1½ C. dried chickpeas, soaked overnight	2 garlic cloves, minced
2 quarts water	2 tbsp. olive oil
¼ C. lemon juice	½ tsp. caraway seeds
¼ C. tahini paste	½ tsp. salt
	1 tsp. cayenne pepper

Directions:
Prepare a water bath and place the Sous Vide in it. Set to 196 F.   Strain the chickpeas and place in a vacuum-sealable bag with 1 quart of water. Release air by the water displacement method, seal and submerge the bag in the water bath. Cook for 3 hours. Once the timer has stopped, remove the bag and transfer into an ice water bath and allow to chill.   In a blender, mix the lemon juice and tahini paste for 90 seconds. Add in garlic, olive oil, caraway seeds, and salt, mix for 30 seconds until smooth. Remove the chickpeas and drain it. For a smoother hummus, peel the chickpeas.   In a food processor, combine the half of chickpeas with the tahini mix and blend for 90 seconds. Add the remaining chickpeas and blend until smooth. Put the mixture in a plate and garnish with cayenne pepper and the reserved chickpeas.

Eggplant Kebab

Ingredients: Servings: 3   Cooking Time: 1 Hour

1 large eggplant, sliced into 1-inch thick slices	1 medium-sized tomato, finely chopped
1 small zucchini, sliced into 1-inch thick slices	1 tsp. red pepper flakes
1 large green bell pepper, seeds	3 tbsp. olive oil
	1 tsp. salt
	Serve with:

removed and sliced

2 garlic cloves, crushed

Sour cream or yogurt

Directions:

Wash the eggplant and zucchini. Slice into 1-inch thick pieces and set aside. Wash the bell pepper and cut in half. Remove the seeds and slice. Set aside. Wash the tomato and finely chop it. Set aside. Now, place all vegetables along with garlic, red pepper, olive oil, and salt in a large Ziploc bag. Seal the bag and cook en sous vide for 1 hour at 185 degrees.

Nutrition: Info Calories: 189 Total Fat: 16g Saturated Fat: 2g; Trans Fat: 0g Protein: 9g; Net Carbs: 9g

Tilapia In Soy Sauce

Ingredients: Servings: 2   Cooking Time: 1 Hour And 15 Minutes;

pound tilapia fillets	½ tsp. sea salt
1 medium-sized carrot, sliced	¼ tsp. black pepper, ground
1 medium-sized red pepper, finely chopped	1 tbsp. fresh parsley, finely chopped
tablespoons soy sauce	Serve with:
tablespoons olive oil	Lamb's lettuce

Directions:

Rub each fillet with soy sauce and sprinkle with salt, pepper, and parsley. Place in a large Ziploc along with sliced carrot and finely chopped red bell pepper. Seal the bag and cook en sous vide for 1 hour and ten Mins. at 131 degrees. Remove from the water bath and set aside. Heat up the olive oil in a large skillet, over medium-high heat. Add fillets and briefly cook for 2 Mins. on each side, until nice golden brown color. Remove from the heat and serve.

Nutrition: Info Calories: 344 Total Fat: 12g Saturated Fat: 9g; Trans Fat: 0g Protein: 46g; Net Carbs: 7g

Carrots & Nuts Stuffed Peppers

Ingredients: Servings: 5   Cooking Time: 2 Hours 35 Mins.

4 shallots, chopped	1 tbsp. soy sauce
4 carrots, chopped	1 tbsp. ground cumin
4 garlic cloves, minced	2 tsp. paprika
	1 tsp. garlic

1 C. raw cashews, soaked and drained	powder
	1 pinch cayenne pepper
1 C. pecans, soaked and drained	4 fresh thyme sprigs
1 tbsp. balsamic vinegar	Zest of 1 lemon
	4 bell peppers, tops cut off and seeded

Directions:

Prepare a water bath and place the Sous Vide in it. Set to 186 F. Combine in a blender the carrots, garlic, shallots, cashews, pecans, balsamic vinegar, soy sauce, cumin, paprika, garlic powder, cayenne, thyme, and lemon zest. Mix until roughly. Pour the mixture into the bell peppers shells and place in a vacuum-sealable bag. Release air by the water displacement method, seal and submerge the bag in the water bath. Cook for 1 hour and 15 minutes. Once the timer has stopped, remove the peppers and transfer to a plate.

Anchovies In Sour Sauce

Ingredients: Servings: 5   Cooking Time: 40 Minutes;

1 lb. anchovies, whole	1 C. olive oil
½ C. freshly squeezed lime juice	3 garlic cloves, crushed
	pepper corns
2 tbsp. fresh thyme, finely chopped	1 C. sour cream
	¼ C. freshly squeezed lemon juice
1 tbsp. dried mint	1 tsp. salt
1 tbsp. fresh rosemary, finely chopped	Serve with:
	Spring onions

Directions:

In a large bowl, combine olive oil with lime juice, fresh thyme, dried mint, rosemary, crushed garlic, and pepper corns. Mix well to combine and submerge fish into this mixture. Refrigerate for one hour. Remove from the refrigerator and transfer to a Ziploc along with the marinade. Cook en sous vide for 40 Mins. at 104 degrees. Remove from the water bath and set aside. In a medium-sized bowl, combine sour cream with lemon juice and salt. Use the mixture to top anchovies. Serve cold.

Nutrition: Info Calories: 628 Total Fat: 58g Saturated Fat: 14g; Trans Fat: 0g Protein: 26; Net Carbs: 7g

Bbq Tofu

Ingredients: Servings: 8   Cooking Time: 2 Hours 15 Mins.

15 oz. tofu	1 tsp. onion
3 tbsp. barbecue sauce	powder
2 tbsp. tamari sauce	1 tsp. salt

Directions:
Prepare a water bath and place the Sous Vide in it. Set to 180 F.   Cut the tofu into cubes. Place it in a plastic bag. Release air by the water displacement method, seal and submerge the bag in water bath.Set the timer for 2 hours.   Once the timer has stopped, remove the bag and transfer to a bowl. Add the remaining ingredients and toss to combine.

Ginger Balls

Ingredients: Servings: 3   Cooking Time: 1 Hour 30 Mins.

1 lb. ground beef	¼ C. fresh mint,
1 C. onions, finely chopped	finely chopped
3 tbsp. olive oil	2 tsp. ginger paste
¼ C. fresh cilantro, finely chopped	1 tsp. cayenne pepper
	2 tsps salt

Directions:
In a large bowl, combine ground beef, onions, olive oil, cilantro, mint, cilantro, ginger paste, cayenne pepper, and salt. Mold patties and refrigerate for 15 minutes. Remove from the refrigerator and transfer to separate vacuum-sealable bags. Cook in Sous Vide for 1 hour at 154 F.

Italian-style Tomato Dipping Sauce

Ingredients: Servings: 10   Cooking Time: 45 Mins.

2 lb. very ripe tomatoes, chopped with juices	Sea salt and ground black pepper, to taste
1 C. scallions, chopped	1 tsp. red pepper flakes
3 cloves roasted garlic, pressed	1 tsp. sugar
2 tsp. dried Italian herb seasoning	2 tbsp. extra-virgin olive oil
2 heaping tbsp.	1 C. Parmigiano-Reggiano cheese, preferably freshly grated

fresh cilantro, roughly chopped

Directions:
Preheat a sous vide water bath to 180 degrees F.   Add all ingredients, minus cheese, to cooking pouches; seal tightly.   Submerge the cooking pouches in the water bath; cook for 40 minutes.   Place the prepared sous vide sauce in a serving bowl; top with grated Parmigiano-Reggiano cheese and serve with breadsticks. Bon appétit!

Nutrition: Info 71 Calories; 3g Fat; 6g Carbs; 3g Protein; 4g Sugars

Radish Cheese Dip

Ingredients: Servings: 4   Cooking Time: 1 Hour 15 Mins.

30 small radishes, green leaves removed	1 C. water for steaming
1 tbsp. Chardonnay vinegar	1 tbsp. grapeseed oil
Sugar to taste	12 oz. cream cheese

Directions:
Make a water bath, place Sous Vide in it, and set to 183 F. Put the radishes, salt, pepper, water, sugar, and vinegar in a vacuum-sealable bag. Release air from the bag, seal and submerge in the water bath. Cook for 1 hour. Once the timer has stopped, remove the bag, unseal and transfer the radishes with a little of the steaming water into a blender. Add cream cheese and puree to get a smooth paste. Serve.

Sous Vide Pickled Rhubarb

Ingredients: Servings: 8   Cooking Time: 40 Mins.

2 lb. rhubarb, sliced	1 tbsp. brown sugar
7 tbsp. apple cider vinegar	¼ celery stalk, minced
	¼ tsp. salt

Directions:
Prepare a water bath and place the Sous Vide in it. Set to 180 F. Place all the ingredients in a vacuum-sealable bag. Shake to coat well. Release air by the water displacement method, seal and submerge the bag in water bath.Cook for 25 minutes. Once the timer has stopped, remove the bag. Serve warm.

Cheesy Taco Dip

Ingredients: Servings: 10   Cooking Time: 2 Hours 5 Mins.

1 lb. pork, ground	3 garlic cloves, chopped
1/2 lb. beef, ground	12 oz. cream of celery soup
1 tsp. Taco seasoning	1 C. processed American cheese
1/2 C. medium-hot taco sauce	Sea salt and ground black pepper, to taste
1 C. shallots, chopped	

Directions:
Preheat a sous vide water bath to 140 degrees F.   Place all ingredients in cooking pouches; seal tightly. Submerge the cooking pouches in the water bath; cook for 2 hours.   Season, adjust the seasonings and serve with veggie sticks or tortilla chips. Enjoy!

Nutrition: Info 195 Calories; 12g Fat; 7g Carbs; 24g Protein; 2g Sugars

Delicious Artichokes with Simple Dip

Ingredients: Servings: 6   Cooking Time: 1 Hour

6 artichokes, trimmed and cut into halves	6 cloves garlic, peeled
1 ½ sticks butter, room temperature	2 tsp. lemon zest
Sea salt and freshly ground black pepper, to taste	1/2 C. sour cream
	1/2 C. mayonnaise

Directions:
Preheat a sous vide water bath to 183 degrees F.   Place trimmed artichokes along with butter, garlic, lemon zest, salt and black pepper in cooking pouches; seal tightly. Submerge the cooking pouches in the water bath; cook for 50 minutes. Remove artichokes from the water bath and pat them dry. Then, blow torch artichokes to get the char marks.   Place artichokes on a serving platter.   In a bowl, mix the sour cream and mayonnaise. Serve artichokes with sour cream-mayo dip on the side. Bon appétit!

Nutrition: Info 314 Calories; 21g Fat; 21g Carbs; 3g Protein; 9g Sugars

Mushroom Beef Tips

Ingredients: Servings: 3   Cooking Time: 8 Hours 15 Minutes;

1 lb. beef stew meat, cubed	1 C. beef stock
1 C. button mushrooms, chopped	½ tsp. salt
	¼ tsp. black pepper, ground
1 small onion, chopped	2 tbsp. olive oil
1 garlic clove, crushed	Serve with: Fresh tomato salad

Directions:
In a medium bowl, combine meat, garlic, onion, olive oil, salt, and pepper. Mix well and place all in a large Ziploc bag. Seal the bag and cook for 8 hours at 185 degrees.   Remove the meat from the water bath and set aside to cool for a while. Transfer all to a heavy-bottomed pot and add beef stock and mushrooms. Stir well and bring it to a boil. Reduce the heat to low and cover with a lid. Add some water if needed and cook for 10 more minutes.

Nutrition: Info Calories: 383 Total Fat: 19g Saturated Fat: 5g; Trans Fat: 0g Protein: 48g; Net Carbs: 6g

Chicken Thighs with Green Beans

Ingredients: Servings: 3   Cooking Time: 1 Hour

1 lb. chicken thighs, boneless	1 tbsp. lemon juice, freshly squeezed
1 C. green beans, chopped	tablespoon olive oil
2 garlic cloves, minced	½ tsp. salt
1 tsp. ginger, ground	1 tsp. fresh mint, finely chopped
1 tbsp. Cayenne pepper, ground	Serve with: Fresh tomatoes

Directions:
Wash the chicken thighs under cold running water and cut into thin slices. Gently rub the meat with salt, Cayenne pepper, and ginger. Set aside.   Wash the beans and chop into bite-sized pieces. Set aside.   Place the thighs along with beans, garlic, lemon juice, olive oil, and fresh mint in a large Ziploc bag. Seal the bag and cook en sous vide for 1 hour at 167 degrees.   Remove the bag from the water bath and set aside to cool for a while before serving.

Nutrition: Info Calories: 471 Total Fat: 33g Saturated Fat: 9g; Trans Fat: 0g Protein: 49g; Net Carbs: 9g

Nutty Baked Sweet Potatoes

Ingredients: Servings: 2   Cooking Time: 3 Hours 45 Mins.

1 lb. sweet potatoes, sliced	¼ C. walnuts
Salt to taste	1 tbsp. coconut oil

Directions:
Prepare a water bath and place the Sous Vide in it. Set to 146 F. Place the potatoes and salt in a vacuum-sealable bag. Release air by the water displacement method, seal and submerge the bag in the water bath. Cook for 3 hours. Heat a skillet over medium heat and toast the walnuts. Chop them.   Preheat the over to 375 F and lined a baking tray with parchment foil. Once the timer has stopped, remove the potatoes and transfer to the baking tray. Sprinkle with coconut oil and bake for 20-30 minutes. Toss once. Serve topped with toasted walnuts.

Sweet And Sticky Tebasaki

Ingredients: Servings: 6   Cooking Time: 4 Hours 10 Mins.

1 ½ lb. chicken drumettes	1 tbsp. Shoyu sauce
Coarse sea salt and freshly ground black pepper, to your liking	1 tsp. granulated garlic
	1 tbsp. black vinegar
	2 tsp. sesame oil
3 tbsp. packed dark brown sugar	2 tbsp. sesame seeds, toasted
1 tsp. ginger juice	
1 tbsp. sake	

Directions:
Preheat a sous vide water bath to 148 degrees F.   Now, season chicken drumettes with salt and black pepper. Place the seasoned chicken drumettes in cooking pouches; seal tightly.   Submerge the cooking pouches in the water bath; cook for 4 hours.   In a saucepan, heat the sugar, ginger juice, sake, Shoyu sauce, and granulated garlic over medium-high heat.   Bring the sauce to a rolling boil; add the vinegar and allow this glaze to cool.   Remove the chicken drumettes from the water bath; pat dry with kitchen towels.   Heat the oil in a cast-iron skillet over medium-high heat; sear the chicken drumettes until well browned on both sides. Transfer the chicken drumettes directly to the bowl of glaze and toss to coat them completely. Serve garnished with toasted sesame seeds. Bon appétit!

Nutrition: Info 345 Calories; 26g Fat; 1g Carbs; 22g Protein; 3g Sugars

Tasty French Toast

Ingredients: Servings: 2   Cooking Time: 100 Mins.

2 eggs	½ tsp. cinnamon
4 bread slices	1 tbsp. butter,
½ C. milk	melted

Directions:
Prepare a water bath and place the Sous Vide in it. Set to 150 F.   Whisk together the eggs, milk, butter and cinnamon. Place the bread slices in a vacuum-sealable bag and pour the egg mixture over. Shake to coat well. Release air by the water displacement method, seal and submerge the bag in water bath.Set the timer for 1 hour and 25 minutes. Once the timer has stopped, remove the bag. Serve warm.

Aromatic Lamb with Dill

Ingredients: Servings: 4   Cooking Time: 6 Hours 15 Minutes;

2 lb. lamb, tender cuts	3 tbsp. fresh dill, finely chopped
1 tbsp. sea salt	2 basil leaves, whole
½ C. vegetable oil	
1 tsp. freshly ground red pepper	Serve with: Sour cream

Directions:
Rinse well the meat and place on a clean working surface. Using a sharp paring knife, cut into 3-inches long and 2-inces thick pieces. Place in a Ziploc along with other ingredients.   Cook en sous vide for 6 hours at 140 degrees. Remove from the water bath and set aside.   Preheat the oven to 400 degrees. Line some baking paper over a baking sheet and place lamb cuts along with sauce.   Bake for 15 minutes, or until lightly charred on top.   Serve with sour cream.

Nutrition: Info Calories: 670 Total Fat: 41g Saturated Fat: 13g; Trans Fat: 0g Protein: 62g; Net Carbs: 6g

Spicy Butter Corn

Ingredients: Servings: 5   Cooking Time: 35 Mins.

5 ears yellow corn, husked	5 tbsp. butter
1 tbsp. fresh parsley	½ tsp. Cayenne pepper
	Salt to taste

Directions:
Prepare a water bath and place the Sous Vide in it. Set to 186 F.   Place 3 ears of corn in each vacuum-sealable

bag. Release air by the water displacement method, seal and submerge the bags in the water bath. Cook for 30 minutes. Once the timer has stopped, remove the corn from the bags and transfer into a plate. Garnish with cayenne pepper and parsley.

Chicken & Mushrooms In Marsala Sauce

Ingredients: Servings: 2   Cooking Time: 2 Hours 25 Mins.

2 chicken breasts, boneless and skinless	1 tbsp. butter
	Salt and black pepper to taste
1 C. Marsala wine	2 garlic cloves, minced
1 C. chicken broth	
14 oz. mushrooms, sliced	1 shallot, minced
½ tbsp. flour	

Directions:
Prepare a water bath and place the Sous Vide in it. Set to 140 F. Season the chicken with salt and pepper and place in a vacuum-sealable bag along with the mushrooms. Release air by the water displacement method, seal and submerge in water bath. Cook for 2 hours. Once the timer has stopped, remove the bag. Melt the butter in a pan over medium heat, whisk in the flour and the remaining ingredients. Cook until the sauce thickens. Add chicken and cook for 1 minute.

Cheesy Pears with Walnuts

Ingredients: Servings: 2   Cooking Time: 55 Mins.

1 pear, sliced	2 C. rocket leaves
1 lb. honey	Salt and black pepper to taste
½ C. walnuts	
4 tbsp. shaved Grana Padano cheese	2 tbsp. lemon juice
	2 tbsp. olive oil

Directions:
Prepare a water bath and place the Sous Vide in it. Set to 158 F. Combine the honey and pears. Place in a vacuum-sealable bag. Release air by the water displacement method, seal and submerge the bag in the water bath. Cook for 45 minutes. Once the timer has stopped, remove the bag and transfer into a bowl. Top with the dressing.

Milky Mashed Potatoes with Rosemary

Ingredients: Servings: 4   Cooking Time: 1 Hour 45 Mins.

2 lb. red potatoes	3 sprigs rosemary
5 garlic cloves	Salt and white pepper to taste
8 oz. butter	
1 C. whole milk	

Directions:
Prepare a water bath and place the Sous Vide in it. Set to 193 F. Wash the potatoes and peel them and slice. Take the garlic, peel and mash them. Combine the potatoes, garlic, butter, 2tbsp of salt, and rosemary. Place in a vacuum-sealable bag. Release air by the water displacement method, seal and submerge the bag in the water bath. Cook for 1 hour and 30 minutes.   Once the timer has stopped, remove the bag and transfer into a bowl and mash them. Stir the blended butter and milk. Season with salt and pepper. Top with rosemary and serve.

Perfect Lil Smokies

Ingredients: Servings: 8   Cooking Time: 2 Hours

2 lb. cocktail sausages	1 /12-oz. bottle chili sauce

Directions:
Preheat a sous vide water bath to 140 degrees F. Add cocktail sausages and chili sauce to cooking pouches; seal tightly. Submerge the cooking pouches in the water bath; cook for 2 hours. Serve with toothpicks and enjoy!

Nutrition: Info 314 Calories; 24g Fat; 18g Carbs; 26g Protein; 5g Sugars

Baby Carrots with Creamy Sesame Dressing

Ingredients: Servings: 6   Cooking Time: 1 Hour

1 ½ lb. baby carrots	1 tbsp. lemon juice
	1 tsp. maple syrup
Sea salt and white pepper, to taste	1/3 C. sesame seeds, toasted
2 tsp. olive oil	1 tbsp. fresh dill leaves, chopped
1 tbsp. fresh parsley, minced	1/2 tsp. mustard powder
1 tbsp. mint, minced	
Dressing:	
1/3 C. sour cream	

Directions:

Preheat a sous vide water bath to 183 degrees F. Add baby carrots, salt, white pepper, olive oil, parsley, and mint to cooking pouches; seal tightly. Submerge the cooking pouches in the water bath; cook for 55 minutes. Now, make the dressing by mixing all ingredients. Dress sous vide baby carrots and serve at room temperature. Enjoy!

Nutrition: Info 129 Calories; 1g Fat; 18g Carbs; 1g Protein; 6g Sugars

French Fries

Ingredients: Servings: 6   Cooking Time: 45

3 lb. potatoes, sliced	Salt and black pepper to taste
5 C. water	¼ tsp. baking soda

Directions:

Prepare a water bath and place the Sous Vide in it. Set to 195 F. Place the potato slices, water, salt and baking soda in a vacuum-sealable bag. Release air by the water displacement method, seal and submerge the bag in water bath.Set the timer for 25 minutes. Meanwhile, heat the oil in a saucepan over medium heat. Once the timer has stopped, remove the potato slices from the brine and pat dry them. Cook in the oil for a few minutes, until golden.

Traditional French Béarnaise Sauce

Ingredients: Servings: 12   Cooking Time: 45 Mins.

4 tbsp. Champagne vinegar	1/2 C. dry white wine
1 tbsp. fresh tarragon, finely chopped	5 egg yolks
	2 sticks butter, melted
3 tbsp. shallots, finely chopped	1 tbsp. fresh lemon juice

Directions:

Preheat a sous vide water bath to 148 degrees F. In a pan, place the vinegar, wine, tarragon, and shallots; bring to a rolling boil. Turn down heat to simmer. Continue cooking for 12 minutes. Strain the mixture through a fine-mesh strainer into a food processor. Fold in the egg yolks and blitz mixture until uniform and smooth. Place the sauce in cooking pouches; seal tightly. Submerge the cooking pouches in the water bath; cook for 25 minutes. Add the contents from the cooking pouches to a mixing dish; add the butter and

lemon juice; mix with an immersion blender until smooth. Serve with your favorite roasted vegetable bites. Bon appétit!

Nutrition: Info 175 Calories; 12g Fat; 1g Carbs; 4g Protein; 3g Sugars

Jarred Pumpkin Bread

Ingredients: Servings: 4   Cooking Time: 3 Hours 40 Mins.

1 egg, beaten	1 tsp. cinnamon
6 tbsp. canned pumpkin puree	¼ tsp. nutmeg
	1 tbsp. sugar
6 oz. flour	¼ tsp. salt
1 tsp. baking powder	

Directions:

Prepare a water bath and place the Sous Vide in it. Set to 195 F. Sift the flour along with the baking powder, salt, cinnamon, and nutmeg in a bowl. Stir in beaten egg, sugar and pumpkin puree. Mix to form a dough. Divide the dough between two mason jars and seal. Place in water bath and cook for 3 hours and 30 minutes. Once the time passed, remove the jars and let it cool before serving.

Chicken Liver Spread

Ingredients: Servings: 8   Cooking Time: 5 Hours 15 Mins.

1pound chicken liver	2 tbsp. soy sauce
	3 tbsp. vinegar
6 eggs	Salt and black pepper to taste
8 oz. bacon, minced	
3 oz. shallot, chopped	4 tbsp. butter
	½ tsp. paprika

Directions:

Prepare a water bath and place the Sous Vide in it. Set to 156 F. Cook the bacon in a skillet over medium heat, add shallots and cook for 3 minutes. Stir in the soy sauce and vinegar. Transfer to a blender along with the remaining ingredients. Blend until smooth. Place all the ingredients in a mason jar and seal. Cook for 5 hours. Once the timer has stopped, remove the jar and serve.

Herby Italian Sausage Pannini

Ingredients: Servings: 4   Cooking Time: 3 Hours 15 Mins.

1 lb. Italian sausage	1 onion, sliced
	1 C. tomato juice

1 red bell pepper, sliced	1 tsp. dried oregano
1 yellow bell pepper, sliced	1 tsp. dried basil
1 garlic clove, minced	1 tsp. olive oil
	Salt and black pepper to taste
	4 bread slices

Directions:

Prepare a water bath and place the Sous Vide in it. Set to 138 F. Place the sausages in a vacuum-sealable bag. Add the garlic, basil, onion, pepper, tomato juice, and oregano in each bag. Release air by the water displacement method, seal and submerge the bags in the water bath. Cook for 3 hours. Once the timer has stopped, remove the sausages and transfer to a hot skillet. Fry them for 1 Min. per side. Set aside. Add the remaining ingredients in the skillet, season with salt and pepper. Cook until water has evaporated. Serve the sausages and the remaining ingredients in between the bread.

Paprika & Rosemary Potatoes

Ingredients: Servings: 4   Cooking Time: 55 Mins.

8 oz. fingerling potatoes	1 tbsp. butter
Salt and black pepper to taste	1 sprig rosemary
	1 tsp. paprika

Directions:

Prepare a water bath and place the Sous Vide in it. Set to 178 F. Combine the potatoes with salt, paprika and pepper. Place them in a vacuum-sealable bag. Release air by the water displacement method, seal and submerge the bag in the water bath. Cook for 45 minutes. Once the timer has stopped, remove the potatoes and cut by the half. Heat the butter in a skillet over medium heat and stir in rosemary and potatoes. Cook for 3 minutes. Serve in a plate. Garnish with salt.

Spinach & Mushroom quiche

Ingredients: Servings: 2   Cooking Time: 20 Mins.

1 C. of fresh Cremini mushrooms, sliced	1 garlic clove, minced
1 C. of fresh spinach, chopped	¼ C. Parmesan cheese, grated
2 large eggs, beaten	1 tbsp. butter
2 tbsp. whole milk	½ tsp. salt

Directions:

Wash the mushrooms under cold running water and thinly slice them. Set aside. Wash the spinach thoroughly and roughly chop it. In a large vacuum-sealable bag, place mushrooms, spinach, milk, garlic, and salt. Seal the bag and cook in sous vide for 10 Mins. at 180 F. Meanwhile, melt the butter in a large saucepan over a medium heat. Remove the vegetable mixture from the bag and add to a saucepan. Cook for 1 minute, and then add beaten eggs. Stir well until incorporated and cook until eggs are set. Sprinkle with grated cheese and remove from heat to serve.

Leek & Garlic Eggs

Ingredients: Servings: 2   Cooking Time: 35 Mins.

2 C. fresh leek, chopped into bite-sized pieces	1 tbsp. butter
	2 tbsp. extra virgin olive oil
5 garlic cloves, whole	4 large eggs
	1 tsp. salt

Directions:

Whisk together eggs, butter, and salt. Transfer to a vacuum-sealable bag and cook in Sous Vide for ten Mins. at 165 F. Gently transfer to a plate. Heat the oil in a large skillet over medium heat. Add garlic and chopped leek. Stir-fry for ten minutes. Remove from the heat and use to top eggs.

Beef with Onions

Ingredients: Servings: 3   Cooking Time: 1 Hour

¾ C. lean beef, tender cuts chopped into bite-sized pieces	1 tsp. soy sauce
	1 tsp. dried thyme
2 large onions, peeled and finely chopped	2 tbsp. vegetable oil
	2 tbsp. sesame oil
¼ C. water	Serve with:
3 tbsp. mustard	Fresh tomatoes

Directions:

Rinse the meat and pat dry with a kitchen paper. Using a kitchen brush, spread the mustard over meat and sprinkle with dried thyme. Place in a Ziploc along with soy sauce, chopped onions, and sesame oil. Cook en sous vide for one hour at 154 degrees. Remove from the water bath and set aside. Heat up the vegetable oil in a large skillet, over medium-high heat. Add beef chops and stir-fry for 5 minutes, stirring constantly. Remove from the heat and serve.

Nutrition: Info Calories: 366 Total Fat: 26g Saturated Fat: 8g; Trans Fat: 0g Protein: 28; Net Carbs: 7g

Panko Yolk Croquettes

Ingredients: Servings: 5   Cooking Time: 60 Mins.

2 eggs plus 5 yolks	¼ tsp. italian
1 C. panko	seasoning
breadcrumbs	½ tsp. salt
3 tbsp. olive oil	¼ tsp. paprika
5 tbsp. flour	

Directions:

Prepare a water bath and place the Sous Vide in it. Set to 150 F. Place the yolk inside the water (without a bag or glass) and cook for 45 minutes, turning over halfway through. Let cool slightly. Beat the eggs along with the other ingredients, except the oil. Dip the yolks in the egg and panko mixture.   Heat the oil in a skillet. Fry the yolks for a few Mins. per side, until golden.

COCKTAILS AND INFUSIONS

Sweet Basil Syrup

Ingredients: Servings: 4   Cooking Time: 1 Hour

2 C. water	1 lime, use the
2 C. basil	rind only
2 C. sugar	

Directions:

Set the Sous vide cooker to 180°F.   Combine all the ingredients into Sous Vide bag and seal using a water immersion technique.   Cook the syrup 1 hour. Prepare ice-cold water bath.   Remove the bag from the cooker and place into ice-cold water bath 30 minutes. Strain the syrup into a clean glass jar.   Serve or store in a fridge.

Nutrition: Info   Per   serving:Calories   411.3, Carbohydrates 102.1 g, Fats 0.1 g, Protein 0.5 g

Eggnog

Ingredients: Servings: x   Cooking Time: 1 Hour
Cooking Temperature: 140°f

8 large eggs	2 C. heavy cream
4 large egg yolks	½ tsp. nutmeg,
4 C. whole milk	freshly grated
1½ C.	Pinch of salt
confectioner'	6 whole cloves
sugar	3 cinnamon sticks
1 tbsp. pure	
vanilla extract	

Directions:

Attach the sous vide immersion circulator to a Cambro container or pot with water using an adjustable clamp and preheat water to 140°F.   For eggnog base: in a stand mixer, beat eggs and egg yolks until thick and pale yellow.   Add milk, cream, sugar, vanilla, powdered sugar, nutmeg, and salt and beat well.   In a large cooking pouch, place base mixture, cloves, and cinnamon. Seal pouch tightly after squeezing out the excess air. Place pouch in sous vide bath and set the cooking time for about 1 hour.   Remove pouch from the sous vide bath and immediately immerse in a large bowl of ice water for at least 20 minutes.   Strain mixture into a sealable pitcher. Discard cloves and cinnamon. Refrigerate for several hours to overnight to chill before serving.

Cherry Manhattan

Ingredients: Servings: 8   Cooking Time: 1 Hour

Bourbon infusion:	To finish:
2 C. bourbon	4oz. sweet
¼ C. raw cacao	vermouth
nibs	Chocolate bitters,
1 C. dried cherries	as desired

Directions:

Make the infusion; preheat Sous Vide to 122°F.   In a Sous Vide bag combine bourbon, cacao nibs, and cherries.   Seal the bag, and cook 1 hour   Remove the bag from the water bath and let cool. Strain the content into a jar.   Fill the tall glasses with ice.   Add chocolate bitters (3 dashes per serving) and 1/8 of the infused bourbon.   Skewer the Sous vide cherries and garnish.

Nutrition: Info   Per   serving:Calories   22.1, Carbohydrates 2.2 g, Fats 1.3 g, Protein 0.4 g

Thyme Liqueur

Ingredients: Servings: 12   Cooking Time: 90 Mins.

Zest of 8 large	1 C. ultrafine sugar
oranges	1 C. water
4 sprigs fresh	1 C. vodka
thyme	

Directions:

Prepare your Sous Vide water bath using your immersion circulator and raise the temperature to 180-degrees Fahrenheit.   Add all the listed ingredients to a heavy-duty resealable zip bag and seal using the immersion method.   Cook for 90 minutes.   Strain the mixture and serve chilled!

Nutrition: Info   Per   serving:Calories: 507 ;Carbohydrate: 110g ;Protein: 2g ;Fat: 8g ;Sugar: 105g ;Sodium: 15mg

Vodka Lemon Meyer

Ingredients: Servings: 6   Cooking Time: 120 Mins.

1 C. granulated sugar
1 C. freshly squeezed Meyer lemon

1 C. vodka
Zest of 3 Meyer lemons

Directions:
Prepare your Sous Vide water bath using your immersion circulator and raise the temperature to 135-degrees Fahrenheit. Take a resealable zip bag and add all the listed ingredients. Seal the bag using the immersion method. Submerge and cook for about 2 hours. Once done, strain the mixture through a fine metal mesh strainer into a medium bowl. Chill the mixture overnight and serve!

Nutrition: Info Per serving:Calories: 354 ;Carbohydrate: 48g ;Protein: 0g ;Fat: 0g ;Sugar: 47g ;Sodium: 6mg

Pineapple Rum

Ingredients: Servings: 12   Cooking Time: 120 Mins.

1 peeled and cored pineapple cut into 1-inch pieces

1 bottle dark rum
1 C. granulated sugar

Directions:
Prepare your Sous Vide water bath using your immersion circulator and raise the temperature to 135-degrees Fahrenheit. Take a resealable zipper bag and add the pineapple, rum, sugar, and seal using the immersion method. Submerge underwater and cook for about 2 hours. Once done, strain the mixture through a metal mesh strainer into a medium bowl. Chill overnight and serve!

Nutrition: Info Per serving:Calories: 442 ;Carbohydrate: 45g ;Protein: 1g ;Fat: 0g ;Sugar: 54g ;Sodium: 8mg

Orange Creamsicle Cocktail

Ingredients: Servings: x   Cooking Time: 3 Hours Cooking Temperature: 130°f

Zest of 3 oranges
2-1/4 tbsp. sugar

½ C. bourbon
1 vanilla bean, split and scraped

Directions:
Attach the sous vide immersion circulator to a Cambro container or pot with water using an adjustable clamp and preheat water to 130°F. Add all ingredients to a sterilized mason jar. Cover with cap tightly. Place jar in sous vide bath and set the cooking time for about 1-3 hours. Carefully remove jar from sous vide bath and open it. Strain vodka into a pitcher. Discard orange zest and vanilla bean. Serve over ice with an orange twist.

Honey Ginger Shrub

Ingredients: Servings: 6   Cooking Time: 120 Mins.

1 C. water
½ C. balsamic vinegar
1 tbsp. freshly grated ginger

½ C. honey
Bourbon whiskey
Club soda
Lemon wedges as required

Directions:
Prepare your Sous Vide water bath using your immersion circulator and raise the temperature to 134-degrees Fahrenheit. Take a resealable zipper bag and add the water, vinegar, honey, ginger, and seal it using the immersion method. Submerge and cook for about 2 hours. Once cooked, strain the mixture through a fine metal mesh strainer into a medium bowl. Chill the mixture overnight. Serve with one-part whiskey and one-part club soda in a glass over ice. Garnish with a lemon wedge and serve!

Nutrition: Info Per serving:Calories: 232 ;Carbohydrate: 54g ;Protein: 1g ;Fat: 0g ;Sugar: 51g ;Sodium: 19mg

Tom Collins Cocktail

Ingredients: Servings: 20   Cooking Time: 1 Hour

7 C. gin
1 C. lemon juice
1 ½ C. granulated sugar

2 C. lemon rind
Soda water, to serve with

Directions:
Preheat Sous Vide to 131°F. In a large Sous vide bag, combine gin, lemon juice, lemon rind, and sugar. Fold the edges of the bag few times and clip to the side of your pot. Cook the cocktail 1 hour. Strain the cocktail into a large glass jug. Place aside to cool completely before use. Serve over ice, and finish off with a soda water. Garnish the cocktail with lemon rind or fresh thyme.

Nutrition: Info Per serving:Calories 71.8, Carbohydrates 17.2 g, Fats 0.2 g, Protein 0.3 g

Rosemary & Lemon Vodka

Ingredients: Servings: 5   Cooking Time: 180 Mins.

1 bottle vodka
Zest of 6 large lemons
5 sprigs fresh rosemary

Directions:
Prepare your Sous Vide water bath using your immersion circulator and raise the temperature to 145-degrees Fahrenheit. Take a heavy-duty resealable zip bag and add all the listed ingredients. Seal using the immersion method and cook for 3 hours. Once done, transfer the contents through a strainer and allow it to cool. Serve!

Nutrition: Info Per serving:Calories: 247 ;Carbohydrate: 23g ;Protein: 2g ;Fat: 16g ;Sugar: 21g ;Sodium: 82mg

Strawberry Infused Tequila

Ingredients: Servings: x   Cooking Time: 2 Hours Cooking Temperature: 165°f

For Tequila:	¼ C. Cointreau
3 C. fresh strawberries, hulled and halved	¼ C. agave syrup
1 bottle tequila	For Garnishing:
1/3 C. white sugar	½ C. fresh strawberries
1/3 C. lime juice	Fresh mint leaves

Directions:
Attach the sous vide immersion circulator to a Cambro container or pot with water using an adjustable clamp and preheat water to 165°F. Place all ingredients in a cooking pouch. Seal pouch tightly after squeezing out the excess air. Place pouch in sous vide bath and set the cooking time for about 2 hours. Remove pouch from the sous vide bath and immediately immerse in a large bowl of ice water for about 15-30 minutes. Strain mixture through a fine-mesh strainer into a pitcher. Fill a lowball glass with ice and add tequila infusion. Garnish with strawberries and mint leaves.

Berry Vodka

Ingredients: Servings: x   Cooking Time: 3 Hours Cooking Temperature: 130°f

2 C. mixed berries /cranberry, blueberry, raspberry and blackberry	Vodka, as required

Directions:
Attach the sous vide immersion circulator to a Cambro container or pot with water using an adjustable clamp and preheat water to 130°F. Place berries in a mason

jar. Add enough vodka to leave about ½-inch space from top and cover with the lid tightly. Place jar in sous vide bath and set the cooking time for about 3 hours. Remove mason jar from the sous vide bath and carefully open it. Strain the mixture and serve over ice.

Honey Lemon Thyme Infusion

Ingredients: Servings: 10   Cooking Time: 1 ½ Hours

2 C. water	2 C. honey
2 organic lemons, sliced	2 bunches lemon thyme

Directions:
Preheat sous Vide cooker to 135°F. Combine all ingredients into Sous vide bag. Seal the bag using water immersion technique. Cook the syrup 1 ½ hours. Prepare ice-cold water bath. Remove the bag from the cooker and place into the water bath. Chill the syrup 30 minutes. Strain into a clean glass jar and serve.

Nutrition: Info Per serving:Calories 229.2, Carbohydrates 57 g, Fats 0 g, Protein 0.3 g

Infused Blackberry Syrup

Ingredients: Servings: 8   Cooking Time: 2 Hours

1.5lb. blackberries	4 C. sugar
4 C. water	4 sprigs basil

Directions:
Preheat Sous vide to 135°F. In a Sous Vide bag combine all ingredients. Seal the bag and submerge in a water bath. Cook 2 hours. Remove the bag from the cooker. Place the bag in an ice-cold water and cool 30 minutes. Strain the infusion into a glass jar. Serve or store in a fridge.

Nutrition: Info Per serving:Calories 441.2, Carbohydrates 108.2 g, Fats 0.4 g, Protein 1.2 g

Irish Iced Coffee

Ingredients: Servings: x   Cooking Time: 6 Hours Cooking Temperature: 165°f

For Coffee:	For Serving:
3 C. bourbon	Ice, as required
½ C. whole coffee beans	2 oz. infused whiskey
2 tbsp. brown sugar	1 oz. heavy cream

Directions:

Attach the sous vide immersion circulator to a Cambro container or pot with water using an adjustable clamp and preheat water to 165°F. Place all ingredients in a cooking pouch. Seal pouch tightly after squeezing out the excess air. Place pouch in sous vide bath and set the cooking time for about 6 hours. Remove pouch from the sous vide bath and shake well. Immediately immerse in a large bowl of ice water for at least 30 minutes. Strain mixture through a fine strainer into a container. For serving: in serving glasses, divide ice and whiskey. Add bourbon mixture in each glass. Top with cream and serve.

Rose Syrup

Ingredients: Servings: x   Cooking Time: 2 Hours
Cooking Temperature: 122°f

3 C. sugar	1 tsp. fresh lemon
1 C. water	rind
½ C. dried roses	

Directions:
Attach the sous vide immersion circulator to a Cambro container or pot with water using an adjustable clamp and preheat water to 122°F. In a cooking pouch or clean mason jar, place all ingredients and mix gently. Seal tightly and place in the sous vide bath. Set the cooking time for about 2 hours.

quick Limoncello

Ingredients: Servings: x   Cooking Time: 3 Hours
Cooking Temperature: 130°f

Zest of 3 lemons	2-1/4 tbsp. sugar
1-3/4 C. vodka	

Directions:
Attach the sous vide immersion circulator to a Cambro container or pot with water using an adjustable clamp and preheat water to 130°F. Add all ingredients to a sterilized mason jar. Cover with cap tightly. Place jar in sous vide bath and set the cooking time for about 1-3 hours. Carefully remove jar from sous vide bath and open it. Strain vodka into a pitcher. Discard lemon zest. Serve over ice with the garnishing of sparkling water and lemon twist.

Cranberry Vodka

Ingredients: Servings: x   Cooking Time: 2 Hours 15
Mins Cooking Temperature: 153°f

For Vodka:	For Simple Syrup:
4 C. vodka	2½ C. water
¾ Of a lb. fresh	2 C. sugar
cranberries	

Directions:
Attach the sous vide immersion circulator to a Cambro container or pot with water using an adjustable clamp and preheat water to 153°F. Place vodka and cranberries in a cooking pouch. Seal pouch tightly after squeezing out the excess air. Place pouch in sous vide bath and set the cooking time for about 2 hours. Remove pouch from the sous vide bath and carefully open it. Through a strainer, strain the mixture and transfer into a stoppered bottle. For simple syrup: in a pot, add water and sugar over medium-high heat and bring to a boil. Simmer for about 15 minutes, stirring occasionally. Remove from heat and keep aside to cool. After cooling, add sugar syrup into vodka and stir to combine.

Pumpkin Spice Bitters

Ingredients: Servings: x   Cooking Time: 2 Hours
Cooking Temperature: 122°f

1/3 C. dark rum	2 cinnamon sticks
3 thumbs of	½ tsp. whole
ginger, peeled	cloves
½ tsp. black	1 nutmeg, roughly
peppercorns	chopped

Directions:
Attach the sous vide immersion circulator to a Cambro container or pot with water using an adjustable clamp and preheat water to 122°F. Place all ingredients in a cooking pouch. Seal pouch tightly after squeezing out the excess air. Place pouch in sous vide bath and set the cooking time for about 2 hours. Remove pouch from the sous vide bath and carefully open it. Strain the mixture and store in a small bitters bottle.

Bloody Mary Vodka

Ingredients: Servings: 20   Cooking Time: 180 Mins.

6 quartered roma	1 bottle vodka
tomatoes	6 whole garlic
1 Anaheim pepper,	cloves, peeled
stemmed and	1 thinly sliced
seeds removed,	jalapeno pepper
sliced into ½ inch	1 tbsp. whole black
pieces	peppercorns
¼ onion, peeled	Zest of 3 large
and sliced into ½-	limes
inch pieces	

Directions:
Prepare your Sous Vide water bath using your immersion circulator and raise the temperature to 145-degrees Fahrenheit. Add all the listed ingredients to

your resealable zipper bag. Seal using the immersion method. Cook for about 3 hours and transfer the contents through a mesh strainer. Serve!

Nutrition: Info Per serving:Calories: 437 ;Carbohydrate: 77g ;Protein: 10g ;Fat: 4g ;Sugar: 44g ;Sodium: 460mg

Orange Cream Cocktail

Ingredients: Servings: x   Cooking Time: 1½ Hours
Cooking Temperature: 130°f

1/4 C. sugar	1 3/4 C. Vodka
Zest of 3 large oranges	1 vanilla bean, seeds from inside the pod

Directions:
Attach the sous vide immersion circulator to a Cambro container or pot with water using an adjustable clamp and preheat water to 130°F. Place all ingredients in a clean mason jar. Seal tightly. Place the jar in the sous vide bath and set the cooking time for about 1½ hours. Remove from the sous vide bath and immediately immerse in a large bowl of ice water. Strain the mixture through a fine mesh sieve. This is to remove the orange zest and vanilla bean pieces Place in a sealed container and store in refrigerator up to 1 month.

Coffee Liquor

Ingredients: Servings: 20   Cooking Time: 180 Mins.

32 oz. strong black coffee	1 bottle vodka
2 C. granulated sugar	½ C. coffee beans
	2 split vanilla beans

Directions:
Prepare your Sous Vide water bath using your immersion circulator and raise the temperature to 145-degrees Fahrenheit. Take a heavy-duty large resealable zip bag and add all the listed ingredients. Seal the bag using the immersion method. Cook for about 3 hours underwater. Once done, transfer the contents through a fine mesh strainer and let it cool. Serve!

Nutrition: Info Per serving:Calories: 216 ;Carbohydrate: 25g ;Protein: 5g ;Fat: 12g ;Sugar: 23g ;Sodium: 92mg

Chili Vodka

Ingredients: Servings: x   Cooking Time: 2 Hours
Cooking Temperature: 153°f

1 /168 fluid ounce, 375 ml bottle of vodka	2 small red chilis

Directions:
Attach the sous vide immersion circulator to a Cambro container or pot with water using an adjustable clamp and preheat water to 153°F. Place all ingredients in a cooking pouch. Seal pouch tightly after squeezing out the excess air. Place pouch in sous vide bath and set the cooking time for about 2 hours. Remove pouch from the sous vide bath and immediately immerse in a large bowl of ice water for about 15-20 minutes. Remove chilis from vodka and transfer back into the vodka bottle.

Tonic Water

Ingredients: Servings: x   Cooking Time: 2 Hours
Cooking Temperature: 158°f

4 tsp. powdered cinchona bark	4 C. fresh water
1 C. lemongrass, chopped roughly	Zest and juice of 1 grapefruit
Zest and juice of 1 orange	1 tsp. allspice berries
Zest and juice of 1 lime	¼ C. powdered citric acid
Zest and juice of 1 lemon	1 tsp. salt
	¾ C. of agave syrup

Directions:
Attach the sous vide immersion circulator to a Cambro container or pot with water using an adjustable clamp and preheat water to 158°F. Place all ingredients in a cooking pouch. Seal pouch tightly after squeezing out the excess air. Place pouch in sous vide bath and set the cooking time for about 2 hours. Remove pouch from the sous vide bath and carefully open it. Strain the mixture through a fine strainer into a container and discard solids.

Chocolate Cherry Manhattan

Ingredients: Servings: x   Cooking Time: 1 Hour
Cooking Temperature: 122°f

For Chocolate Bourbon Infusion:	For Chocolate Cherry Manhattan:
1 C. dried cherries	3 dashes chocolate bitters
2 C. bourbon	1 oz. sweet vermouth
¼ C. cacao nibs	3 sous vide cherries
2 oz. cherry chocolate bourbon infusion	

Directions:

Attach the sous vide immersion circulator to a Cambro container or pot with water using an adjustable clamp and preheat water to 122°F. For cherry infusion: place all ingredients in a cooking pouch. Seal pouch tightly after squeezing out the excess air. Place pouch in sous vide bath and set the cooking time for about 1 hour. Remove pouch from the sous vide bath and bath and immediately immerse in a large bowl of ice water. Strain the mixture and reserve cherries for garnishing. For 1 serving: fill a short glass with ice. Add bourbon, bitters, and vermouth and stir to combine. Garnish with reserved cherries and serve.

Cucumber Lemongrass Cocktail

Ingredients: Servings: x   Cooking Time: 3 Hours
Cooking Temperature: 122°f

1 fresh lemongrass stalk, bruised and chopped	5 fresh mint sprigs, bruised
	¾ C. cane sugar
½ Cucumber, thinly sliced	2 C. gin
	3 C. water
Rind of 1 lime	Juice of 2 limes

Directions:

Attach the sous vide immersion circulator to a Cambro container or pot with water using an adjustable clamp and preheat water to 122°F. Place all ingredients in a cooking pouch. Seal pouch tightly after squeezing out the excess air. Place pouch in sous vide bath and set the cooking time for about 3 hours. Remove pouch from the sous vide bath and carefully open it. Strain mixture through a fine-mesh sieve. Mix with tonic or fizzy water and serve.

Ginger Syrup

Ingredients: Servings: 10   Cooking Time: 55 Mins.

1 C. Ginger, sliced thinly	2 ½ C. Water
1 large White Onion, peeled	¼ C. Monk Fruit Powder

Directions:

Make a water bath, place a Sous Vide cooker in it, and set it at 185°F. Place the onion in a vacuum-sealable bag. Release air by the water displacement method, seal and submerge the bag in the water bath. Set the timer for 40 minutes. Once the timer has stopped, remove and unseal the bag. Transfer the onion with 4 tbsp. of water to a blender and puree to smooth. Place a pot over medium heat, add the onion puree and the remaining listed ingredients. Bring to a boil for 15 minutes. Turn off heat, cool, and strain through a fine

sieve. Store in a jar, refrigerate, and use for up to 14 days. Use it as a spice in other foods.

Nutrition: Info Per serving:Calories 33.3, Carbohydrates 8.27g, Fats 0.01 g, Protein 0.04 g

Old Fashioned

Ingredients: Servings: x   Cooking Time: 3 Hours
Cooking Temperature: 130°f

Zest of 1 orange	Morello or maraschino cherries, as required
1-3/4 C. bourbon	
2-1/4 tbsp. sugar	

Directions:

Attach the sous vide immersion circulator to a Cambro container or pot with water using an adjustable clamp and preheat water to 130°F. In a sterilized mason jar, add all ingredients. Cover with cap tightly. Place jar in sous vide bath and set the cooking time for about 1-3 hours. Carefully remove jar from sous vide bath and open it. Strain bourbon into a pitcher. Discard orange zest. Serve over ice with an orange twist and cherries.

Lavender Syrup

Ingredients: Servings: 4   Cooking Time: 60 Mins.

1 C. water	1 tbsp. culinary grade dried lavender
1 C. sugar	

Directions:

Prepare your Sous Vide water bath using your immersion circulator and raise the temperature to 135-degrees Fahrenheit. Take a heavy-duty resealable zipper bag and add the water, lavender, and sugar. Seal it using the immersion method. Submerge it underwater and cook for about 1 hour. Once done, let it cool down to room temperature and strain through a metal mesh. Serve chilled!

Nutrition: Info Per serving:Calories: 112 ;Carbohydrate: 101g ;Protein: 0g ;Fat: 0g ;Sugar: 218g ;Sodium: 2mg

Mojito

Ingredients: Servings: x   Cooking Time: 1½ Hours
Cooking Temperature: 158°f

17 fluid oz. silver rum	2/3 C. fresh mint leaves, plus extra for serving
Simple syrup, as required	Lemon-lime soda, as required
Fresh lime juice, as required	

Directions:
Attach the sous vide immersion circulator to a Cambro container or pot with water using an adjustable clamp and preheat water to 158°F. In a pan of boiling water, blanch mint leaves for about 10-15 seconds. Strain mint leaves and transfer into a bowl of ice water. Place mint leaves and rum in a cooking pouch. Seal pouch tightly after squeezing out the excess air. Place pouch in sous vide bath and set the cooking time for about 1½ hours. Remove pouch from the sous vide bath and bath and immediately immerse in a large bowl of ice water. Strain the mixture. For 1 serving: in a rocks glass, place 2½ oz. infused rum with simple syrup, lime juice and 2-3 fresh mint leaves and stir to combine. Fill glass with carbonated soda and serve with a garnish of a watermelon chunk.

VEGETABLES & SIDES

Mediterranean Vegetable Platter

Ingredients: Servings: 6   Cooking Time: 40 Mins.

1/2 lb. broccoli	1 heaping tbsp.
1/2 lb. cauliflower	fresh parsley,
1 lb. eggplant	roughly chopped
1 lb. green beans	1/4 C. tahini paste,
2 bay leaves	preferably
1 tsp. mixed whole	homemade
peppercorns	1 lemon, thinly
Sea salt, to taste	sliced

Directions:
Preheat a sous vide water bath to 183 degrees F. Place your veggies along with bay leaves and peppercorns in cooking pouches; seal tightly. Submerge the cooking pouches in the water bath; cook for 35 minutes. Remove your veggies from the cooking pouch; pat them dry with kitchen towels and season with salt. Arrange the vegetables on a nice serving platter; scatter chopped parsley over them. Afterwards, garnish the vegetables with tahini and lemon slices and serve.

Nutrition: Info 101 Calories; 5g Fat; 18g Carbs; 4g Protein; 8g Sugars

Blueberry Jam

Ingredients: Servings: 10   Cooking Time: 1 Hour 30 Mins.

2 C. blueberries	2 tbsp. lemon
1 C. white sugar	juice

Directions:
Preheat the water bath to 180°F. Put the ingredients into the vacuum bag and seal it. Cook for 1 hour 30 Mins. in the water bath. Serve over ice cream or cake, or store in the fridge in an airtight container.

Nutrition: Info Per serving:Calories 74, Carbohydrates 13 g, Fats 2 g, Protein 1 g

Cinnamon Poached Pears

Ingredients: Servings: 8   Cooking Time: 30 Mins.

4 Bosc pears /firm yet ripe	1 C. tawny port
½ C. granulated sugar	2 wide strips lemon zest, 2 inches long and ½ inch wide
2 wide strips orange zest, 2 inches long and ½ inch wide	½ tsp. ground cinnamon
	Ice cream for flavor

Directions:
Set your Sous Vide immersion circulator to a temperature of 180-degrees Fahrenheit, and prepare your water bath Peel the pears and add them in a heavy-duty zip bag, together with the remaining ingredients Seal using the immersion method and cook for 30 Mins. Cool for 30 Mins. and pour the liquid into a pan. Place it over medium heat and reduce the liquid by 2/3 Remove the heat and wait until the liquid is cooled Core the pears diagonally and create fan shapes Carefully transfer the pears to your serving plate and pour the previously prepared sauce on top Serve with a topping of your favorite ice cream

Nutrition: Info Calories: 383 Carbohydrate: 97g Protein: 1g Fat: 0g Sugar: 85g Sodium: 12mg

Whiskey Infused Apples

Ingredients: Servings: 4   Cooking Time: 1 Hour

4 Gala apples	2 tbsp. maple
2 tbsp. brown sugar	whiskey

Directions:
Preheat your Sous Vide cooker to 175°F Peel, core, and slice apples. Place the apple slices, sugar, and whiskey into Sous Vide bag. Vacuum seal and submerge in water. Cook 1 hour. Remove the bag from the water. Serve apples with ice cream while hot.

Nutrition: Info Per serving:Calories 86.9, Carbohydrates 20.4 g, Fats 0.5 g, Protein 0.2 g

Spinach Cheese Dip

Ingredients: Servings: x   Cooking Time: 1 Hour Cooking Temperature: 180°f

1 lb. cream cheese, cubed	1 garlic clove, peeled and pressed
½ C. beer	
2 oz. smoked Gouda cheese, grated	1 tbsp. Dijon mustard
½ Medium red bell pepper, seeded and chopped	1 tsp. Herbs de Provence
	1 tsp. salt
	½ tsp. ground white pepper
½ C. fresh baby spinach leaves, chopped	1 sourdough round loaf, for serving

Directions:
Attach the sous vide immersion circulator to a Cambro container or pot with water using an adjustable clamp and preheat water to 180°F. Place all ingredients except bread in a cooking pouch. Seal pouch tightly after squeezing out the excess air. Place pouch in sous vide bath and set the cooking time for about ½-1 hour. Remove the pouch from the sous vide bath and carefully massage it to mix the dip mixture. Return pouch to sous vide bath until cheese melts completely. Meanwhile, with a bread knife, remove the top from the loaf of bread. Carefully hollow out the middle of loaf to make a bread bowl. Cut the interior bread into bite-sized pieces. Remove the pouch from the sous vide bath and carefully open it. Immediately, transfer dip into the bread bowl. Serve with bread pieces.

Brown Rice Pilaf

Ingredients: Servings: x   Cooking Time: 3 Hours Cooking Temperature: 180°f

1 tbsp. extra-virgin olive oil	Kosher salt, to taste
1 medium leek /white and light green portion, halved and thinly sliced	¼ C. currants
	1 C. brown rice, rinsed
	2 C. vegetable broth
1 garlic clove, minced	¼ C. walnuts, toasted and chopped

Directions:
Attach the sous vide immersion circulator to a Cambro container or pot with water using an adjustable clamp and preheat water to 180°F. In a small pan, heat the olive oil over medium heat and cook leek, garlic, and ½ tsp. of salt until fragrant, stirring occasionally. Remove from heat and stir in currants and rice. Place rice mixture and broth in a cooking pouch. Seal pouch tightly after squeezing out the excess air. Place pouch in

sous vide bath and set the cooking time for about 3 hours. Remove pouch from the sous vide bath and carefully open it. Transfer rice mixture into a serving bowl and season with salt. Sprinkle with walnuts and serve.

Wine Maple Poached Fruits

Ingredients: Servings: 4   Cooking Time: 1 Hour

1 lb. ripe peaches, peeled, pitted and halved	1 C. maple syrup
	1 tsp. whole cloves
	1 vanilla pod
1 C. white wine	2 sticks cinnamon
2 C. water	1/3 C. almonds, blanched
1 /1-inch piece fresh ginger, peeled	

Directions:
Preheat a sous vide water bath to 170 degrees F. Place all ingredient, except for almonds, in a large-sized cooking pouch; seal tightly. Submerge the cooking pouch in the water bath; cook for 50 minutes. Pour the cooking liquid into a pan that is preheated over a moderate flame. Bring to a rolling boil. Immediately turn the heat to medium. Continue to cook an additional 6 minutes, or until the sauce is slightly thickened and syrupy. To serve, arrange peach on a serving plate; spoon the wine/maple syrup over them; garnish with blanched almonds. Bon appétit!

Nutrition: Info 294 Calories; 3g Fat; 71g Carbs; 9g Protein; 64g Sugars

Whiskey Sugared Sweet Potatoes

Ingredients: Servings: x   Cooking Time: 1 Hour 25 Mins Cooking Temperature: 150°f

½ C. brown sugar	1 tsp. salt
½ tsp. cinnamon	¼ C. American whiskey
½ tsp. ground allspice	
¼ tsp. cayenne pepper	4 sweet potatoes, peeled, and cut into ½-inch cubes
Pinch of granulated onions	4 tbsp. butter
Pinch of granulated garlic	1 tbsp. cider vinegar

Directions:
Attach the sous vide immersion circulator to a Cambro container or pot with water using an adjustable clamp and preheat water to 150°F. In a bowl, mix together sugar, spices, and salt. Set aside. In a small pan, bring whiskey to a boil. Cook until it reduces by half. Add sugar mixture and cook until a paste is formed.

Transfer sugar paste into a large bowl. Add sweet potato cubes and butter to the bowl and mix until well combined. Place sweet potato mixture in a cooking pouch. Seal pouch tightly after squeezing out the excess air. Place pouch in sous vide bath and set the cooking time for about 1 hour. Preheat oven to 400°F. Line a baking sheet with parchment paper. Remove pouch from the sous vide bath and carefully open it. Remove sweet potato cubes from pouch, reserving cooking liquid in a pan. Place sweet potato cubes onto prepared baking sheet. Roast for about 25 minutes, stirring once after 15 minutes. Meanwhile, cook reserved cooking liquid until desired thickness. Remove sweet potatoes from oven and transfer into a bowl. Add thickened sauce and vinegar and toss to coat well. Serve immediately.

Sous Vide Tomato Sauce

Ingredients: Servings: 4   Cooking Time: 15 Mins.

4 C. cored and halved fresh tomatoes	Salt to taste
½ onion, chopped	Freshly ground black pepper, to taste
¼ C. fresh basil	5 tbsp. extra-virgin olive oil
2 garlic cloves, minced	

Directions:
Prepare the Sous Vide water bath using your immersion circulator and raise the temperature to 176-degrees Fahrenheit. Take a heavy-duty large resealable zip bag and add in the tomatoes, ¼ C. basil, garlic, onion, and oil. Seal using the immersion method. Submerge it underwater and let it cook for 15 minutes. Once cooked, transfer the contents to a blender and puree for about 1 minute. Add a bit of salt and pepper and serve.

Nutrition: Info Calories: 117 Carbohydrates: 26g Protein: 5g Fat: 1g Sugar: 14g Sodium: 470mg

Easy Garden Green Beans

Ingredients: Servings: 4   Cooking Time: 45 Mins.

1 ½ lb. fresh green beans, trimmed and snapped in half	Flaky salt and lemon pepper, to taste
2 tbsp. olive oil	3 cloves garlic, minced

Directions:
Preheat a sous vide water bath to 183 degrees F. Place the green beans, 1 tbsp. of olive oil, salt, and lemon pepper in a large cooking pouch; seal tightly. Submerge the cooking pouch in the water bath; cook for 40 minutes. In the meantime, heat the remaining tbsp. of olive oil in a pan; sauté the garlic for 1 Min. or until aromatic. Add the green beans to the pan with garlic, stir, and serve immediately. Enjoy!

Nutrition: Info 100 Calories; 6g Fat; 1g Carbs; 1g Protein; 4g Sugars

Asparagus Vinaigrette

Ingredients: Servings: 2   Cooking Time: 15 Mins.

1 Bunch large asparagus	1 tsp. red wine vinegar
Salt and pepper as needed	1 hard-boiled egg, cooled and roughly chopped
¼ C. extra-virgin olive oil	Fresh parsley, chopped
1 tsp. Dijon mustard	

Directions:
Prepare the Sous Vide water bath using your immersion circulator and increase the temperature to 185-degrees Fahrenheit Slice up the fibrous bottom of the asparagus and discard it Peel the bottom three-quarters of the stalks and place them, in a single layer, in a zip bag Season with salt and pepper and seal using the immersion method and cook for 15 Mins. For the vinaigrette, put the olive oil, vinegar and Dijon mustard in a bowl and mix them well Season with salt and transfer to a mason jar. Seal tightly and shake until emulsified Remove the bag and transfer to an ice bath Discard the cooking liquid and serve with a topping of egg, parsley, and the vinaigrette

Nutrition: Info Calories: 139 Carbohydrate: 9g Protein: 5g Fat: 10g Sugar: 4g Sodium: 469mg

Butter Radish

Ingredients: Servings: 4   Cooking Time: 45 Mins.

1 lb. radish, halved	1 tsp. sea salt
3 tbsp. unsalted butter	½ tsp. freshly ground black pepper

Directions:
Prepare the Sous Vide water bath using your immersion circulator and raise the temperature to 180-degrees Fahrenheit Put all the listed ingredients into a medium-sized zip bag Seal using the immersion method and allow it to cook underwater for about 45 Mins. Once done, remove the bag and transfer the contents to a platter Serve!

Nutrition: Info Calories: 248 Carbohydrate: 56g Protein: 1g Fat: 1g Sugar: 53g Sodium: 535mg

Sous Vide Garlic Tomatoes

Ingredients: Servings: 4   Cooking Time: 45 Mins.

4 pieces cored and diced tomatoes
3 minced garlic cloves
1 tsp. dried oregano
2 tbsp. extra-virgin olive oil
1 tsp. fine sea salt

Directions:
Prepare the Sous-vide water bath using your immersion circulator and raise the temperature to 145-degrees Fahrenheit.   Add all the listed ingredients to the resealable bag and seal using the immersion method. Submerge underwater and let it cook for 45 minutes. Once cooked, transfer the tomatoes to a serving plate. Serve with some vegan French bread slices.

Nutrition: Info Calories: 289 Carbohydrates: 44g Protein: 11g Fat: 8g Sugar: 2g Sodium: 326mg

Tangerine Ice Cream

Ingredients: Servings: 6   Cooking Time: 24 Hours And 30 Mins.

1 C. mandarin (only juice and pulp)
2 C. heavy cream
6 fresh egg yolks
½ C. milk
½ C. white sugar
¼ C. sweet condensed milk
A pinch of salt

Directions:
In a big bowl, combine all ingredients and whisk well until even.   Carefully pour the mixture into the vacuum bag and seal it.   Cook for 30 Mins. in the water bath, previously preheated to 185°F.   When the time is up, quick chill the vacuum bag without opening it. To do this, put it into big bowl or container, filled with ice and water.   Refrigerate the vacuum bag with ice-cream for 24 hours.   Carefully transfer the mixture to an ice-cream machine and cook according to the instructions.

Nutrition: Info   Per   serving:Calories   152, Carbohydrates 17 g, Fats 8 g, Protein 3 g

Pickled Mixed Veggies

Ingredients: Servings: 4   Cooking Time: 40 Mins.

12 oz. beets, cut up into ½-inch slices
½ Serrano pepper, seeds removed
2/3 C. white vinegar
2/3 C. filtered water
2 tbsp. pickling spice

1 garlic clove, diced

Directions:
Prepare the Sous-vide water bath using your immersion circulator and raise the temperature to 190-degrees Fahrenheit.   Take 4-6 ounces' mason jar and add the Serrano pepper, beets, and garlic cloves   Take a medium stock pot and add the pickling spice, filtered water, white vinegar, and bring the mixture to a boil Remove the stock and strain the mix over the beets in the jar.   Fill them up.   Seal it loosely and submerge it underwater. Cook for 40 minutes.   Allow the jars to cool and serve!

Nutrition: Info Calories: 174 Carbohydrates: 34g Protein: 4g Fat: 2g Sugar: 19g Sodium: 610mg

Pickled Radishes

Ingredients: Servings: x   Cooking Time: 45 Mins Cooking Temperature: 190°f

2/3 C. water
2/3 C. white wine vinegar
2 garlic cloves, sliced in half lengthwise
3 tbsp. sugar
1 bay leaf
1 tbsp. salt
½ tsp. yellow mustard seeds
¼ tsp. coriander seeds
½ tsp. whole peppercorns
12 oz. /3/4 lb. of radishes, trimmed and quartered

Directions:
Attach the sous vide immersion circulator to a Cambro container or pot with water using an adjustable clamp and preheat water to 190°F.   In a pot, add all ingredients except radishes and bring to a boil, stirring continuously until sugar melts.   Place radishes in a single layer in a cooking pouch. Pour sugar mixture over radishes. Seal pouch tightly after squeezing out the excess air. Place pouch in sous vide bath and set the cooking time for about 45 minutes.   Remove pouch from the sous vide bath and immediately immerse in a bowl of ice water. After cooling, remove radishes from pouch and serve immediately.   Radishes can be stored in the refrigerator in an airtight container.

Schmaltzy Brussels Sprouts

Ingredients: Servings: 4   Cooking Time: 30 Mins.

¼ C. schmaltz /such as rendered chicken, duck or goose fat
½ tsp. salt
1 lb. Brussels sprouts
Pepper as needed

Directions:

Prepare the Sous Vide water bath using your immersion circulator and increase the temperature to 183-degrees Fahrenheit Trim the Brussels to halve and quarter them Put them in a zip bag and season with salt and pepper Add the schmaltz and mix well Seal the bag using the immersion method Submerge and cook for 30 Mins. Remove from the bag and serve!

Nutrition: Info Calories: 246 Carbohydrate: 23g Protein: 12g Fat: 13g Sugar: 4g Sodium: 351mg

Sesame Broccoli And Cauliflower

Ingredients: Servings: 4   Cooking Time: 45 Mins.

1 lb. cauliflower, cut into florets	1/4 tsp. ground black pepper
1 lb. broccoli, cut into florets	2 tsp. extra-virgin olive oil
1 tsp. dried parsley flakes	1 tbsp. black sesame seeds
Sea salt, to taste	

Directions:

Preheat a sous vide water bath to 185 degrees F.   Place the cauliflower, broccoli, parsley flakes, black pepper, sea salt, and 1 tsp. of olive oil in cooking poaches; seal tightly.   Submerge the cooking pouches in the water bath; cook for 40 minutes.   Remove your veggies form the cooking pouches. Drizzle the remaining tsp. of olive oil over your veggies.   Sprinkle with black sesame seeds just before serving. Enjoy!

Nutrition: Info 86 Calories; 3g Fat; 2g Carbs; 2g Protein; 6g Sugars

Pickled Carrots

Ingredients: Servings: 1   Cooking Time: 90 Mins.

1 C. white wine vinegar	½ C. beet sugar
3 tbsp. kosher salt	10-12 pieces' petite carrots, peeled with the stems trimmed
1 tsp. black peppercorns	
1/3 C. ice cold water	4 sprigs fresh thyme
	2 peeled garlic cloves

Directions:

Prepare the Sous-vide water bath using your immersion circulator and raise the temperature to 190-degrees Fahrenheit.   Take a medium-sized saucepan and add the vinegar, salt, sugar, and peppercorns and place it over medium heat.   Then, let the mixture reach the boiling point and keep stirring until the sugar has

dissolved alongside the salt   Remove the heat and add the cold water.   Allow the mixture to cool down to room temperature.   Take a resealable bag and add the thyme, carrots, and garlic alongside the brine solution and seal it up using the immersion method.   Submerge underwater and cook for 90 minutes.   Once cooked, remove the bag from the water bath and place into an ice bath.   Carefully take the carrots out from the bag and serve !

Nutrition: Info Calories: 127 Carbohydrates: 24g Protein: 2g Fat: 1g Sugar: 16g Sodium: 54mg

Cheesy Grits

Ingredients: Servings: x   Cooking Time: 3 Hours Cooking Temperature: 180°f

1 C. old fashioned grits	4 oz. /1/4 lb. cheddar cheese, grated, plus extra for garnish
3 C. vegetable broth	
1 C. cream	Salt and freshly ground black pepper, to taste
2 tbsp. cold butter, cut into small pieces	
	Paprika for garnish

Directions:

Attach the sous vide immersion circulator to a Cambro container or pot with water using an adjustable clamp and preheat water to 180°F.   In a large bowl, add grits, broth, and cream and beat until well combined. Add butter and gently stir.   Place grits mixture in a cooking pouch. Seal pouch tightly after squeezing out the excess air. Place pouch in sous vide bath and set the cooking time for about 2-3 hours.   Remove pouch from the sous vide bath and carefully open it. Transfer grits into a bowl. Immediately, add cheese and beat until well combined. Stir in salt and black pepper.   Serve immediately with a sprinkling of extra cheese and paprika.

queso Blanco Dip

Ingredients: Servings: x   Cooking Time: 30 Mins Cooking Temperature: 175°f

1½ C. Asadero or Chihuahua cheese, shredded finely	1 Serrano pepper, stemmed and chopped finely
¼ C. half-and-half cream	2 tbsp. onion, grated
4 oz. /1/4 lb. green chilies, chopped	2 tsp. ground cumin
	½ tsp. salt

Directions:

Attach the sous vide immersion circulator to a Cambro container or pot with water using an adjustable clamp and preheat water to 175°F. Place all ingredients except bread in a cooking pouch. Seal pouch tightly after squeezing out the excess air. Place pouch in sous vide bath and set the cooking time for about 30 minutes. Remove pouch from bath occasionally and massage mixture to mix. Remove the pouch from the sous vide bath and carefully open it. Immediately, transfer dip into a bowl and serve.

Sous-vide Golden Beets

Ingredients: Servings: 2   Cooking Time: 90 Mins.

1 C. freshly squeezed orange juice	1 lb. golden beets, cut up into ¼ inch thick slices
¼ C. freshly squeezed lemon juice	1 tsp. freshly ground black peppercorns
4 tbsp. unsalted vegan butter	1 tsp. kosher salt
1 tbsp. agave nectar	

Directions:
Prepare the Sous-vide water bath using your immersion circulator and raise the temperature to 180-degrees Fahrenheit. Add the listed ingredients to a resealable zip bag and seal using the immersion method. Cook for 1 ½ hours Once done, remove the bag and take the beets out and set them aside. Pour the cooking liquid into a saucepan and bring it to a simmer over medium-high heat. Keep simmering until the liquid is lowered by half. Remove from the heat and stir in beets. Serve!

Nutrition: Info Calories: 169 Carbohydrates: 7g Protein: 1g Fat: 16g Sugar: 4g Sodium: 112mg

Pickle In A Jar

Ingredients: Servings: 6   Cooking Time: 15 Mins.

1 C. white wine vinegar	½ C. beet sugar
2 tsp. kosher salt	2 English cucumbers sliced up into ¼ inch thick slices
1 tbsp. pickling spice	½ white onion, thinly sliced

Directions:
Prepare the Sous-vide water bath using your immersion circulator and raise the temperature to 180-degrees Fahrenheit. Take a large bowl and add the vinegar, sugar, salt, pickling spice and whisk them well.

Transfer to a heavy-duty resealable zipper bag alongside the cucumber and sliced onions and seal using the immersion method. Submerge underwater and let it cook for 15 minutes. Transfer the bag to an ice bath Pour the mixture into a 4-6 oz. mason jar Serve or store!

Nutrition: Info Calories: 117 Carbohydrates: 27g Protein: 1g Fat: 1g Sugar: 19g Sodium: 304mg

Sweet Potato Casserole

Ingredients: Servings: 6   Cooking Time: 2 Hours

2 lb. sweet potatoes, peeled and cut into 1-inch cubes	1 tsp. vanilla
	1/4 C. butter, softened
1/4 tsp. ground allspice	1/2 C. finely chopped pecans, divided
Salt and white pepper, to taste	2 C. miniature marshmallows
4 tbsp. sour cream	

Directions:
Preheat a sous vide water bath to 180 degrees F. Add sweet potatoes, allspice, vanilla, salt, and white pepper to a large cooking pouch; seal tightly. Submerge the cooking pouch in the water bath; cook for 1 hour 45 minutes. Then, mix sweet potatoes with sour cream. Spoon the mixture into a casserole dish. Combine the butter with pecans; top the casserole with this butter mixture. Spread miniature marshmallows over the top. Preheat the oven to 380 degrees F. Bake for 15 Mins. or until the top is golden brown. Bon appétit!

Nutrition: Info 307 Calories; 16g Fat; 48g Carbs; 5g Protein; 12g Sugars

Momofuku Styled Brussels

Ingredients: Servings: 8   Cooking Time: 50 Mins.

2 lbs. Brussels sprouts, stems trimmed and slice in half	2 tbsp. water
	1 tbsp. rice vinegar
	1½ tsp. lime juice
2 tbsp. extra-virgin olive oil	12 pieces thinly sliced Thai chilis
¼ tsp. kosher salt	1 small minced garlic clove
¼ C. fish sauce	Chopped fresh mint
1½ tbsp. granulated sugar	Chopped fresh cilantro

Directions:
Prepare the Sous Vide water bath using your immersion circulator and raise the temperature to 183-degrees

Fahrenheit   Put the Brussel sprouts, olive oil and salt in a heavy-duty, resealable bag   Seal using the immersion method   Cook for 50 Mins.   Put the fish sauce, sugar, water, rice vinegar, lime juice, garlic, and chilis in a small bowl and mix them to prepare the vinaigrette   Once done, put the Brussels on an aluminum foil, lined baking sheet and heat up your broiler   Broil the Brussels for 5 Mins. until they are charred   Transfer to a medium-sized bowl and add the vinaigrette   Toss well and sprinkle with mint and cilantro

Nutrition: Info Calories: 610 Carbohydrate: 38g Protein: 10g Fat: 5g Sugar: 20g Sodium: 684mg

Garlic & Paprika Sweet Potatoes

Ingredients: Servings: x   Cooking Time: 1 Hour Cooking Temperature: 185°f

7 tbsp. salted butter, softened	2 tsp. fresh thyme, chopped
4½ tbsp. maple syrup	2 tsp. smoked paprika
10 roasted, smoked garlic cloves	2 lb. /1 kg sweet potatoes, peeled and chopped
Sea salt, to taste	

Directions:
Attach the sous vide immersion circulator to a Cambro container or pot with water using an adjustable clamp and preheat water to 185°F.   In a bowl, add all ingredients except sweet potatoes and mix until well combined.   Place sweet potatoes and butter mixture in a cooking pouch. Seal pouch tightly after squeezing out the excess air. Place pouch in sous vide bath and set the cooking time for about 45-60 minutes.   Remove pouch from the sous vide bath and carefully open it. Remove sweet potatoes from pouch.   Heat a sauté pan and cook sweet potatoes until golden brown.

Pickled Jalapeño Peppers

Ingredients: Servings: x   Cooking Time: 30 Mins Cooking Temperature: 180°f

1 C. white wine vinegar	6 jalapeño peppers, sliced crosswise ¼-inch thick
3 tbsp. ultrafine sugar	
2 tsp. kosher salt	½ White onion, thinly sliced

Directions:
Attach the sous vide immersion circulator to a Cambro container or pot with water using an adjustable clamp and preheat water to 180°F.   In a large bowl, add

vinegar, sugar, and salt and beat until sugar is dissolved. Place jalapeño peppers, onion, and vinegar mixture in a cooking pouch. Seal pouch tightly after squeezing out the excess air. Place pouch in sous vide bath and set the cooking time for about 30 minutes.   Remove pouch from the sous vide bath and immediately immerse in a large bowl of ice water to cool. Remove peppers from pouch and serve immediately.

Cardamom Apricots

Ingredients: Servings: 4   Cooking Time: 1 Hour

1 pint small apricots, halved	½ tsp. ground ginger
1 tbsp. unsalted butter	A pinch of smoked sea salt
1 tsp. cardamom seeds, freshly ground	Fresh basil for garnishing, chopped

Directions:
Prepare your Sous Vide water bath by increasing the temperature to 180-degrees Fahrenheit using an immersion circulator   Put the butter, apricots, ginger, cardamom, and salt in a large, heavy-duty plastic bag, and mix them well   Carefully seal the bag using the immersion method and submerge it in the hot water Let it cook for 60 Mins. and remove the bag once done Put the apricots in serving bowls   Garnish by topping it up with basil   Serve!

Nutrition: Info   Per   serving:Calories: 270 ;Carbohydrate: 60g ;Protein: 1g ;Fat: 0g ;Sugar: 49g ;Sodium: 33mg

Miso Roasted Celeriac

Ingredients: Servings: 6   Cooking Time: 2 Hours

1 tbsp. miso paste	1 tbsp. mustard seeds
1 whole celeriac, carefully peeled and cut into small bite-sized pieces	Juice of ¼ a large lemon
6 cloves garlic	5 cherry tomatoes roughly cut
5 sprigs thyme	Chopped up parsley
1 tsp. onion powder	8-oz. vegan butter
3 tbsp. feta cheese	1 tbsp. olive oil
	8 oz. cooked quinoa

Directions:
Prepare the Sous Vide water bath using your immersion circulator and raise the temperature to 185-degrees Fahrenheit   Take a large-sized pan and place it over medium heat, add the garlic, thyme, feta cheese, and

dry fry them for 1 and a ½ Min. Add the butter and keep stirring until slightly browned Add the onion powder and keep the mixture on the side and allow it to cool at room temperature Add the celeriac to a zip bag alongside the cooled butter mixture Submerge and cook for 1½ to 2 hours Transfer the mixture to a hot pan (place over medium heat) and stirring it until golden brown Season with miso paste Add the oil to another pan and place it over medium heat, add the tomatoes, mustard seeds and re-heat the quinoa Carefully add the lemon and parsley to the previously made tomato mixture Assemble your platter by transferring the celeriac and tomato mix Serve!

Nutrition: Info Per serving:Calories: 200 ;Carbohydrate: 5g ;Protein: 12g ;Fat: 15gt ;Sugar: 1g ;Sodium: 36mg

Parsnips

Ingredients: Servings: x   Cooking Time: 1 Hour 40 Mins Cooking Temperature: 185°f

2-3 parsnips, peeled and cut into thick rounds	Vegetable broth, enough to cover parsnips in cooking bag
2-3 tsp. fresh thyme leaves	Butter, as required

Directions:
Attach the sous vide immersion circulator to a Cambro container or pot with water using an adjustable clamp and preheat water to 185°F. In a cooking pouch, place parsnip rounds, thyme, and enough broth to cover. Seal pouch tightly after squeezing out the excess air. Place pouch in sous vide bath and set the cooking time for about 45 Mins. and no more than 90 minutes. Remove pouch from the sous vide bath and carefully open it. Remove parsnips from pouch, reserving broth in a bowl. with paper towels, pat dry parsnip rounds completely. In a non-stick frying pan, melt butter over high heat and cook parsnip rounds until browned on both sides. Add reserved broth with some water over high heat and cook until sauce becomes thick, basting parsnips occasionally with sauce. Serve parsnips with pan sauce.

Root Vegetable Soup with Pita Chips

Ingredients: Servings: 4   Cooking Time: 55 Mins.

2 shallots, peeled and chopped	1 C. turnip, chopped
2 parsnips, chopped	2 tbsp. olive oil
2 celery stalks,	2 C. baby spinach
chopped	2 heaping tbsp.
2 carrots, chopped	fresh parsley, chopped
2 cloves garlic, minced	1 sprig fresh rosemary,
4 C. vegetable broth, preferably homemade	chopped
	1 C. pita chips

Directions:
Preheat a sous vide water bath to 185 degrees F. Place the shallots, parsnips, celery, carrots, turnip, garlic, vegetable broth, and olive oil in cooking pouches; seal tightly. Submerge the cooking pouches in the water bath; cook for 50 minutes. Now, empty the contents into a serving bowl; add baby spinach, parsley, and rosemary. Serve with pita chips and enjoy!

Nutrition: Info 178 Calories; 9g Fat; 23g Carbs; 3g Protein; 6g Sugars

Braised Fennel with Peas And Caramelized Onion

Ingredients: Servings: 4   Cooking Time: 1 Hour

1 tbsp. olive oil	1 ½ tbsp. chickpea flour
1 yellow onion, slice into rings	1/2 tsp. granulated garlic
A pinch of salt	
1/2 lb. fresh peas	1 bay leaf
1/2 C. fennel	1/2 tsp. dried dill
1/2 C. double cream	1 tsp. cayenne pepper
1/2 C. broth, preferably homemade	Salt and ground black pepper, to taste
3 tbsp. ghee	

Directions:
Preheat a sous vide water bath to 183 degrees F. Heat the olive oil in a nonstick skillet over a moderate flame until it is shimmering. Sauté the onions with a pinch of salt until they are caramelized. Add all ingredients, including the caramelized onions, to cooking pouches; seal tightly. Submerge the cooking pouches in the water bath; cook for 50 minutes. Remove the cooking pouches from the water bath; ladle the vegetables into serving bowls and serve with garlic croutons, if desired. Bon appétit!

Nutrition: Info 217 Calories; 13g Fat; 12g Carbs; 1g Protein; 3g Sugars

Orange Compote

Ingredients: Servings: 4   Cooking Time: 3 Hours

4 blood oranges, quartered and thinly sliced
2 C. granulated sugar
½ vanilla seed pod

1 lemon, juice and zest
1 tsp. beef gelatin powder or agar agar

Directions:
Set the Sous Vide cooker to 190°F. Combine all ingredients in a Sous Vide bag. Seal using water immersion technique. Cook the oranges 3 hours. Remove the bag from the cooker and place into an ice-cold water bath. Once cooled transfer into a food processor. Add the gelatin and process until smooth. Allow cooling completely before serving.

Nutrition: Info Per serving:Calories 502.7, Carbohydrates 123.1 g, Fats 0.3 g, Protein 1.9 g

Crunchy Apple Salad with Almonds

Ingredients: Servings: 4   Cooking Time: 40 Mins. + Chilling Time

3 crisp eating apples, cored, and sliced
2 tbsp. honey
1/2 C. dried cranberries
1 C. almonds
6 oz. package mixed spring greens
1/4 C. sour cream

1/4 C. mayonnaise
1 tsp. yellow mustard
1/2 tbsp. lime juice
1 tbsp. sugar
Salt and white pepper, to your liking

Directions:
Preheat a sous vide water bath to 160 degrees F. Add the apples and honey to a cooking pouch; seal tightly. Submerge the cooking pouches in the water bath; cook for 35 minutes. Remove the apples from the cooking pouch and let them cool completely. Transfer the apples to a nice salad bowl. Add the cranberries, almonds, and greens. In a mixing bowl, whisk the sour cream, mayonnaise, mustard, lime juice, sugar, salt, and pepper. Whisk until sugar is dissolved. Dress the salad and serve well-chilled. Bon appétit!

Nutrition: Info 193 Calories; 9g Fat; 39g Carbs; 3g Protein; 28g Sugars

Spicy Summer Medley

Ingredients: Servings: 6   Cooking Time: 1 Hour 20 Mins.

1 lb. kabocha pumpkin, cut into wedges
1/2 lb. eggplants, sliced
1/2 lb. cabbage
4 tbsp. sesame oil
4 cloves garlic, minced
1 tsp. fresh ginger, grated
2 shallots, peeled and cut into wedges
1 red bell pepper, seeded and thinly sliced

1 yellow bell pepper, seeded and thinly sliced
1 serrano pepper, seeded and thinly sliced
1/4 C. sake
1/4 C. water
2 tbsp. ketchup
2 ripe tomatoes, chopped
Salt and ground black pepper, to taste
1/2 tsp. cayenne pepper
2 tbsp. miso
2 tsp. sugar

Directions:
Preheat a sous vide water bath to 183 degrees F. Place kabocha pumpkin, eggplants, and cabbage in separate cooking pouches; add 1 tbsp. of sesame oil to each pouch; seal tightly. Submerge the cooking pouches in the water bath; cook for 45 minutes. When the timer goes off, remove the pouch with eggplants; reserve. Set the timer for a further 20 minutes. Remove the pumpkin and cabbage from the cooking pouches; reserve. Heat the remaining tbsp. of sesame oil in a pot over a moderate heat. Now, sauté the garlic, ginger, shallots and peppers until just softened. Pour in sake to deglaze your pan. Add the water and bring the mixture to a rolling boil for 5 minutes. Add the rest of above ingredients, including the reserved vegetables. Now, decrease the heat to low to maintain a simmer; simmer approximately 8 Mins. to allow the flavors to develop. Ladle into individual bowls and serve warm. Bon appétit!

Nutrition: Info 216 Calories; 9g Fat; 25g Carbs; 8g Protein; 11g Sugars

Acorn Squash

Ingredients: Servings: x   Cooking Time: 1 Hour Cooking Temperature: 194°f

2 tbsp. butter
Pinch of dried rosemary
Pinch of salt

1 acorn squash, seeded and cut into wedges

Directions:
Attach the sous vide immersion circulator to a Cambro container or pot with water using an adjustable clamp and preheat water to 194°F. In a pan, melt butter over medium heat until light brown specks appear, stirring

occasionally. Stir in rosemary and salt and remove from heat.   Place acorn squash in a cooking pouch. Pour brown butter over squash wedges evenly. Seal pouch tightly after squeezing out the excess air. Place pouch in sous vide bath and set the cooking time for about 1 hour. Remove pouch from the sous vide bath and carefully open it. Transfer squash wedges onto a serving platter and serve.

Whiskey & Poached Peaches

Ingredients: Servings: 4   Cooking Time: 30 Mins.

2 peaches, pitted and quartered
½ C. rye whiskey
½ C. ultrafine sugar
1 tsp. vanilla extract
A pinch of salt

Directions:
Prepare your Sous Vide water bath using your immersion circulator and raise the temperature to 180-degrees Fahrenheit   Place all the ingredients in a heavy-duty zip bag   Seal it using immersion method and submerge it in the hot water   Let it cook for about 30 Mins.   Once the timer runs out, take the bag out and transfer it to an ice bath   Serve!

Nutrition: Info   Per   serving:Calories: 656 ;Carbohydrate: 162g ;Protein: 13g ;Fat: 3g ;Sugar: 147g ;Sodium: 8mg

Southern Buttery Grits

Ingredients: Servings: x   Cooking Time: 3 Hours Cooking Temperature: 180°f

½ C. roughly ground grits
1 tbsp. unsalted butter
½ tsp. kosher salt
2 C. water

Directions:
Attach the sous vide immersion circulator to a Cambro container or pot with water using an adjustable clamp and preheat water to 180°F.   Place all ingredients in a cooking pouch. Seal pouch tightly after squeezing out the excess air. Place pouch in sous vide bath and set the cooking time for about 3 hours.   Remove pouch from the sous vide bath and carefully open it. Transfer grits into a bowl and serve immediately.

Potato Confit

Ingredients: Servings: 4   Cooking Time: 1 Hour

1 lb. small red potatoes
1 tsp. chopped fresh rosemary
1 tsp. kosher salt
¼ tsp. ground white pepper
2 tbsp. whole butter
1 tbsp. corn oil

Directions:
Prepare the Sous Vide water bath using your immersion circulator and increase the temperature to 190-degrees Fahrenheit   Then cut the potatoes in half, carefully season the potatoes with rosemary, salt and pepper   Mix the potatoes with butter and oil   Transfer them to a heavy-duty, resealable bag and seal using the immersion method   Submerge underwater and cook for 60 Mins.   Once done, add them into a large bowl, add the extra butter and serve

Nutrition: Info   Per   serving:Calories: 314 ;Carbohydrate: 53g ;Protein: 8g ;Fat: 10g ;Sugar: 6g ;Sodium: 306mg

Carrots with Butter

Ingredients: Servings: x   Cooking Time: 25 Mins Cooking Temperature: 185°f

Baby carrots
Olive oil, as required
Pinch of salt
Butter, as required

Directions:
Attach the sous vide immersion circulator to a Cambro container or pot with water using an adjustable clamp and preheat water to 185°F.   Place carrots in a single layer in a cooking pouch. Add a little olive oil and salt. Seal pouch tightly after squeezing out the excess air. Place pouch in sous vide bath and set the cooking time for about 25 minutes.   Remove pouch from the sous vide bath and carefully open it. Remove carrots from pouch. with paper towels, pat dry carrots completely Serve immediately with a topping of butter.

OTHER FAVORITE RECIPES

Chicken Noodle Soup

Ingredients: Servings: 8   Cooking Time: 50 Mins.

2 1/2 lb. chicken
2 sliced carrots
2 sliced celery stalks
1 chopped onion
2 tbsp. olive oil
5 chopped garlic cloves
1/4 C. dry white wine
cup chicken stock
2 1/2 C. cooked noodles
3 tbsp. chopped parsley
2 tbsp. chopped dill
2 tbsp. lemon juice
Salt, pepper as per taste

Directions:

Set the sous vide machine to 195 degrees Fahrenheit. Take the chicken pieces in the sous vide bag and seal it. Place this bag in the water bath for 10 minutes. Take oil in a pan. Cook carrots, onion, celery and garlicuntil softened. Sprinkle salt and pepper. Add wine and cook for 1 minute. Add cooked chicken and chicken stock and simmer for 35 minutes. Remove the chicken, shred it into bite-size pieces and put it back into the pot. Lastly, add the noodles and cook for 5 minutes. Season with lemon juice, parsley, dill and serve hot.

Nutrition: Info calories 128kcal, fats 3g, carbs 7g, protein 18g.

Light Vegetarian Frittata

Ingredients: Servings: 5   Cooking Time: 1 Hour 40 Mins.

1 tbsp. olive oil	1 C. butternut
1 medium onion, chopped	squash, peeled and diced
Salt to taste	6 oz. oyster
4 cloves minced garlic	mushrooms, chopped
1 daikon, peeled and diced	¼ C. parsley leaves, freshly
2 carrots, peeled and diced	minced
1 parsnip, peeled and diced	A pinch of red pepper flakes
	5 large eggs
	¼ C. whole milk

Directions:

Prepare a water bath and place the Sous Vide in it. Set to 175 F. Grease a few jars with oil. Set aside. Heat a skillet over high heat with oil. Add the onion sweat for 5 minutes. Add garlic and cook for 30 seconds. Season with salt. Combine carrots, daikon, squash and parsnips. Season with salt and cook 10 Mins. more. Add the mushrooms and season with the pepper flakes and parsley. Cook for 5 minutes. In a bowl, whisk the eggs and milk Season with salt. Separate the mixture amongst the jars with the vegetables. Seal and submerge the jars in the water bath. Cook for 60 minutes. Once the timer has stopped, remove the jars. Let cool and serve.

Crispy Sous Vide Egg Yolks

Ingredients: Servings: 4   Cooking Time: 65 Mins.

4 + 1 egg	½ tsp. fine salt
4 tbsp. all-purpose flour	¾ tsp. black truffle salt
1/3 tsp. baking	
powder	Salt and pepper,
½ C. breadcrumbs	to taste

Directions:

Fill and preheat Sous Vide cooker to 148°F. Cook four eggs 60 minutes. Let the eggs cool in cold water 10 minutes. Carefully peel the eggs, and let the egg white drips out. Reserve egg yolks. Heat 1-inch oil in a skillet over medium heat. While the oil is heating, whisk flour, baking powder, and salt in a bowl. Beat remaining egg in a small bowl. Dredge egg yolks through flour and dip into beaten egg. Finally, roll in breadcrumbs. Fry in heated oil until golden brown. Drain the egg yolks on a paper towel. Sprinkle with black truffle salt. Serve.

Nutrition: Info Per serving:Calories 160, Carbohydrates 16.3 g, Fats 6.3 g, Protein 9.5 g

Eggs Benedict

Ingredients: Servings: 4   Cooking Time: 1 Hour

4 slices, Canadian bacon	1 teaspoon, water
4 eggs	1 teaspoon, lemon juice
2 English muffins	1 egg yolk
Fresh parsley, chopped	4 tbsp. of butter
Butter	Salt to taste
Hollandaise	Pinch, cayenne
½ shallot, diced	

Directions:

Preheat your water bath to 148°F Add all the hollandaise ingredients to a large Ziploc bag then place the bag in the water bath to remove air through water displacement. Seal the bag and place it in the water bath Add 4 eggs into the same water bath in another Ziploc bag or direct. Cook for an hour. Sear the Canadian bacon until done, over medium heat. Slice the 2 English muffins in half then toast them. If need be, place the seared bacon and toasted muffins into an oven preheated to 250°F to keep warm as you finish making the sauce. Remove the hollandaise from the Ziploc bag once done cooking and pour into your blender. Blend until the mixture becomes smooth light yellow on medium speed – this is because the mixture will be quite separated when you remove it from the water bath. Crack the poached eggs with a spoon and do away with the excess egg whites or place in a bowl. Place each of the poached egg onto each muffin slice, which is topped with bacon. Top generously with hollandaise sauce and chopped parsley.

Nutrition: Info Per serving:Calories 433, Carbohydrates 25 g, Fats 21 g, Protein 36 g

Cherry Tomato Eggs

Ingredients: Servings: 6 Cooking Time: 40 Mins.

10 eggs	½ C. milk
1 C. cherry	½ tsp. nutmeg
tomatoes, halved	1 tsp. butter
2 tbsp. sour cream	1 tsp. salt
1 tbsp. chives	

Directions:
Prepare a water bath and place the Sous Vide in it. Set to 170 F. Place cherry tomatoes in a large vacuum-sealable bag. Whisk the eggs with the remaining ingredients and pour over the tomatoes. Release air by the water displacement method, seal and submerge the bag in water bath. Set the timer for 30 minutes. Once done, remove the bag and transfer to a plate.

Soft And Chili Eggs

Ingredients: Servings: 5 Cooking Time: 60 Mins.

1 tbsp. chili	Salt and black
powder	pepper to taste
5 eggs	

Directions:
Prepare a water bath and place Sous Vide in it. Set to 147 F. Place eggs in a vacuum-sealable bag. Release air by the water displacement method, seal and submerge in the bath. Cook for 50 minutes. Once the timer has stopped, remove the bag and place them in an ice bath to cool and peel. Sprinkle the eggs with the spices and serve.

Meatballs In Spaghetti Nests

Ingredients: Servings: 24 Cooking Time: 20 Mins.

1/2 C. spaghetti	1 egg whites
1/2 C. shredded	24 meatballs
Parmesan	1 C. marinara
1/4 C. shredded	sauce
mozzarella	Salt and Pepper

Directions:
Set the sous vide machine to 195 degrees Fahrenheit. Place the meatballs in the Ziploc bag and apply vacuum. Submerge this bag in water bath for 5 minutes. Cook the pasta as described on the pack. Strain the water and rinse. Take a large mixing bowl and add egg whites, salt and whisk thoroughly. Add mozzarella and Parmesan cheese and mix. Grease the muffin pan with butter or cooking spray. Put the above mixture in the muffin C. and arrange such that it takes the shape of the cup. Preheat oven to 400 degrees Fahrenheit and heat this muffin C. for 15 minutes. Toss the cooked

meatballs in the marinara sauce. Place a meatball in each spaghetti nest. Top it with grated Parmesan and serve.

Nutrition: Info calories 70kcal, fats 4g, carbs 6g, protein 3g.

Herb Flavored Roasted Turkey

Ingredients: Servings: 8 Cooking Time: 45 Hours

1 turkey	3 garlic heads
3 onions	2 carrots
6 sprigs rosemary	2 stalks celery
6 sprig sage	3/4 C. chicken
2 tbsp. olive oil	broth
	Salt and pepper
	per taste

Directions:
Clean the turkey, dry the main cavity and stuff half quantity of onion, herbs and garlic into it. Rub olive oil over the turkey and sprinkle salt. Set the sous vide machine to 195 degrees Fahrenheit. Take a large ziplock bag and place the stuffed turkey in it. Apply vacuum to remove the air. Place this bag in the water bath for 2 hours. In a cooking pan, cook the vegetables with the broth. Remove the turkey. Remove the contents of the turkey cavity. Add these contents into the vegetable mix. Use this as the gravy. Carve the turkey and serve hot.

Nutrition: Info calories 441kcal, protein 92g.

Chicken Stir-fry

Ingredients: Servings: 4 Cooking Time: 25 Mins.

2 chopped bell	1 sliced scallions
peppers	1 tbsp. honey
1 chopped onion	1 tbsp. sriracha
1 lb. boneless	1 tsp. sesame oil
chicken chunks	2 garlic cloves
2 tbsp. soy sauce	1-inch ginger
3 tbsp. cornstarch	1 tbsp. toasted
2 tbsp. rice	sesame seeds
vinegar	Salt and pepper as
	per taste

Directions:
Heat oil in a pan and cook the onion, bell peppers, and scallion until they are tender. Keep this aside. Toss the chicken with cornstarch Set the sous vide machine to 195 degrees Fahrenheit. Place this chicken in the ziplock bag and remove the air. Submerge this bag in water bath and cook for 10 minutes. In a bowl mix soy sauce, vinegar, honey, sriracha, sesame oil and add cooked chicken. Add the cooked vegetables, water and

simmer for 2 minutes. Sprinkle sesame seeds. Serve hot with rice.

Nutrition: Info calories 495kcal, fats 13g, protein 32g, carbs 60g.

Squash And Lentil Stew

Ingredients: Servings: 6   Cooking Time: 35 Mins.

1 lb. green lentils	1 tsp. coriander
2 sliced shallots	powder
1 butternut squash	1/2 tsp. cardamom
cups baby spinach	powder
cups vegetable	1 tbsp. vinegar
broth	Salt and pepper
1 tbsp. chopped	
ginger	

Directions:
Take the squash and peel it. Cut it into 1 1/2" pieces. Set the sous vide machine to 165 degrees Fahrenheit. Take the lentils, squash in the sous vide bag. Place the bag in sous vide and cook for 5 minutes. Transfer it to a cooking pan. Add shallot, ginger, oil,cardamom powder, coriander powder,salt and vegetable broth. Cook on high flame for 12 minutes. Add spinach, vinegar, salt, pepper and serve hot.

Nutrition: Info calories 325kcal, carbs 57g, proteins 19g, fats 4g, fiber 15g.

Ground Beef Omelet

Ingredients: Servings: 3   Cooking Time: 35 Mins.

1 C. lean ground	½ tsp. dried
beef	oregano, ground
¼ C. finely	Salt and black
chopped onions	pepper to taste
¼ tsp. dried	1 tbsp. olive oil
thyme, ground	

Directions:
Preheat the oil in a skillet over a medium heat. Add onions and stir-fry for about 3-4 minutes, or until translucent. Add ground beef and cook for 5 minutes, stirring occasionally. Sprinkle with some salt, pepper, thyme, and oregano. Stir well and cook for a Min. more. Remove from the heat and set aside. Prepare a water bath and place the Sous Vide in it. Set to 170 F. Whisk the eggs in a medium bowl and pour in a vacuum reseleable bag. Add ground beef mixture. Release air by the water displacement method and seal the bag. Immerse the bag in the water bath and set the timer for 15 minutes. Using a glove, massage the bag every 5 Mins. to ensure even cooking. Once the timer stopped, remove

the bag from the water bath and transfer the omelet to a serving plate.

Poached Eggs

Ingredients: Servings: 4   Cooking Time: 65 Mins.

4 C. water	Salt and black
4 eggs paprika	pepper to taste
1 tbsp.	
mayonnaise	

Directions:
Prepare a water bath and place Sous Vide in it. Set to 145 F. Place eggs in a vacuum-sealable bag. Release air by the water displacement method, seal and submerge bath. Set the timer for 55 minutes. Once the timer has stopped, remove the bag and transfer to an ice bath to cool and peel. Meanwhile, bring the water to a boil in a saucepan. Lace the peeled eggs inside and cook for a minute. While the eggs are cooking, whisk together the remaining ingredients. Drizzle over the eggs.

Tofu Crisps

Ingredients: Servings: 4   Cooking Time: 60 Mins.

1 3/4 C. tofu	3 tbsp. cornstarch
1/2 sliced red	2 tbsp. vegetable
onion	oil
1/4 C. red wine	1 C. cooked quinoa
vinegar	2 tbsp. roasted
1/4 C. Thai chili	cashews
sauce	Parsley leaves and
1 tbsp. olive oil	salt
1 chopped	
cucumber	

Directions:
Make slices of tofu and press it between the paper towels. In a bowl make a mixture of onions, vinegar, Thai sauce, olive oil, cucumber. Apply cornstarch to both sides of tofu. Set the sous vide machine to 180 degrees Fahrenheit. Take the pieces of tofu in a large Ziploc bag. Seal it using vacuum. Place the bag in sous vide and cook for 60 minutes. Serve the tofu with quinoa, salad, cashews and parsley.

Nutrition: Info calories 440kcal, proteins 18g, carbs 45g, fats 20g, fibers 5g.

Skewed Chicken Satay

Ingredients: Servings: 4   Cooking Time: 15 Mins.

1 3/4 lb. diced	1 1/2 tbsp.
boneless chicken	coriander powder
1 1/2 tsp. lime zest	1 tsp. cumin

1 1/2 tbsp. lime juice
1 tbsp. coconut oil
2 tbsp. tamari
1 1/2 tbsp. fish sauce
3 crushed garlic cloves
1 1/2 tbsp. grated ginger
1 1/2 tbsp. turmeric powder

powder
Salt, pepper, coriander leaves
For Sauce:
3/4 C. cashews
1/2 C. almond butter
2 tbsp. grated ginger
2 tbsp. tamari
2 chopped red chili
1 tbsp. sesame oil
1 tbsp. maple syrup

Directions:
Mix all the dry ingredients needed for chicken. Toss the chicken cubes in it with little oil and marinate for 2 hours. Set the sous vide machine to 195 degrees Fahrenheit. Place this chicken in the zoplock bag. Seal the bag under vacuum. Place it in the water bath for 10 Mins. Mix all the ingredients needed for the sauce to form a smooth blend. Preheat the grill. Thread the chicken pieces to the skewers and grill for 5 Mins. until brown from all sides. Serve hot with cashew sauce.

Nutrition: Info calories 200kcal, fats 10g, protein 25g.

Duck Cacciatore

Ingredients: Servings: 4   Cooking Time: 90 Mins.

1 duck cut into 8 pieces
4 smashed garlic cloves
2 chopped carrots
2 chopped celery
1 chopped yellow onion

1 C. dry red wine
3 C. crushed tomatoes
3/4 lb. mushrooms
4 tbsp. butter
2 sprigs parsley
Salt, pepper, flour, olive oilas per need.

Directions:
Sprinkle salt, pepper and flour on the duck. Set the sous vide machine to 195 degrees Fahrenheit. Take a ziplock bag and place these duck pieces in it. Apply vacuum to remove the air. Place this bag in the water bath for 30 minutes. In a cooking pan add carrots, celery, onion, red wine, garlic and cook for 5 minutes. Add tomatoes, mushroom and stir. Place the duck on the cooked vegetables and top with parsley and butter. Cover and cook for 1 hour. Serve hot.

Nutrition: Info calories 450kcal, fats 25g, carbs 13g, protein 42g.

Arugula & Prosciutto Omelet

Ingredients: Servings: 2   Cooking Time: 25 Mins.

4 thin slices prosciutto
¼ C. fresh arugula, finely chopped

5 large eggs
¼ C. sliced avocado
Salt and black pepper to taste

Directions:
Prepare a water bath, place Sous Vide in it, and set to 167 F. Whisk the eggs with arugula, salt, and pepper. Transfer to a vacuum-sealable bag. Press to remove the air and then seal the lid. Cook for 15 minutes. Once the timer has stopped, remove the bag, unseal and transfer the omelet to a serving plate and top with avocado slices and Prosciutto.

Chicken Noodles

Ingredients: Servings: 4   Cooking Time: 20 Mins.

1 1/2 C. chopped boneless chicken
3 C. chopped red cabbage
1 C. shredded carrots
2 chopped garlic cloves

1/4 C. vinegar
2/4 C. peanut butter
1/4 soy sauce
1/4 C. chicken broth
1 C. rice noodles
Salt, pepper, peanuts, cilantro

Directions:
Cook the rice noodles as per the instructions given on the package. Take a large mixing bowl. Add chicken, cabbage, carrots, garlic and oil. Set the sous vide machine to 195 degrees Fahrenheit. Place this mixture in the ziplock bag. Remove air and seal the bag. Place this bag in the water bath for 10 Mins. Take a large sauce pan. Take the cooked chicken and vegetables. Add vinegar, chicken broth, peanut butter and soy sauce and simmer for 10 minutes. Add noodles to the chicken and mix. Serve hot.

Nutrition: Info calories 520kcal, protein 28g, carbs 61g, fats 19g.

Kung Pao Brussel Sprouts

Ingredients: Servings: 1   Cooking Time: 35 Mins.

2 lb. Brussels sprouts
2 tbsp. olive oil
1 tbsp. sesame oil
2 cloves garlic
1 tbsp. corn-starch

1/2 C. soy sauce
1/2 C. water
2 tsp. vinegar
2 tsp. garlic chili sauce
1 tbsp. brown

sugar
Salt, pepper, green
onion

Directions:

Cut the Brussels in half and toss them with olive oil, salt and pepper. Set the sous vide machine to 195 degrees Fahrenheit. Take the above mixture in the sous vide bag. Remove air from the bag and seal. Submerge this bag in water bath and heat for 20 minutes. Heat sesame oil and add garlic, cornstarch, soy sauce, water, vinegar, sugar, chili paste, salt, pepper. Simmer for 3 minutes. Pour this sauce over the Brussels, garnish with green onions and serve hot.

Nutrition: Info calories 90kcal, carbs 22g, protein 11g, fats 5g.

Beef Lettuce Pineapple Wraps

Ingredients: Servings: 6   Cooking Time: 20 Mins.

1 lb. frozen beef	1 grated garlic
1/4 C. pineapple	clove
juice	1 tbsp. honey
2 tbsp. soy sauce	1 tbsp. sesame oil
1/2 tsp. red	2 tbsp. canola oil
pepper flakes	Salt, pepper,
1 tbsp. grated	lettuce leaves,
ginger	sticky rice

Directions:

Mix garlic, pineapple juice, soy sauce, ginger, red pepper flakes, sesame oil and honey. Make thin slices of beef and apply the above mixture. Marinate for 30 Mins. or refrigerate for 3 hours. Set the sous vide machine to 195 degrees Fahrenheit. Place the slices of beef in a ziplock bag. Apply vacuum and remove the air from the bag. Seal the bag. Submerge this bag in water bath for 20 Mins. Serve the beef with lettuce leaves and sticky rice

Nutrition: Info calories 190kcal, fats 14g, protein 15g.

Egg Soufflé with Avocado And Toast

Ingredients: Servings: 4   Cooking Time: 50 Mins.

8 large eggs	1 tbsp. olive oil
¼ tsp. salt	Additional:
¼ tsp. black	
pepper	1 sliced avocado
½ C. grated	Toasted bread
parmesan	

Directions:

Fill and preheat Souse Vide cooker to 172°F. In a bowl, beat eggs with salt and pepper. Fold in parmesan and

olive oil. Divide the mixture among four 4oz. jars. Attach two-part canning lids "fingertip tight." Do not over tight because the pressure will not be able to escape and the jar will shatter. Submerge jars in water bath 50 minutes. Remove jars from water bath. Loosen outer edge with a knife. Invert soufflé onto toasted bread. Serve with avocado slices.

Nutrition: Info Per serving:Calories 216, Carbohydrates 5.3 g, Fats 24 g, Protein 14.7 g

Avocado Bacon Turkey Sandwich

Ingredients: Servings: 1   Cooking Time: 15 Mins.

4 slices of turkey	1 tbsp.
breast	mayonnaise
2 slices of toasted	4 slices bacon
bread	1/2 sliced avocado
1 slice provolone	1/2 sliced tomato
cheese	1 lettuce leaf

Directions:

Set the sous vide machine to 195 degrees Fahrenheit. Take the slices of turkey breast and bacon in separate ziplock bags and seal these bags. Place these bags in the water bath for 15 minutes. Apply mayonnaise to one side of each slice of bread. Top the slice bread slice with cheese, bacon, turkey, avocado, tomato and lettuce. Cover this with another slice of the toasted bread. Cut it into pieces and serve.

Nutrition: Info calories 578kcal, fats 35g, carbs 38g, protein 31g.

Juicy Chicken Nuggets

Ingredients: Servings: 20 Nuggets   Cooking Time: 15 Mins.

2 lb. boneless	2 eggs
chicken	1/4 C. water
1 garlic clove	Pepper, salt,
1 lemon	paprika, coconut
1/4 C. tapioca	oil
flour	

Directions:

Cut the chicken into bite-sized nuggets. Take a mixing bowl. Mince the garlic and lemon together. Add water and mix. Add chicken to this and marinate for more than an hour in a refrigerator. Remove the chicken pieces from the marinade. Set the sous vide machine to 195 degrees Fahrenheit. Take these chicken pieces in a ziplock bag and seal it. Place the bag in the water bath for 5 Mins. In a bowl, mix paprika, tapioca flour, salt, pepper. In another bowl beat the eggs. Dip the chicken in the powder mix and then into the eggs.

Take oil in a pan and shallow fry the nuggets until golden brown. Transfer onto the paper towel to remove excess oil and serve.

Nutrition: Info calories 48kcal, fats 3g, carbs 3g, protein 3g.

Mushroom Orzo Green Soup

Ingredients: Servings: 6   Cooking Time: 35 Mins.

1 C. sliced mushroom	cups vegetable broth
1 C. orzo	1 1/4 C. celery
3 C. sliced spinach	1/2 C. shallots
3 C. broccoli	1/4 C. garlic
2 tbsp. olive oil	Salt, pepper and basil pesto

Directions:
In a large cooking pan mix the celery, shallots, garlic, salt and oil.   Set the sous vide machine to 175 degrees Fahrenheit.   Take the above mix in a ziplock pouch. Seal it under vacuum or under water.   Place the bag in sous vide and cook for 8 minutes.   Take the cooked vegetables in a skillet and add vegetable broth and broccoli. Simmer for 15 minutes.   Add mushroom, orzo, spinach and simmer again for 10 Mins. until all vegetables soften.   Sprinkle salt, pepper, basil pesto and serve hot.

Nutrition: Info calories 230kcal, proteins 7g, carbs 34g, fats 8g, fibers 5g.

quinoa Mushroom Burger

Ingredients: Servings: 5   Cooking Time: 45 Mins.

chopped mushroom caps	1 clove garlic
1/2 C. walnuts	1 C. cooked quinoa
1/4 C. chopped red onion	1/2 C. cornstarch
2 tbsp. canola oil	1/2 C. mayonnaise
3 chopped green onions	2 tsp. rice vinegar
	Burger buns
	Salt and pepper

Directions:
In a bowl mix mushrooms, walnut, garlic with oil, salt and pepper.   Set the sous vide machine to 195 degrees Fahrenheit.   Take the above mix in the sous vide bag and seal it by removing all the air.   Place the bag in sous vide and bake for 20 minutes.   Pulse together the onions, mushroom mixture and vinegar to form a paste. Add cornstarch and quinoa to form dough. Refrigerate for 2 hours.   Make patties of this dough and cook them till they turn brown on both sides.   Serve these patties on the bun with mayonnaise.

Nutrition: Info calories 495kcal, carbs 49g, protein 9g, fats 31g, fiber 7g.

Ginger-honey Chicken Wings

Ingredients: Servings: 4   Cooking Time: 45 Mins.

16 chicken wings	1/4 C. soy sauce
1/2 C. honey	2 tbsp. grated ginger
1/4 C. lime juice	3 minced garlic cloves
1 tbsp. lime zest	2 sliced scallions
3 tbsp. sesame oil	Salt and pepper

Directions:
In a small bowl, mix all ingredients apart from chicken wings. Keep aside 2/3 of this mixture.   Take 1/3 of the mixture in a ziplock bag, add the chicken wings. Remove the air and marinate in the refrigerator for 6 hours.   Bring it to room temperature.   Set the sous vide machine to 195 degrees Fahrenheit.   Place the same ziplock in the water bath for 40 Mins.   Preheat the oven to 400 degrees Fahrenheit.   Pour the remaining marinade and cook for 5 minutes.   Serve hot.

Nutrition: Info calories 210kcal, fats 12g, carbs 7g, protein 19g.

Avocado & Egg Sandwich

Ingredients: Servings: 4   Cooking Time: 70 Mins.

8 slices of Bread	1 tsp. paprika
4 eggs	1 tbsp. chopped parsley
1 avocado	Salt and black pepper to taste
4 tsp. Hollandaise sauce	

Directions:
Prepare a water bath and place the Sous Vide in it. Set to 145 F. Scoop out the avocado flesh and mash it. Stir in sauce and spices. Place the eggs in a vacuum-sealable bag. Release air by the water displacement method, seal and submerge the bag in water bath. Set the timer for 1 hour.   Once done, immediately place in an ice bath to cool. Peel and slice the eggs. Spread half of the egg slices with the avocado mash and top with egg slices. Top with the remaining bread slices.

Ham And Manchego Egg Bites

Ingredients: Servings: 6   Cooking Time: 1 Hour

1 cup, chopped ham	6 pieces, eggs
1/2 cup, Manchego	Pepper, taste
	Salt to taste

cheese
½ cup, heavy
cream

Butter for
brushing

Directions:
Place the cheese, heavy cream and eggs in a blender and process until smooth. Season with pepper and salt. Brush the interior of the canning jars (bottles) with butter then place the chopped ham inside. Add in the egg mixture then cover the jars and cook in a water bath with your precision cooker set to 170°F for 1 hour.

Nutrition: Info Per serving:Calories 343, Carbohydrates 25 g, Fats 11 g, Protein 36 g

Apple Yogurt with Raisins

Ingredients: Servings: 4   Cooking Time: 4 Hours

4 C. milk	½ C. Greek yogurt
½ C. sweet apples, peeled, cored and chopped into small pieces	1 tsp. cinnamon
	4 tsp. small raisins
	2 tbsp. honey

Directions:
Pour the milk into a pan and heat it to 180°F. Cool it down to the room temperature. Preheat the water bath to 113°F. Mix in the yogurt, add the apples, cinnamon, honey, raisins, and pour the mixture into canning jars. Cover the jars with the lids and cook in the water bath for 3 hours. When the time is up, cool down the jars to the room temperature and then refrigerate before serving.

Nutrition: Info Per serving:Calories 99, Carbohydrates 6 g, Fats 3 g, Protein 12 g

Eggs with Roasted Peppers

Ingredients: Servings: 6   Cooking Time: 1 Hour

6 large eggs	3 roasted peppers, peeled and seeded
½ C. grated Gouda cheese	Salt and pepper, to taste

¼ C. cream
cheese

Directions:
Set the cooker to 172°F. In a food blender, blend eggs, Gouda cheese, cream cheese, salt, and pepper. Slice the peppers into thin strips. Place the peppers in the bottom of six 4oz. Jars, making sure they go up the sides a bit. Pour the egg mixture. Attach two-part canning lids "fingertip tight." Submerge in a water bath and cook 1 hour. Remove the jars from a water bath. Slide a knife around the peppers and eggs and remove carefully, or invert onto a plate. Serve with warm bread.

Nutrition: Info Per serving:Calories 158.3 Carbohydrates 6.1 g, Fats 10.7 g, Protein 9.4 g

Asparagus And Shiitake Tacos

Ingredients: Servings: 4   Cooking Time: 20 Mins.

1 C. shiitake mushrooms	1 bunch green onions
1 lb. Asparagus	1 C. guacamole
3 tbsp. canola oil	1 cloves garlic
1 tsp. ground chipotle chile	corn tortillas
	Salt, pepper, cilantro, lime

Directions:
Take a large mixing bowl. Add shiitakes, asparagus, and green onions and toss with oil, garlic, chipotle and salt. Set the sous vide machine to 145 degrees Fahrenheit. Take the asparagus in a ziplock bag and seal it under vacuum. In another ziplock take onions and shiitakes and seal. Submerge both of these bags in water bath and heat for 5-6 Mins. Transfer these vegetables on the chopping tray and cut into 2" pieces. Serve these with guacamole, corn tortillas, cilantro, lime wedges and hot sauce.

Nutrition: Info Calories 350kcal, protein 7g, carbs 36g, fats 21g, fiber 11g.

Recipe index

Chicken with Sun-dried Tomatoes 44

Chili Beef Meatballs 34

Chili Chicken & Chorizo Tacos with Cheese 47

Chili Chicken 47

Chili Lamb Steaks with Sesame Seed Topping 31

Chili Vodka 86

Chocolate & Ricotta Mousse 25

Chocolate Cherry Manhattan 86

Chocolate Chili Cake 21

Cilantro-garlic Beef Roast 30

Cinnamon Poached Pears 88

Cinnamon Poached Pears with Ice Cream 22

Cinnamon-apple Flavored Balsamic Vinegar 64

Citrus Corn with Tomato Sauce 73

Citrus Yogurt 25

Classic Chicken Cordon Bleu 41

Coconut Cream Sea Bass 50

Coconut Potato Mash 69

Cod In Tom Yum Broth 56

Coffee Butter 65

Coffee Liquor 86

Crab Zucchini Roulade & Mousse 52

Cranberry Vodka 85

Creamy Tomato Soup 59

Créme Brûlée 23

Crème Fraiche 62

Crispy Chicken with Mushrooms 37

Crispy Salmon with Sweet Ginger Glaze 53

Crispy Sous Vide Egg Yolks 98

Crispy Tilapia with Mustard-maple Sauce 51

Crunchy Apple Salad with Almonds 96

Crusted Tuna Fish 52

Cuban Shredded Beef 35

Cucumber Lemongrass Cocktail 87

D

Dark Chocolate Mousse 22

Delicious Artichokes with Simple Dip 77

Delightful Tofu with Sriracha Sauce 70

Dill Mackerel 54

Doce De Banana 20

Duck Breast A La Orange 39

Duck Breast with Balsamic Fig Jam 48

Duck Cacciatore 101

Duck Leg Confit 40

E

Easy Garden Green Beans 90

Easy Spiced Hummus 74

Easy Two-bean Salad 71

Effortless Pickled Fennel with Lemon 72

Egg And Chorizo Toast 15

Egg Soufflé with Avocado And Toast 102

Eggnog 82

Eggplant Kebab 74

Eggplant Lasagna 67

Eggplant Parmesan 74

Eggs Benedict 98

Eggs with Roasted Peppers 104

F

Flank Steak with Chimichurri Sauce 36

Fragrant Canadian Bacon 16

French Fries 80

French Scrambled Eggs 16

French Toast 16

G

Garlic & Paprika Sweet Potatoes 94

Garlic Basil Rub 67

Garlic Rack Of Lamb 35

Garlic Shrimps 54

Germany's Potato Salad 70

Ginger Balls 76

Ginger Syrup 87

Ginger Tamari Brussels Sprouts with Sesame 68

Ginger-honey Chicken Wings 103

Gnocchi Pillows And Caramelized Peas with Parmesan 68

Grand Marnier 24

Greek Flavored Chicken Meatballs 43

Greek Meatballs 38

Green Chicken Curry with & Noodles 49

Green Pea Cream with Nutmeg 68

Ground Beef Omelet 100

Grouper with Beurre Nantais 56

P

Panko Yolk Croquettes 82
Paprika & Rosemary Potatoes 81
Paprika Tenderloin with Herbs 37
Parmesan Omelette 15
Parsley Prawns with Lemon 57
Parsnips 95
Pasteurized Mayonnaise 66
Peppercorn Veal Chops with Pine Mushrooms 28
Perfect Curried Squash 71
Perfect Lil Smokies 79
Perfect Soft-boiled Eggs 19
Persimmon Butter 63
Pheasant Confit 41

Pickle In A Jar 93
Pickled Carrots 92
Pickled Cucumbers Pots 72
Pickled Jalapeño Peppers 94
Pickled Mixed Veggies 91
Pickled Radishes 91
Pineapple Compote with Rum & Mint 64
Pineapple Rum 83
Poached Eggs 100
Poached Pears 23
Pork & Bean Stew 31
Pork & White Beans Stew 59
Pork & Zucchini Ribbons 36

Pork Carnitas 33
Pork Chop with Spiced Coffee Sauce 37
Pork Knuckles 34
Pork Medallions 27
Pork Osso Bucco 32
Pork Steaks with Creamy Slaw 26
Potato & Date Salad 68
Potato Confit 97
Provencal Tomato Sauce 61
Provolone Cheese Grits 69
Pulled Pork(2) 35
Pumpkin Spice Bitters 85

Q

quail Legs 28
queso Blanco Dip 92

quick Limoncello 85
quinoa Mushroom Burger 103

R

Radish Cheese Dip 76
Raspberry Infused Vinaigrette 61
Red Cabbage & Potatoes with Sausage 29
Rhubarb & Thyme Syrup 24

Rich Orange Curd 26
Ricotta Cheese 63
Rolled Beef 31
Root Vegetable Soup with Pita Chips 95

Rose Syrup 85
Rosemary & Lemon Vodka 83
Rosemary Chicken Stew 39
Rosemary Russet Potatoes Confit 69

S

Sage Salmon with Coconut Potato Mash 51
Salmon Egg Bites 54
Salmon Soba Noodles 50
Saucy Veal with Port Wine 30
Savory Buttery Lobster Tails 55
Savory Creamy Cod with Parsley 49
Scallops with Lemon Meyer Glaze 55
Schmaltzy Brussels Sprouts 91
Seafood Stock 64
Seared Tuna Steaks 52

Sensuous White Chocolate Cheese Cake 20
Sesame Broccoli And Cauliflower 92
Sherry Braised Pork Ribs 33
Shrimp Appetizer 74
Shrimp Cocktail Slider 55
Shrimp Penne 53
Shrimp Salad 50
Simple Lemon Jam 25
Skewed Chicken Satay 100
Soft And Chili Eggs 99
Sous Vide Burgers 36

Sous Vide Coconut Congee 15
Sous Vide Garlic Tomatoes 91
Sous Vide Pickled Rhubarb 76
Sous Vide Tomato Sauce 90
Sous Vide Yummy Cream Topped Banana 17
Sous-vide Golden Beets 93
Southern Buttery Grits 97
Soy Chili Sauce 62
Spicy Adobo Chicken 48
Spicy Butter Corn 78
Spicy Fish Tortillas 52
Spicy Summer Medley 96

CPSIA information can be obtained
at www.ICGtesting.com
Printed in the USA
BVHW011559240122
627019BV00003B/105